Johann Wilhelm von Archenholz

A Picture of England

Containing a Description of the Laws, Customs and Manners of England

Johann Wilhelm von Archenholz

A Picture of England
Containing a Description of the Laws, Customs and Manners of England

ISBN/EAN: 9783337232115

Printed in Europe, USA, Canada, Australia, Japan

Cover: Foto ©ninafisch / pixelio.de

More available books at **www.hansebooks.com**

A

PICTURE

OF

ENGLAND.

A

PICTURE

OF

ENGLAND.

CONTAINING

A DESCRIPTION OF THE LAWS, CUSTOMS AND MANNERS OF ENGLAND.

Interfperfed with curious and interefting Anecdotes of

Prefent K. Denmark	General Smith	Mrs. Abington
Prince of Wales	Lord Camden	Mr. Wedgewood
Late E. M. Therefa	Lord Thurlow	Chevalier D'Eon
Louis XV.	Lord Kenyon	Lord Stormont
Duke de Choifeul	D. of Bridgewater	Mr. Villette
Late D. of Bedford	Lord Chatham	General Ganfell
Dut. Dow. Bedford	Lord Sackville	Late Mr. Garrick
D. Northumberland	General Burgoyne	Mr. Foote
Dut. of Devonfhire	Mr. Luttrell	Mrs. Cornelys
Lord Bute	Mr. Wilkes, and	Mrs. Siddons
Lord North	feveral other al-	Barry
Lord Mansfield	dermen	Woodward
Mr. Fox	Mr. Burke	Wefton
Mr. Pitt	Mr. Horne Tooke	Henderfon
Lord Sandwich	Late Lord Clive	Palmer
Admiral Keppel	Mr. Gibbon	Mr. Kelly, &c. &c.

By M. D'ARCHENHOLZ,

Formerly a Captain in the Service of the King of Pruffia.

TRANSLATED FROM THE FRENCH.

DUBLIN:

PRINTED BY P. BYRNE, No. 103, GRAFTON-STREET.

1790.

CHAPTER. I.

CHAPTER II.

CHAP.

CHAPTER III.

CHAPTER IV.

CHAPTER V.

CHAPTER VI.

CHAP-

CHAPTER VII.

CHAPTER VIII.

CHAPTER IX.

CHAPTER. X.

CHAPTER XI.

A

PICTURE

OF

ENGLAND.

———

CHAPTER I.

View of Great Britain—Manner of thinking in England—Privileges and Liberty of the Nation—Courts of Justice—Duchess of Kingston—Colonel de la Mothe—General Elections—Rights of the Sovereign—Outlines of the Character of Geo. III.——Ministerial Projects——Lord George Germaine—National opinions of Equality, Honour, Dishonour, and unequal Matches—Mr. Luttrell—General Burgoyne—Saratoga.

THE island of Great Britain is so different from all the other states of Europe, in the form of its government, its laws, its customs, its manners, and the mode of thinking and of acting adopted by its inhabitants, that it seems rather to belong to some other globe than that on which we live. The contrast is uncommonly striking when one passes directly from France to England. On that occasion

B   a stranger

a ſtranger imagines himſelf tranſported to another planet, the voyage is ſo ſhort, and performed in ſuch a ſmall ſpace of time.

No country in the world ought more to intereſt the philoſophical obſerver than that kingdom, of which ſo much is ſaid and ſo little underſtood. This indeed will be always the opinion of every impartial man, who has reſided there ſufficiently long to learn the language of the country, and acquire the knowledge neceſſary to form a proper opinion.

The uncommon revolution that has taken place in England within the two laſt centuries, in the manners, the ſciences and the arts, in commerce, religion, and above all in the political conſtitution, is worthy of exciting the greateſt aſtoniſhment. Notwithſtanding the ancient privileges which the nation acquired with great difficulty, and which even in barbarous times aſſumed the name of liberty, the government was ſtill tyrannical. Of this the hiſtory of the reign of Henry VIII. and of the cruel Mary, his daughter, will furniſh the moſt inconteſtible proofs. However, in more proſperous times, they paſſed rapidly from the extreme of oppreſſion to the moſt unbridled liberty in both civil and religious affairs. It is out of the boſom of this independence that thoſe characters ariſe whoſe originality ſo much ſurpriſes us. A rich Engliſhman, and in general every inhabitant of that fortunate iſland, knows no other reſtraint on his conduct than the laws, and his own inclination.—If he does not infringe on the juriſprudence of his country, he is entirely maſter of his own actions. From thence proceed thoſe numerous follies, and thoſe extravagancies, at which the nations among whom they are unknown ſeem ſo much ſhocked, for want of being able to inveſtigate the cauſe, which would make them rather aſtoniſhed that they are not more

numerous

numerous. *The opinion of the world,* so formidable in other countries, is there disregarded. Nobody consults any thing but his own judgment; and they all despise the sentiments of those from whom they have nothing either to hope or to fear.

There, as every where else, they laugh at a ridiculous person, but they treat him with a great deal of indulgence; and they do not esteem a gentleman less on account of his oddity, provided he hurts no one; for it is one of the particular features of an an Englishman's character, never to lose sight of the laws of his country. I shall hereafter shew, by means of the most remarkable examples, the influence this has on the national character.

The English have adopted in their literature this liberty, or rather this propriety of thinking and of acting; and it is to this that we are indebted for so many bold systems, so many spirited and useful truths, with which their philosophers and mathematicians have enriched human nature. From thence also proceed that daring flight of genius, and those new paths which their historians and their poets have opened, and with which they have as it were enlarged the world of ideas.

That country has so many attractions, that no stranger ever remains there any time without being attached to it by some secret charm: there are two things, however, first necessary; the one, that he should understand English: and the other, that he should have plenty of money, to enable him to live comfortably in a country where every thing is dear. He will then, whatever may be his taste, his age, or his manner of thinking, find every thing necessary to his satisfaction. This charm extends to all conditions, from the highest to the most wretched. During the residence of the present king of Denmark in France, all the arts were employed to amuse him: they made entertainments for him

hitherto

hitherto unknown; they even illuminated the forests, to give him the pleasure of the chace by torch-light. Every witty expression which he said, or did not say, became at once the subject and the burthen of some new song. In one word, the nation strove on his account to metamorphose Paris into an Elisium. Nevertheless London, where he enjoyed none of these pleasures, where no one, not even a common sailor, gave the wall to him, appeared much more charming.

It is proved by more than one example, that those of the most distinguished rank are not always sorry to feel that they are but men. A powerful prince of the Empire, who was too conscious of his high birth to deign ever to forget it, happening to visit England, found the Britons treat him with less respect than he had experienced from his own subjects. He began at first to complain; but reflecting that it was only what he had a right to expect he ended by joking at the circumstance; and although he had not afterwards any more occasion to be pleased with the attentions of the court than with the politeness of the people, this did not prevent him from still thinking that his stay was agreeable.

The English themselves know so well how to appreciate the blessings enjoyed in their native country, that those malefactors who conceive the slightest hope of escaping from punishment, rather choose to be exposed to the perils attendant on a criminal process than to expatriate themselves. Exile is, in their eyes, a species of death little less dreadful than a violent end; for one always sees, at their public executions, wretches who might have easily escaped by flight.

Notwithstanding that this country differs in so many respects from all others, and, according to the opinion of Montesquieu, is blessed with a more perfect government than any other; yet it so happens
that

that its excellence is little known, nay, is often abufed, even by thofe who pafs for philofophers. From hence proceed thofe foolifh doubts concerning the preference of an abfolute monarchy, or a limited one like that of Great-Britain. I envy not any man thofe chains which he glories in; by comparifon they may appear light, and even honourable; but he muft furely not only be unjuft, but even mad, who wifhes, by means of fophiftry, to raife the condition of the fubject of a monarchy above that of an Englifhman.

Whoever will take the trouble to read the aftonifhing actions, recounted in this work, when I treat of the conftitution, the laws, and the general welfare, will then perhaps ceafe to think the following fpeech of the Nabob of Arcot hyperbolical, on introducing colonel Smith to the victorious Soubah of the Decan: " Great prince! receive my " prefent: it is a warrior with whom I give you " the friendfhip of the Englifh, who are a nation " of kings!"

A German philofopher, of whom I fhall hereafter make mention, gives this excellent definition of political liberty: " I call that ftate free," fays he, " where there is no greater reftraint on human " actions, than what is abfolutely neceffary for the " prefervation of the commonwealth; a ftate where " nothing is regulated with partiality, but by gene- " ral acquiefcence, and with the full view of aug- " menting the general good; a ftate which, in the " privileges of any individual or any condition, " has no refpect but for the moft diftinguifhed me- " rit; a ftate, in one word, *where the greateft* " *powers can at once difplay themfelves, and act in* " *concert.*" I fhall prove, by inconteftible facts, that all this is more peculiar to England than any other country.

Notwith-

Notwithſtanding the inteſtine diſſenſions inevi-
table in a republic, and which even appear neceſſary
to its preſervation, ſince, furniſhing food to the de-
mocratical ſpirit, they keep the ſtate in health by
giving it life and activity; notwithſtanding the
unhappy iſſue of the American war; notwithſtanding the enormous debt and devouring luxury of the
nation; in fine, notwithſtanding all the vices and
imperfections which are the unhappy lot of human
nature; the people of England ſtill poſſeſs a felicity
worthy to be envied, and of which perhaps other
nations can ſcarce have a conception: ſo difficult it
is, in living under the mildeſt yoke, to form juſt
ideas of a national liberty grounded on the rights
of humanity.

Nothing ever appeared more jocular to the Engliſh than that paſſage in the manifeſto of France,
publiſhed at the beginning of the laſt war, where
it is ſaid, " that the moſt chriſtian king found him-
" ſelf under the neceſſity of protecting the Ameri-
" cans, whoſe *liberty and privileges had been at-*
" *tacked.*" In their anſwer, the miniſtry did not
teſtify a ſmall ſhare of aſtoniſhment, that they ſhould
make uſe of expreſſions in France which could not
in that kingdom be underſtood.

It is a truth which will not admit of doubt, that
no poliſhed nation was ever ſo free as the Engliſh
are at this day; and thoſe who are acquainted with
the conſtitution of ancient and modern kingdoms
will not heſitate to ſubſcribe to this opinion. We
cannot but pardon his patriotiſm, when a Dutchman
or a Swiſs flatters himſelf with poſſeſſing as much
liberty as an Engliſhman. A ſuccinct account of
Britiſh liberty, by affording a compariſon, will render my argument apparent.

Without mentioning the great number of fran-
chiſes and immunities of every kind, which the great
charter and many favourable revolutions have at
different

different times procured to the nation, we may arrange the rights of the people under six classes, viz.

The Liberty of the Press,
The Habeas Corpus Act,
Public Courts of Justice,
The Trial by Jury,
The Right of being represented in Parliament.
The Privilege of Public Remonstrances.

LIBERTY OF THE PRESS.

It is with great reason that the English boast of the liberty of the press, and regard it as the *palladium* or safe-guard of their civil liberty. It is true that it is often abused by the publication of foolish pasquinades, and shameful libels; but this inconvenience is amply indemnified by the immense advantages produced from it*

- The most hardened servant of the crown, who in the cabinet and in parliament blushes not to propose the most pernicious plans, and who knows how to endure with the utmost coolness the most outrageous contradictions and reproaches, is stopped in the midst of his audacious enterprises by the public voice. Hitherto no English minister has dared to forget or despise this voice. It is this which often renders his bad designs abortive, and destroys his best concerted projects.

The liberty of the press is also favourable to those popular assemblies so necessary in a free state ; for the newspapers inform the public of the time, the place, and generally the object of those meetings, which they detail in a particular manner to the whole nation. In them every one enjoys the most

B 4   entire

---

* I must say, to the honour of our country, that, except England, there is no other kingdom in the world where an honest man may write so many bold truths, and discover so many abuses, as in Germany.

entire liberty of fpeech ; the members of parliament themfelves, who often go to them, fometimes find matters better difcuffed there than in either houfe of parliament. The ftatefman whofe meafures have been difapproved, and the minifter who has been difmiffed, there find a free accefs ; there they employ their friends and their credit, and bring all the arts they are mafters of into play to gain the people to their interefts.

Without the liberty of the prefs, it would have been impoffible for a ftate in which the king is the difpofer of all the offices, dignities, and in a manner of all the riches of the country, to have maintained its independence fo long. The moft infignificant attempt of a minifter, which in its remoteft confequence gives an appearance of a defign on the national liberty, immediately fets the nation in movement ; the people become clamorous ; the minifter trembles, and the projeat is abandoned. If the public were lefs attentive to trifles, the crown would foon extend its prerogative, and at laft infenfibly arrive at the end which it aims at—abfolute power.

HABEAS CORPUS ACT.

This fhelters the loweft fubjeat in the ftate from oppreffion. By means of this, neither the minifter, nor even the king himfelf, can keep any Englifhman in prifon if the caufe of his detention is not affigned in a few days ; it alfo provides that he fhall be produced before fome public tribunal, face to face with his accufer. By its means, one of the loweft of the people is perfeatly fecure againft the greateft grandee in the ftate, although he may be aided by the fovereign authority. Can there be a greater contraft, than betwixt this act and the famous *letters de cachet*, of which the minifters of France were hitherto fo prodigal ? It was fufficient to have offended the under clerk of fome ftatefman, to have been fent to the Baftile and buried alive. If we may believe
Linguet

Linguet, this infernal cuſtom is ſtill in vogue. This ſingular man, during his firſt viſit to England, tortured his genius to abuſe in his Annals the liberty enjoyed by the Engliſh. Now better inſtructed in the ſchool of the Baſtile, he thinks differently, and regards England as the moſt ſacred aſylum. He publicly deplores his fooliſh patriotiſm, and aſſures us in this Journal that his cure is radical.

· By means of the hiſtory of Wilkes, in part forgotten, and in part unknown in Germany, I ſhall hereafter ſhew the great advantages of the act in queſtion.

PUBLIC COURTS OF JUSTICE.

Theſe are a neceſſary appendage to a free ſtate. In ancient Greece and Rome, all ſuits and proceſſes were diſcuſſed and determined in public. In ſuch a ſituation it is difficult to be evidently unjuſt, when the auditory conſiſts of a whole people, who obſerve the ſligheſt action and cenſure the leaſt improper word. There never was any judge but the decemvir Appius, ſo audacious as to bully a whole nation, and become guilty of an open injuſtice.

During the proceſs againſt the ducheſs of Kingſton in 1777, a circumſtance occured which clearly demonſtrates the excellence of a public trial. This lady being the wife of a peer of the realm, was conſequently tried before the Houſe of Lords. All the peers of England were her judges, under the direction of a lord high ſteward, named for that purpoſe by the king, his dignity ending with the trial. The theatre of this auguſt ſcene was Weſtminiſter-hall, whoſe ſpacious incloſure was not ſufficient for the crowd of ſpectators. The principal evidence on the ſide of the ducheſs was a bed-ridden old man, whom it was impoſſible to carry out of his chamber. However, the depoſition of this man was ſo favourable to the ducheſs, that it was indiſpenſably neceſſary towards the gaining of her cauſe. What was to

be done ? She demanded of her judges, that they
would pleafe to appoint a judicial deputation to receive his teftimony at his own houfe. This was indeed a favour uncommon in England : it appeared,
however, fo equitable to a number of the peers, that
they were about to make a decree to that purpofe

The earl of Mansfield, lord chief juftice of England, a man, who to the eloquence of Cicero unites
the moft profound knowledge of the laws of his
country, feeing the intention of the houfe, rofe from
his feat. After having informed them that it was
his wifh to allow to the accufed all proper means of
juftification, he painted in the moft lively colours
the prejudicial confequences of fuch an illegal favour ; he obferved, that a precedent like this, the
authority of which is always fo powerful in the Englifh courts of law, would induce and even oblige
them to confent to fimilar demands ; that, in all proceffes of great importance, there are fick witneffes
who wifh to be privately examined ; and would it
not be cafy, added he, to deceive or feduce a fmall
number of men entrufted with fuch a commiffion,
or even perhaps to procure the election to fall on a
chofen few ?   He ended by faying, that this innova-
tion would open the docr to venality and feduction ;
that it would give a mortal ftroke to the national
liberty ; that it would endanger the right of property fo facred in this ifland, and even the lives of their
fellow citizens.

To comprehend the force of this reafoning it is
neceffary to obferve, that in all the Englifh courts
of juftice the fentence almoft entirely depends on the
depofition of witneffes, and that the oral teftimony
of one fingle evidence is of more avail than a thoufand documents. The fpeech of lord Mansfield
made the moft lively impreffion on his audience.
Thofe of the peers who were the moft zealous
friends of the duchefs immediately defifted from
their

their demand, and her eloquent defenders became silent. Was not this an interesting scence to a philosophical observer?

TRIAL BY JURY.

Twelve sworn citizens, whom they call a jury, give judgment in all the courts of justice. They actually acquit or condemn. It is true, they are assisted by one or more judges, whose business it is to hear the witnesses, take care of the legality of the procedure, sum up the evidence, and pronounce the sentence according to the tenor of the law. Besides this, to prevent the inconvenience that must naturally arise from the pretended criminal's being dragged before a court of justice on slight suspicions, every accusation is first examined by a grand jury, whose decision either annihilates or continues the process. The petty juries, who give a final sentence, must be unanimous, and are shut up in a chamber until they bring in their verdict: on the other hand, the proceedings of the grand jury are regulated by a plurality of voices. If one of the twelve jurymen dies, after the arraignment and before the conviction of the supposed criminal, he is immediately released; because no person can be tried twice for the same offence.

The great impartialty of the English courts of justice is interwoven with the very constitution of the government. Never has the most powerful minister, however great his authority, or however profligate his conduct, attempted to bid defiance to the laws. Whatever may be his power, and however numerous his adherents, if he but attempt to oppress the least of his fellow-citizens, a process will immediately issue against him, and he will be obliged to appear before the judges in person. Whoever knows the value of such an inestimable privilege, will not fail to admire the administration of justice in England, which can never indeed be imitated but in a state equally free.

Every

Every inhabitant houfe-keeper, at the end of two years, is obliged to undertake in his turn certain parochial employments gratis, and is alfo to ferve on juries. Foreigners, although they have not been naturalized, are likewife liable to thefe offices as well as the natives. The twelve neceffary for the determination of any procefs, are chofen out of a very large number; which renders intrigues impoffible; and indeed there has been no example of an attempt of this kind. By thefe means, the trials, are at once quick and impartial. Linguet himfelf, who before he fmarted for his patrioifm, had undertaken the tafk of reviling every thing in England, was forced againft his own inclination to pay to thefe juridical cuftoms the tribute of his admiration. In a criminal trial, if the accufed be a foreigner, the jury is compofed of fix Englifhmen and fix foreigners, whofe names are communicated to him before hand, to the end that he may be enabled to reject, without explaining his reafons, any of them whom he fufpects to be his enemies.

Nothing is more aftonifhing than the mildnefs and humanity with which criminals are here treated, whether they be thieves, murderers, or incendiaries. Even if their guilt is evident, the bar, the jury, and the judges, all feem to confpire for their acquittal. They fearch the indictment for fome trifling fault that may render it equivocal; a falfe furname, an indeterminate date, a fingle letter omitted; all thefe are fatal to the procefs, and will immediately put an end to it. The counfel defend the culprit with zeal, and the witneffes againft him are queftioned with much ftrictnefs, and fometimes with much feverity. His own confeffion is never demanded, and he can be convicted by the evidence of credible witneffes alone. It is repugnant to human nature to fee a man bear teftimory againft himfelf; and this philofophical maxim affords a ftrange contraft to the practice of thofe tribunals of which torture is the
grand

grand refource. When all the evidence is ended, it is permitted the accufed to make his defence ; and the greateft attention is paid to every thing he fays. If he is found guilty, a judge announces to him the punifhment which the law inflicts on his offence, in a fpeech which, fo far from being compofed of reproachful and reviling words, is generally filled with tender and compaffionate expreffions.

Colonel de la Mothe, the French fpy, executed at London in 1782, who in his own country had been confidered as a defpicable wretch, was not a little furprifed at the indulgence he experienced here. They fent to him while in prifon the heads of the accufation, that he might have time to prepare an anfwer. The moft celebrated advocates undertook his defence without any fee. He received a lift of the jury who were to try him ; and, in a word, he was treated in fuch a manner as if the public welfare was interefted in his prefervation. The prefiding judge, after having with great mildnefs ftated the care which the laws had fhewn to his fituation, ended with thefe words: " It is thus, fir, that you " have been ufed in a country, where you had no " right to expect the leaft favour: but fuch are the " cuftoms of a people whofe deareft interefts you " have attempted to invade." Are not fuch examples fufficient to deftroy thofe vulgar prejudices, by which we are taught to believe that the manners of the Englifh are barbarous ? This is not the act of a few individuals, but of a nation, difplayed in its conftitution, its manners, its ufages, and its law. Whoever fearches into facts, and examines them with attention, muft perceive the fuperiority of the laws of England.

THE RIGHT OF BEING REPRESENTED IN PARLIAMENT.

Every freeholder, poffeffed of the annual rent of forty fhillings per annum, has a right to vote at the election

e Ation of the members of parliament for his own
county. This right, however, is not always founded on the same claim, in the cities and boroughs.
In some of them, every proprietor of a house has a
vote; in others, only the members of the corporation. Some are allowed to name representatives
without poffeffing any land at all. The two univerfities of Oxford and Cambridge poffefs this privilege,
merely from the refpect that the nation pays to
learning and the fciences.

The means of corruption give the court great influence at general elections: however, the laft king
could not prevent the patriotic party from making
the moft efficacious laws againft this fhameful abufe,
which is ftill continued with impunity. For example, the candidate goes among the electors, buys all
kinds of trifles, and pays for them very dearly; for
inftance, five guineas have been given for a whiftle,
a fowl, &c. &c. The fhop-keepers know what this
fignifies, pocket the money, and give their votes in
return. As this is entirely a matter of fpeculation,
it often happens that the candidate waftes prodigious
fums in vain, when the influence of his rival happens
to be greater than his own. Fordyce, the famous
banker, expended 30,000l. in an attempt of this
kind; and then, imagining that injuftice had been
done him, had the folly to embark in a procefs equally expenfive, in confequence of which many hundreds of the inhabitants were fent to London to appear as evidence. This fecond attempt, however,
had the fame fate as the firft, and did not a little
contribute to his total ruin. The regard in which
a member of parliament is held there, and his influence on public affairs, more efpecially if he poffeffes
eloquence—that eloquence which leads to the firft
offices of the ftate—have fuch powerful attractions
to an Englifhman, that they induce him to make

aftonifhing

astonishing efforts to obtain a place in the senate of his country. One of the principal reasons of modern venality proceeds from the great number of nabobs, who, on their return from India, attempt at any price to purchase a seat in parliament; and this is also the cause of the impunity which they experience, for the enormous crimes committed in that part of the world.

There cannot be a more astonishing contrast between any two civilized nations, than that with respect to Italy and England. The Italians celebrate almost every day in the year a religious holiday; the English, a political festival. The latter is as little known in Italy, as the former in England. Nothing is more common in that island than meetings, processions, and other testimonies of public joy, which interest in a very lively manner all those who are acquainted with the reasons of them; but the finest and most extraordinary of all is, without contradiction, a general election. One may then behold the same scenes which were exhibited in ancient Rome, when the people chose their new magistrates. Those of the very first rank, who by their wealth and their talents deserve to be reckoned among the chief persons in the state, go about soliciting the meanest of the people for their votes.— The handsome duchess of Devonshire herself was not ashamed to entreat the lowest shopkeepers in Westminster, in behalf of Mr. Fox. That charming lady's motive was not to oblige this unquiet and turbulent statesman, but to please the Prince of Wales, who interested himself in his election.

The appointed day being arrived, all the electors assemble in bodies, and range themselves under their respective colours. The candidates walk in procession accompanied by a crowd of their friends, and the different parties are distinguished from each other by the ribbands worn in their hats. Before

each

each are carried colours, on which the name of the
candidate and his device are painted. Thefe pro-
ceffions, confifting of fome thoufands of men, and
which, in London in particular, have always a
hundred thoufand fpectators, are made without the
affiftance of armed foldiers, or the officers of juftice,
the prefence of whom is regarded as indifpenfable in
other countries, who for the moft part, do more ill
than good.

The candidates having afcended a kind of amphitheatre, covered with tapeftry, and erected on
purpofe, harangue the people as the Roman orators
did formerly in the forum. After this the names of
the electors are regiftered without diftinction of
rank or age, and a majority of their votes determines
the election of him who, by his new dignity, is empowered to watch over the interefts and fafety of
the ftate, and to enact or annul the laws of his country. On thefe occafions, however great the tumult
may be among a people who enjoy fo much liberty,
there very feldom happens any ferious affray, fo
much difference is there between a people accuftomed to abandon themfelves entirely, and without fear,
to the impulfe of their own breafts, and thofe unfortunate men, who, bending under the yoke of a
frightful defpotifm, fall into the moft guilty excefs
the moment that they perceive their chains either
broken or relaxed. One neither perceives the glit-
tering of fwords or of piftols in the political lifts of
the Englifh, however great the animofity of the
combatants.

The choice being made, the victorious candidate
is brought to his own houfe in trumph. On his
election Mr. Fox, in allufion to his fupport from the
fair fex, dedicated a banner to them with this
motto, " *Sacred to female patriotifm.*"

I myfelf was prefent, and never beheld a fpecta-
cle which affected me fo much, or which, in my
opinion,

opinion, was capable of conveying to the human mind fuch a noble degree of energy. A celebrated French author, who was alfo there, obferves, "My "fatisfaction was complete, when I recollected "that this univerfal homage was paid to a fimple "individual, without dignities and without power, "fupported only by his own courage, his own zeal, "and the attachment of his friends; that the fame "man, the object of this cavalcade and of thefe "honours, thus recompenfed for his fervices to the "people, and his oppofition to the minifters of the "crown, would, in every other country, have "groaned under perfecutions; that he would, per-"haps, have terminated his life in a dungeon; that "in place of this pomp, which feemed to elevate "him above mortality, an arbitrary order would "have precipated him, with the greateft ignominy, "into the abyffes of a Baftile or a Spandau, or ex-"iled him into the deferts of Siberia. What a "leffon! How truly does it juftify the pride of "Englifhmen! How well does it excufe that pre-"ference which fo many great men have even in-"voluntarily given to their conftitution above all "others!"

It is a certain fact, that thofe elections greatly augment the haughtinefs of the Englifh, and infpire them with high ideas of equality. I was witnefs, at a conteft for the town of Newcaftle, to a very fingular circumftance. Two candidates had offered themfelves for this place: the one was the friend and relation of the late duke of Northumberland, who went there on purpofe to affift him, and engage the people in his interefts: the other was patronized by a merchant of London, of the name of Smith, who had acquired a fortune of 100,000l. in the coal-trade, and had a confiderable intereft among the inhabitants. The duke of Northumberland, who befides the advantages of his rank and fortune, had also occupied some of the most distinguished situations in the state, did not imagine that such a man could oppose him with any probability of success. However, on his arrival at Newcastle he was soon convinced of his mistake. In consequence of this he sent for Mr. Smith, who observed, that he had no business with the duke, and that his grace must wait upon him. The duke actually complied, and said, that if he would allow his relation to represent the borough, his friend should be returned for a town in the neighbourhood that was entirely at his own disposal. Smith upon this roughly refused his grace's proposition, saying, " I have promised " my friend that he shall represent this place, and " no other; and I am not in the habit of breaking " my word." " Very well," replied the duke, " it " only remains that we should try our strength," and immediately departed. In fine, each used his utmost efforts; but the coal-merchant's candidate was elected in spite of all the interest of the Lord Lieutenant of the county, whose little credit became the subject of ridicule.

In regard to parliament, the great abuse consists in the inequality of the representation of the people in the House of Commons. Venality exists but in a small degree in the great cities, and is but of little consequence. What man is able to corrupt an almost innumerable crowd, who live at their ease, who are as rich, and oftentimes more so, than the candidates who solicit them? It was a project truly patriotic, and well worthy of the son of the great William Pitt, to attempt a reformation in regard to the little boroughs. Is it not the height of folly to behold towns which have 40,000 inhabitants, and sometimes even more, without a single member, while a few miserable hamlets have a representation equal to the most considerable cities? London, which ought to send forty members, sends only four,

Manchester,

Manchester, Birmingham, and a great number of other places whose manufactures and commerce render England so flourishing, send not even one. This scheme of Mr. Pitt, which tended to support the political constitution of his country, then on the brink of ruin, was evidently dictated by the greatest propriety. Lord North, and his colleagues, however opposed him: for corruption would have been been annihilated, and all their power had this fatal system for its basis. As long as the sovereign does not seek to extend the privileges of the crown so as to infringe on the constitution, this reformation can never do him any hurt. During the glorious administration of the immortal Chatham, he never had recourse to ministerial authority or the tricks of office; he scorned the arts of influence and corruption.

PRIVILEGE OF PUBLIC REMONSTRANCES.

In the year 1775, the king wished that a criminal condemned to death should not suffer at Tyburn, but be executed out of town, and before the very house where he had committed the burglary. His majesty's desire was notified accordingly by the secretary of state to the sheriffs of the county of Middlesex. In all other countries, they would have regarded with mere indifference the place where the culprit was to have been executed; but they think differently in England. The sheriffs refused to obey. An order drawn up with more precision had not a better effect; on the contrary, they presented an humble remonstrance to the king, wherein they gave the most solid reasons for their disobedience. They said, among other things, that if the place of punishment was changed at pleasure, this would by and by produce an abuse which would sap the fundamental laws of the realm. These executions might be made, sometimes in town, sometimes in the country;

try ; in a public place, in this or that ſtreet, and at laſt even in a houſe ; from whence it would happen, that they might ſoon ceaſe to be public, a circumſtance ſo neceſſary in a free country. The ſheriffs accordingly perſiſted in their refuſal, and their conduct well deſerved the thanks of the whole nation.

They are deceived who imagine that the ſituation of a king of England is diſagreable : on the contrary, if it were ever poſſible that a crown could confer happineſs on the wearer, a ſovereign of England, *if he ſo inclines*, may enjoy this advantage in a peculiar manner. He poſſeſſes great and extraordinary privileges ; indeed, the chief magiſtrate of no free people, either ancient or modern, ever had ſuch extenſive rights. Without appealing to remote times, let us only mention the ſtadtholders of Holland, the predeceſſors of the preſent king of Sweden, and the ſovereigns of Poland ; with theſe let us compare an Engliſh monarch, and we ſhall immediately perceive the difference.

He is empowered, without conſulting his parliament, to contract alliances, to declare war, and to make peace ; to receive and appoint ambaſſadors and miniſters, and to enliſt troops : he can aſſemble parliament when he pleaſes, prorogue it, appoint the place for it to meet in, and even diſſolve it entirely. All new laws muſt have his ſanction : if they have been acceded to by both the other branches of the legiſlature, the refuſal of his conſent immediately annihilates them ; nor is it neceſſary that he ſhould aſſign any reaſon for his conduct. He poſſeſſes the excluſive privilege of appointing the officers by ſea and land ; the magiſtrates, the miniſters, the judges of the crown ; the archbiſhops, biſhops, and other eccleſiaſtics ; he can ennoble ; grant

grant a pardon to criminals; found univerfities, colleges, hofpitals, and eftablifh fairs: he has the fole privilege of iffuing proclamations: he is the guardian of all the fools in the kingdom, and he inherits the eftates of all thofe who die without heirs. All the wrecks of which the owners are unknown belong to him, as well as the land left by the receding of the ocean. He can enact ecclefiaftical laws, eftablifh ceremonies for the church, convoke provincial and national fynods, &c. When a king of England is contented with the peaceable enjoyment of thefe eminent advantages, without trenching on thofe of the nation, he may entirely confide in the adminiftration of his minifters, who are anfwerable for every thing. *" That the king can do no wrong,"* is a maxim among the Englifh minifters.

As the attacks upon them are almoft always accompanied with the moft poignant perfonalities, it is evident that a great portion of phlegm is in this country one of the greateft virtues in a minifter. Lord North poffeffed this in an eminent degree. During his long adminiftration he feems to have adopted the principle of the duke of Orleans, regent of France: " Let them fpeak as long as they al-" low us to act." It is afferted, that a party in oppofition to the court is abfolutely neceffary in the Englifh parliament: this is what made the celebrated Sir Robert Walpole affirm, " That if fuch " a party had not been already formed, he would " have raifed one with the public money."

The leaft perfonal offence offered to the king, is high treafon. He himfelf is fo little bound down in the exercife of his prerogative, that, without confulting any one, he can appoint a common failor to be lord high admiral of England, and tranflate a country curate to the fee of Canterbury. But if the power of the fovereign is unbounded in doing good, on the other hand it is ftrictly limited as to evil.

evil. He dares not, without infringing the laws, command one of his postillions to be chastised. Neither can he tack conditions to the favours which he grants; nor add to the quantum of punishment which he orders to be inflicted.

This line of demarcation is without doubt the ground-work of the constitution. The sovereign, having the executive power in his own hands, can apply to the management of public affairs both celerity and dispatch, and exhibit a salutary uniformity in the exercise of the laws. When we compare with this the slowness and prolixity with which other free states manage their affairs, we shall perceive the numerous advantages resulting from such a constitution.

At no period since the Revolution, have so many and such successful attempts been made in favour of the prerogative as during the present reign. From the commencement of lord North's administration, till his dismission in 1782, the parliament was entirely governed by the crown, and every proposition of the minister confirmed by a decided majority. Such a constant acquiescence on the part of the Commons, and that too at a time, when the people were discontented, is a circumstance unexampled in their history. The character of the sovereign was the sole cause of all this. It is also probable, that it was a trait of this singular character which seldom occurs in a subject, and still less frequently on a throne, that gave to lord Bute such an ascendancy over him. This nobleman, who at the beginning of the present reign was placed at the head of affairs, is perhaps, the sole cause of all the misfortunes which have happened to England for these last twenty years.

Without being either generous or attached to wealth, the king has nevertheless a decided aversion to luxury. No sovereign in Europe is so badly lodged,

keeps

keeps fo poor a table, or facrifices fo little to his pleafures. The economy of the court is fuch, that I
myfelf was prefent at a ball at St. James's, when
the appartments were lighted with tallow candles,
which for a long time have been banifhed from
all the genteel houfes in London.

With a revenue of 900,000l. fterling per annum,
which belongs to the civil lift, to which may be
added 300,000l. arifing from his foreign dominions,
and other contingencies, one may be tempted
to imagine that the king poffeffes immenfe treafures *, notwithftanding he feems, from time to
time, to be overwhelmed with debts, which the parliament is obliged to pay. Behold then that enigma
explained, without which it would have been neceffary to have added a commentary.

Lord North adopted the plan of the earl of Bute,
and, during eleven years of a fhameful adminiftration, precipitated his country, from the flourifhing
ftate in which he found it, into the unhappy condition in which it ftill languifhes. This ftatefman is
not eminent for his eloquence, and far lefs for the
greatnefs of his defigns ; but he excels in little artifi-
ces, and talents peculiarly calculated for intrigue.
By means of thefe he at laft governed the parliament
and realized his own projects of ambition. He was
feconded in all his fchemes by the other minifters,
who were in every point of view worthy of their
chief. Who has not heard of a Germaine, branded
and difhonoured by a council of war, a Sandwich,
a Rigby, and many others, whofe real characters the
king alone feemed to be unacquainted with ? A
writer of fome celebrity has attempted to inveftigate
the reafons, and has narrated a number of fingular
anecdotes to explain the caufe of the reciprocal
averfion

* Certain circumftances have occurred fince the publication of the original, which fully confirm the conjectures of
M. d'Archenholz.

averfion that now exifts between the king and lord
North. It is, however, unneceffary to fearch for
the fecret and extraordinary reafons of an 'enmity,
of which the motives are fo perceptible.

The king for a long time imagined that he at laft
poffeffed in his lordfhip a minifter who was attached to his interefts ; and he could not be perfuaded
to the contrary, fo long as his lordfhip was at the
head of affairs: he was, however, fcarcely difmiffed, when his majefty received the moft convincing proofs of his venal adminiftration. The efteem
which the fovereign had till that moment entertained for him, immediately changed to contempt ; and
this change was the more infupportable to the ex-
minifter, as he had received hopes that he might one
day be again admitted into power. On this he immediately threw off his difguife, and fhowed himfelf
as it were for the firft time, in his own proper form.

The idea of liberty, and the confcioufnefs of protection from the laws, are the reafons why the people in general teftify but little refpect for their fupe-
riors, and even for thofe in the higheft offices, unlefs they have acquired their affections by affable
and popular manners. That perfect equlaity, with
which nature has formed mankind, is apparent in all
the words and actions of thefe iflanders ; neither
dignities nor riches are able to efface it. The very
majefty of the throne is not always fufficiently ref-
pected. The Englifh confider the fovereign as
only the firft magiftrate in their fervice.

The nobility, who in all other countries claim refpect and fubmiffion from their inferiors, dare not
form fuch pretenfions there. The fpirit of liberty,
which that clafs of men fuck in with their very milk,
teaches them to regard all the privileges of their
fellow fubjects as facred.

No minifter (notwithftanding the very caprices
of fuch men often decide in other countries the fate
of

of a whole nation) no grandee of the kingdom will
pretend to make any of the populace give way to
him in the ftreet ; and, notwithftanding this, they
every day walk through the moft crowed part of the
metropolis, where they find themfelves fplafhed,
fqueezed, and elbowed, without having the leaft wifh
to complain. The vaineft Englifhman will converfe
freely with the loweft of his fellow citizens; he will
take part in their diverfions ; and as in England they
do not meafure the difference of conditions by our
fcale, it is not at all unufal to fee two perfons quar-
relling, between whofe fituations in life there is the
greateft difparity.

It is true, that thofe of the firft rank in the ftate
have occafion for the good offices of the loweft of its
members, to enable them to realize their ambitious
hopes ; and it is not at all rare, at the election of
members of parliament, to fee the pooreft citizens
receive letters from the moft illuftrious candidates,
in which their votes are requefted with the utmoft
obfequioufnefs ; and when they have yielded to
thefe folicitations, they are always fure of receiving
others expreffive of thanks. Have we not lately beheld the duchefs of Devonfhire beftowing her gold
and her kiffes for this purpofe ? that very duchefs,
of whom the celebarted Angelica Kauffman has
faid, that fhe looks fo like one of the Graces, as to
realize in her own perfon all the ideas of the moft
fervid imagination.

This affectation of popularity, which fo much
aftonifhes ftrangers, proceeds from the very nature
of the conftitution of a free ftate. The Greeks and
the Romans experienced the fame while their republics fubfifted. Does it not proceed from this,
that the nobility of England are the moft intelligent
in Europe ? They converfe familiarly with men
of learning and artifts, and recompenfe their labours
in the moft generous manner. But that which ren-

C

ders them the moſt worthy of praiſe, is the noble
manner in which they ſupport their diſgrace at court:
on theſe occaſions the zeal and attachment of their
friends, inſtead of being diminiſhed, ſeems to be re-
doubled; and ſo far from loſing them with the favour of the ſovereign, they teſtify greater eſteem
and attachment than before. It was thus that lord
Chatham, who was obliged to reſign when the preſent king mounted the throne, was almoſt idolized
by the people, who eſteemed and loved him before
he loſt his place. His portrait was placed in every
houſe, as a kind of tutelary divinity; the ſtreets,
the taverns, the coffee-houſes, and the tea-gardens
were called after his name, and the eye of every
paſſenger was ſtruck with inſcriptions in honour of this
great benefactor to the nation.

The Engliſh in general form a quite different idea
of honour and infamy from other Europeans. A
man who is arreſted and impriſoned does not experience any inſult on that account, nor is the family
of a criminal who has been put to death, ever rendered infamous. The laſt duke of Lancaſter but
one, eſpouſed the daughter of an oſtler; ſhe ſur-
vived him for ſome years with the title of ducheſs
dowager. The honour of the duke was not im-
peached on this account, and the ducheſs continued
to frequent court like any other lady of quality. A
man of diſtinction retorts one inſult by another, and
pardons it without either being revenged, or fight-
ing with the perſon who inſults him. The late
duke of Bedford, after having occupied the firſt
ſituation in the ſtate, was unmercifully horſe-whip-
ped at a horſe-race*. Nevertheleſs, this did not prevent

---

* George the II. was but imperfectly acquainted with the
Engliſh language. Having received a letter from admiral
Sir Edward Hawke, after his celebrated victory over the
French fleet, in which he informed his majeſty, in the blunt
but expreſſive language of a Britiſh tar, that he had given
the enemy a " DRUBBING ; " the king requeſted of lord Cheſ-

vent him in 1762 from being appointed ambaſſa-
dor extraordinary to the court of France, where he
ſigned the famous peace of Verſailles. The populace
among us, who poſſeſs a very different idea of honour,
would not ſcruple to aſſert that this manner of thinking proceeds from a want of dedicacy, and a preva-
lence of rude and ſavage manners. The philoſopher, on the contrary, who is able to diſcover among
the Engliſh a high degree of this very delicacy, who
finds it carried even to the higheſt pitch of perfection, and who diſcovers no tincture of rudeneſs in
the manners of this enlightened people—the philoſopher, I ſay, will, like them, view the laws of honour
in a different light.

Every ſubject in a monarchy trembles on account
of the moſt trifling circumſtance. The moſt indifferent action, a ſingle word, ſometimes even a
ſuppoſition, are ſufficient to deprive the miſerable
wretch of his ſubſiſtence ; nay, it often coſts him his
fortune, ſometimes his life. Upon the leaſt of theſe
events the welfare and exiſtence of a family depend :
they, therefore, affect an uncommon refinement in
manners ; and from thence it appears, that the moſt
ridiculous prejudices often regulate the laws of that
phantom to which they give the name of honour.

But in a republic, where theſe ideas loſe a great
deal of their force, where the citizen is ignorant of
a thouſand conſiderations of which the ſubject of a
monarchy never dares to loſe ſight ;—in a republic
this is entirely different. It is to the Greeks and the
Romans that I ſhall appeal : at a time when their
civilization was at the higheſt degree of perfection,
they thought exactly on that ſubject as the people of
England do at the preſent day.

C 2

The

terfield that he would explain the word. The witty earl, to
this queſtion, pointing to the duke of Bedford, whoſe enemy
he was, gravely aſſured his majeſty, that no man in the kingdom could better ſatisfy his curioſity in regard to that article
than his grace.

The English look on hypocrify as the moft defpi-
eable of all vices ; and from this proceeds that boldnefs of fpeech, which, if not foftened a little by the
choice of expreffions, would pafs for rudenefs. It is
to their excellent conftitution that they owe a franknefs of character which is at once fo rare and fo ineftimable, and which, among them, is generally
accompanied with an unfhaken courage and a determined refolution. It is not uncommon to hear expreffions both in their courts of juftice and in parliament, for which one would be tempted to imagine
that the party attacked could never be revenged but
by the blood of his adverfary : thefe circumftances,
however, are feldom attended with unhappy confequences. How, indeed, could the parliament of
England exift without this ? The ftranger who
thinks that fuch fallies are blameable, has furely never
reflected on the nature of a free fenate, where the ufeful muft neceffarily be preferred to the agreeable ;
where they do not meet to hear cold and formal
fpeeches dictated by cuftom ; and where it is impoffible for the true patriot, whofe foul is filled with
the importance of the fubject, to moderate his eloquence, ard confine himfelf within the uneafy
fhackles of a fervile complaifance.

One of the moft violent of thefe parliamentary
orators is captain Luttrell, a younger brother of the
dutchefs of Cumberland. This forgetfulnefs of all
the laws of politenefs was fo common to him, that,
in a fpeech in the year 1777, he concluded by wifh-
ing, that all kinds of barbarous and cruel tortures,
which are the difgrace of nations where they are
ftill practifed, might be introduced into England, becaufe lord North could not then efcape the wheel ;
and it would be, added he, " a real pleafure for me to
" fee his bones broken by the hands of the executio-
rer." Lord North, who was prefent, rofe with his
ufual coolnefs, and contented himfelf by faying,
with

with a figh, " that he had better feize the prefent
" opportunity of fpeaking, before he fhould be put
" to the rack."

This fame Mr. Luttrell, the very next year, was
engaged in a new quarrel with lord George Germaine. This nobleman, who after the battle of
Minden had been difhonoured by the fentence of a
court-martial, knew fo well how to procure again
the favour of the then government, that, unhappily
for this country, he was appointed to a place in the
miniftry, and formed that ridiculous plan of operations for general Burgoyne, which occafioned the
the lofs of all his army at Saratoga. Luttrell re-
proached him in full parliament with having been
declared infamous; afferted that he had behaved,
during the German war, with all the cowardice of
a woman; and accompanied thefe reproaches with
fo many acrimonious reflections, that at faft old
Germaine loft all patience: however, amidft all the
tranfports of his rage, he contented himfelf with
calling him a *buffoon*. His opponent's behaviour,
however, was fo contrary to the rules of the houfe,
that it occafioned a great difturbance. Luttrell,
who forefaw the confequence, left his feat, and mingled with the crowd in the gallery, from whence
he could hear what paffed below. The fpeaker befought the members to help him to appeafe the tumult. Germaine acquiefces, but his adverfary is
gone. His abfence augments the noife, until at laft
he is difcovered. He is then ordered to defcend ;—
he obeys, but refufes to make any apology to lord
George Germaine. At this refufal, obftinately perfifted in on his part, a member of parliament gives
it as his opinion, that he ought to be fent to the
Tower if he does not comply ; but as it is impoffible to put fuch a motion to the vote, without being
feconded, and as no one was at this moment difpofed
to do fo, Luttrell himfelf exclaims, " *I fecond the*
" *motion.*"

" *motion*." On this mutual excufes took place, and every thing remained quiet.

It is not at all uncommon to fee two perfons, who have been abufing each other, converfing in the moft familiar manner after their departure from the houfe. It is only the heads of parties who are confined to rules, from which they never depart, and who deteft each other with the utmeft cordiality. The celebrated Edmund Burke, who has always fhewn himfelf a man of principle, during the American war exhaufted all the metaphors of his brilliant imagination againft the adminiftration which conducted it ; he one day finifhed one of his violent fpeeches, with the moft dreadful maledictions againft the miniftry, and affured them, that the firft thing he would teach his grand-children, when they began to lifp, would be alfo to curfe fuch wretches. After having pronounced thefe words of peace, he left the affembly.

The lofs which the Englifh fupported with the greateft difficulty, during the whole American war, was that of their army at Saratoga ; for they had conceived not only the higheft opinion of it, but alfo of the general who had the command. The unhappy cataftrophe attending its captivity, was alfo the caufe why France threw off the mafk, and declared the Americans a free people.

Burgoyne was permitted to return to Europe on his parole, to undertake his own defence ; but was denied the liberty of feeing the fovereign, under pretence of being a prifoner. This circumftance was even urged to prevent him from taking a feat in the Houfe of Commons : however, the latter attempt proved unfuccefsful. Burgoyne there tried to juftify his conduct, but in a general and vague manner, as he ftill wifhed to fcreen the minifters : they, however, being anxious alone for their own prefervation, kept no meafures with him, and forced
this

this unfortunate man, who is one of the few Englifh officers who underftand any thing of military tac-tics, to refign all his employments.

Burgoyne upon this appealed to the nation at large, in a memorial which is a mafter-piece, not only on account of the matter which it contains, but alfo from the affecting manner in which it is compofed. In this production he fully developes the ignorance and bafenefs of the minifters. He had before re-prefented the impoffibility of penetrating with his little army through the woods of America; but fo far from attending to his judicious remonftrances, they were pleafed to reiterate their orders, in the moft pofitive terms, to attempt the undertaking. Burgoyne was a foldier;—he faw himfelf ruined beyond hope, but he felt it his duty to obey. He imagined that, by thus facrificing himfelf and his little army, the minifters intended to realife fchemes of a much greater importance to the nation. As a citizen, his own private feelings were loft in the interefts of the ftate; and as a warrior, he was obliged to confole himfelf with the idea, that the brave commanders had of ten experienced the fame fate.

This production of general Burgoyne's accompa-nied with documents which prove all that he has afferted, ftill remains unanfwered.

CHAPTER II.

THE national pride of the English is a natural consequence of a political constitution, by which every citizen is exempted from any other dependence than that imposed by the laws

This pride is carried among them to a great length. Indeed, how is it possible to know and to feel all the merit of such a system of liberty, without attaching an uncommon value to it? This same sentiment, with which we so violently reproach the English of the present times, has always been felt by the most enlightened nations in the world.

The Greeks and Romans carried it still farther. This laudable pride, which with them was united to a lively and fervid patriotism, occasioned those heroic actions which will for ever be engraved in the records of immortality. If the modern history of
England

England be equally filled with glorious achievements, it is to a love of their country that all this ought to be ascribed ; a love which, carried to the extreme, as it has been, by those haughty islanders, cannot be conceived without a certain degree of of contempt for those nations who do not possess similar sensations.

This fault, if it is one, is still more common amongst the Spaniards than them ; but being founded on no solid grounds, it has become very justly a subject of ridicule. The English themselves are hated on this account, although their very enemies, at the bottom of their hearts, pay tribute to their extraordinary merit.—Envy will glide into nations, as well as individuals.

There are, perhaps, no people in Europe who possess so much natural pride as the French : it will be easy, with a little penetration, to reconcile this with that urbanity and those polite manners for which they are so distinguished. It is under this mask that the sly Frenchman conceals those marks of envy with which he views his English neighbours.

It was this offensive pride of the English that so many nations strove to humble during the American war. Many even of the states of Germany, among whom the spirit of imitation exercises such a despotic rule, that they neither think, live, nor exist but after the French, were animated with the same desire. They carried their madness so far as to forget the blood and the treasures, which that nation, in the present century, had sacrificed for the advantage and repose of their country. They even wished, without knowing why, to see the source of her greatness dried up.

It ought, however, to be remarked, that the principal members of the empire, guided by a more sound and judicious policy, trembled for England ;

even

even Switzerland, which was neither connected
with her by politics nor commerce, offered up continual vows for her preservation.

A traveller, more especially if he passes immediately from France into Great Britain, in looking
for that politeness at once so splendid and so trifling,
which he has been used to, will not fail to imagine
the English rude and uncultivated; and this merely
because he does not give himself the trouble to
search beyond the surface of their characters.

Grosley, a member of the French academy, recounts, with some humour, in one of his letters, a
circumstance that happened to him. He had gone
to England, prejudiced with the idea, that he was
about to visit the most unpolished nation in Europe.
A few days after his arrival he went to the theatre.
The pit was very crowded; and being there alone,
and exceedingly inquisitive, he began to recollect
the little English of which he was master, and put
several questions to the person next him. His
neighbour, who did not understand a word of the
jargon which he uttered, rises precipitately, turns
his back to him and departs. Grosley was but
little surprised at this conduct, so extremely ungenteel
in appearance, and which, for some moments, only
served to confirm him in his former opinion: but
he was soon put to the blush when he saw the Englishman return. This good-natured man had perceived at the other end of the pit, one of his friends
who spoke French; and having pierced the crowd
which separated them, he returned with much difficulty, leading him in his hand.—I ask, whether
this is true politeness or not? A Frenchman, by
paying him a handsome compliment, would have
imagined that he had done enough; the Englishman on the contrary, thought that he ought to do
more, and he accordingly did it. If it is then in actions, and not in simple words that real urbanity
consists

confifts, one is obliged to confefs that the Englifh are the moft polifhed nation in Europe.

The principle of fuch actions is there alfo more pure, becaufe a beggar has no occafion to humble himfelf before the moft wealthy, and a citizen in eafy circumftances knows no bounds to his independence.

The moral character of the Englifh has indeed degenerated, but, notwithftanding this, it is ftill eftimable: for it is not from its parliaments, its oriental depredators, and the crews of its privateers, who all aim at a certain end, that we ought to judge of the nation. Many members of parliament afpire at eminent fituations, and allow themfelves to be corrupted; fo alfo do the adventurers who leave Europe with an intention to plunder Afia; and it is the very nature of pirates to rob and flaughter.

Is it from the refufe of a community that we are to imbibe our opinions of the moral character of a people, or from a multitude of godlike actions, which are performed every day, by thoufands in this ifland?

An extraordinary event, which occurred a few years fince, will ferve to elucidate the noble and generous manner of thinking among the Englifh. The emigrations from the empire, of which fuch fad complaints are made, even at this day, and which are founded on reafons partly juft, and partly imaginary, gave an opportunity to a German gentleman to form a very fingular fcheme.

The name of this projector and his intentions, are ftill unknown; the arts alfo which he practifed to put in execution fuch a well-concerted plan, are equally obfcure: it is however, certain, that a common genius durft never imagine, far lefs be able to p in execution, an enterprife of this nature. In the year 1765, he went to England at the head of

800

300 adventurers, consisting of men, women, and children, whom he had collected in the Palatinate, Franconia, and Suabia, by promising them that they would be much more happy in the English colonies.

On their arrival at the port of London, this singular man disappeared, and has never since been heard of.

At once miserable and disappointed, these unfortunate wretches, neither knowing the language, nor being acquainted with any of the inhabitants, and with only a few rags to cover them, were entirely bewildered in that extensive capital. Without any asylum, without even bread for their children, who asked for it with the most piercing cries, they knew not to whom they could address themselves.

In hopes of a less cruel destiny, they lay down in the open air, in the midst of those streets nearest to the wharf where they had been landed. In every other city, even in Paris itself, the unexpected arrival of a colony of eight hundred persons, would have been talked of every where, and proper measures taken accordingly : but the landing of such a numerous body was for a long time unknown in London. The inhabitants, indeed, of that part of the town, and also the passengers, were greatly astonished at the appearance of this singular groupe, who bewailed their misfortunes in an unknown languge; but not being able to discover the cause, they gave themselves but little concern on the subject.

Two days passed in this manner, and these poor people remained exposed to the inclemency of the elements, and the cravings of hunger. Some died for want, on the third day. Their misery was now at the extreme, for their arrival was unknown any where else than in this little corner of the suburbs : not a single word of it had transpired either in the city or Westminister.

The

The inhabitants in the neighbourhood were not, however, unfeeling spectators of so many calamities : they aided them as far as they were able ; but what are the feeble succours of poverty at such a crisis ? The bakers were accustomed to send their servants every morning loaded with baskets of bread, which they distributed according to the directions of their masters. One of these happening to pass near the place where these emigrants were encamped, heard that they had been several hours without any subsistence. "If it is so," says he, at the same time placing his pannier in the midst of them, "our "customers must have patience to-day ; were my "master to lose them all, he would not be angry. I "will," added he, "aid these poor creatures, if I "pay for it out of my own wages."—I trust that the behaviour of this man does not need a commentary.

The reverend Mr. Waschel, a clergyman of the German church, who lived near to them, at last resolved to advertise this singular event in the newspapers. In a letter which he inserted, and which was signed with his own name, he particularizes, in a most affecting detail, the misery of his countrymen, and implores in their behalf the generous compassion of the English, on which these wretches had so much relied when they left their native country. The effect of this was incredible and beyond expectation.

The morning papers are generally printed at eight o'clock ; by nine a man arrives on horseback from one of the most distant parts of Westminster, and brings to Mr. Waschel a bank note for 100l. sterling. The messenger would not mention the donor, but it was afterwards found to be the old countess of Chesterfield, who performed so charitable an action.

This might be called the earnest of the whole nation. It seemed to rain bank-notes and guineas

upon

upon the good priest. Coffee-houses were opened for subscriptions, attendants were appointed to supply them with necessaries, as they themselves were not able to buy them ; physicians and apothecaries were assigned, and nurses and interpreters appointed to them : in a word, the wants of this deserted band were satisfied, their forlorn situation removed, and they themselves inspired with the sweet hope of better prospects before the middle of that very day.

In the mean time the subscriptions continued open, and there never, perhaps, was such a general contribution. There were but few rich people, of a certain rank, in all the kingdom, who did not assist on this occasion. I myself have read the list of those benefactors to my countrymen, and have counted more than twenty who gave a hundred pounds each, and some even more. The sum total is unknown to me ; it was, however, sufficient to entertain this numerous body of people, during five months, in London ; at the end of that period they were carried to Carolina, in vessels hired for the purpose, and provided with proper necessaries. They had a very excellent passage to America, and received, at the instant of their arrival, not only every thing necessary for their establishment, but also the remainder of the money which had been collected for them.

It may be imagined that the Germans, settled in London, shewed themselves equally generous towards their countrymen as the English.—Not only those in easy circumstances, but even pulent people, to whom the nation had confided the care of these unfortunate wretches, received money for their services out of the fund arising from the subscriptions, and charged at the highest rate !

It has been observed that the common people in England are more intelligent and judicious than in any other country. The free and unrestrained

manner

manner in which they speak and write, on every
subject, is the real cause of this. One is astonished
to hear some of the very lowest of the populace
reason concerning the laws, the right of property,
privileges, &c.

If the English * newspapers generally contain a ✓
large portion of dull and trifling matter, on the
other hand they often abound with passages worthy
to be read and preserved. Sometimes a politician
will insert an essay on a subject which concerns the
welfare of the whole nation, and every body, even
a fish-woman, is able to comprehend it. It is not
at all uncommon. to observe such persons reading
and commenting on the public prints.

Besides original intelligence, the prodigious number of advertisements make them entertaining, and
are often attended with the strangest consequences.

I know a woman. who ran away from her husband after having robbed him. Without the assistance of the newspapers the despair of this repentant
wife would have been unknown, and the dishonour
of her spouse made public ; but a lucky advertise-
ment informed them of each other's situation, and
their reconciliation was equally quick and secret.
The husband having given out that his wife was
gone into the country, addressed a letter to her,
without either inserting her name or residence, but
couched in such terms, that she could readily comprehend it. In this he promised to forget and for-
give all that had happened ; and she having ac-
cidentally read the paper, sent an answer by the
same conveyance, mentioning her terms, and at the
end of three days returned to him without having
occasioned the least suspicion by her absence. The
printer is paid for this kind of correspondence, and
in general all articles which rather interest individuals

---

* In the year 1780, in London alone, 63,000 were printed ＼
every week.

duals than the public. He neither inquires concerning the name, the bufinefs, the intentions, or place of refidence of the advertifer. Thofe fpeculations which are written on national affairs and articles of intelligence are inferted gratis. The author is always fure of remaining undifcovered, by means of a box which opens towards the ftreet, and through which any perfon may thruft a manufcript. If you choofe to make yourfelf known to the printer, he is obliged to obferve fecrecy. Nothing can force him to violate this, for were he to do fo, he would not only lofe his bufinefs, but alfo have his houfe expofed to the fury of the populace.

He is obliged to anfwer for every thing he prints, whether it be a libel, a piece of fcandal, or a pafquinade. The offence, in any of thefe cafes, will fubject him to a procefs. If the king or parliament is attacked, the attorney-general is the accufer ; and on fuch occafions it is not unufual to fee the publifher defended by the moft famous advocates at the bar.

Woodfall, the printer of the Public Advertifer, once the moft famous newfpaper in London, was tried on account of Junius's celebrated letter to the king, which is a mafter-piece of eloquence, boldnefs and truth. All England was interefted in the iffue, and the moft famous lawyers were employed, not fimply to defend an individual, but to fupport that inviolable liberty which every Englifhman arrogates, of fpeaking or writing openly and without referve his fentiments of public affairs. Woodfall was declared innocent, and the procefs was terminated in fuch a manner, as made it impoffible to difcover the ingenious author, whofe name remains unknown to this very day. The critics pretend that it is the moft perfect profe compofition in the Englifh language. Certain expreffions, and a peculiar kind of genius.

genius exhibited throughout the whole, have made some suppose that the celebrated Edmund Burke is this same Junius.

It is not at all uncommon to see a printer put in the pillory, or dragged to gaol: by naming the author they escape these indignities: this, however, they never do without his consent. The reverend Mr. Horne Tooke, curate of Brentford, was so generous as to avow himself on an occasion of this kind in the year 1778.

This singular person, who, as a man, a patriot, and an orator, has acquired such high claims to the general esteem, and to the remembrance of his fellow-citizens in particular, as the founder of that celebrated * society, the end of which was to support the rights and privileges of the nation, had, in a newspaper, described the last war in America as a massacre; and the court party, who instituted and supported it, as so many assassins. The printer being prosecuted, and urged by the author, named him; and the intrepid clergyman was sentenced to twelve months imprisonment. Respect for his profession saved him from the pillory.

The manner in which the people often use the wretches condemned to this kind of punishment, renders it equally dangerous and disgraceful. Sometimes, however, so far from being infamous, it becomes glorious and honourable. I myself saw such a scene. It was a printer, who, while in the pillory, was attended by an innumerable multitude, by whom he was saluted with the utmost respect, and hailed with repeated acclamations. They brought him refreshments, and, as he could not use his hands, they themselves helped him. The pillory, which was crowned with garlands of flowers, was surrounded by persons of the first rank, who discoursed familiarly

* The bill of Rights.

familiarly with this lucky criminal; to whom, if I may fo exprefs myfelf, the pillory feemed a triumphal car ; and however conftrained the pofition in which he was obliged to ftand for an hour, that hour might be efteemed, perhaps, the moft agreeable in his life.

In the year 1779, 4,500 numbers of the Public Advertifer were printed every day during the winter, and 3,000 during the fummer; and of the Daily Advertifer, which contains little elfe but advertifements, no lefs than 5,000 were circulated. This kind of bufinefs is extremely lucrative, and maintains, in the city of London alone, a prodigious multitude of perfons : one with great propriety may fay, that a number of idlers are by this means brought up to do nothing. Among thefe may be reckoned the paragraph writers, who go to the coffee-houfes and public places to pick up anecdotes and the news of the day, which they reduce into fhort fentences, and are paid in proportion to their number and authenticity. The fpeeches in parliament are taken by a certain clafs of men who are known in no other country than England. The proficients in this art will not forget a fingle word, however faft the member may fpeak : their manner of writing is by means of certain figns, which not only exprefs words, but alfo whole fentences.

A newfpaper is alfo printed by the court, under the title of the Gazette. It is dearer, and at the fame time lefs interefting, than any of the others. The editor of this is a man of fome confequence, and generally a member of parliament, who repays the emoluments attached to his office by voting with the miniftry.

The Gazette contains all the acts of parliament ; the petitions ; the addreffes of the counties and villages ; the king's proclamations ; a lift of the promotions

in

in the army and navy ; the appointment to vacant employments, and all news of which they wiſh the people to be informed. During a war they inſert there the diſpatches from their generals and admirals, when they are flattering, taking care, however, to ſuppreſs all articles which may tend obliquely to cenſure themſelves. Every thing againſt their own party is ſuppreſſed.

Such was the practice of lord North. Lord Chatham followed an oppoſite method during his glorious adminiſtration. All the letters from the commanding officers were printed word for word, without the leaſt amendment or reſtriction : the public were informed of every thing even in the middle of the night. This manner of acting, at once ſo juſt and ſo candid, neceſſarily inſpired the nation with the moſt entire confidence in this great man.

It is to this paſſion among the Engliſh for reading, daily, the prodigious number of newſpapers and political pamphlets, that their extreme gravity and inſociable diſpoſition ought to be attributed.

In general nothing is more difficult than to make an Engliſhman ſpeak ; he anſwers to every thing by *yes* or *no*; addreſs him, however, on ſome political ſubject, and he is ſuddenly animated ; he opens his mouth, and becomes eloquent : for this ſeems to be connected from his infancy with his very exiſtence.

A foreigner will find himſelf exactly in the ſame predicament after a long reſidence in England. The ſame cauſe produces the ſame effect. I have known ſome, who, on their arrival in London, were entirely ignorant of politics, and who ſoon afterwards carried this taſte to enthuſiaſm. This matter is eaſily explained : it is in quality of the citizen of a free ſtate and as a rational creature, that one becomes ſolicitous about public affairs. Many are often

personally

perfonally interefted either by means of themfelves others; fome fearch into the charaĉters of
thofe who hold the reigns of government; thers
are conneĉted with them in the moft intimate manner. Nothing but politics is heard in any fociety:
they talk of nothing but about meetings to confider
of the affairs of the ftate, deputations to prefent
petitions, remenftrances, &c.

You may infert your opinions on any public
matter in the newfpapers, with a certainty of being
read a thoufand times. All thefe circumftances together infpire one with a lively intereft in the concerns of the kingdom, and occafion the reading of
the daily prints to be aĉtually an epidemical paffion
among the Englifh.

It is the cuftom no where but in England, to converfe with every body about thefe publications.
Strangers, therefore, are not qualified to judge of the
excellence of thefe communications, but by the good
effeĉts that refult from them. The anecdote of the
German emigrants, which I have before mentioned,
is a very convincing proof of this. If compaffion had
been ftimulated from every pulpit, or charity requefted by found of drum, fuch a generous dona-
tion could never have been obtained, as by means of
a fimple letter, read in all parts of London. The
whole of that extenfive capital was at one and the
fame inftant informed of this melancholy circumftance, whereas a fimple hearfay being always obfcure and equivocal, people of fenfe would have paid
no attention to it.

How many times have not the fame means been
employed to ferve the purpofes of patriotifm, and
to fupport fchemes combined with equal wifdom and
fagacity ! The greateft bleffings, unfortunately,
from the very nature of things, have their con-
comitant difadvantages, and fo it is with the newfpapers.

Without

Without adverting to the circumſtance of lord George Gordon, that dangerous fool, who, in 1780, made uſe of this means to aſſemble a mob, and put London in the moſt imminent danger, there are a number of rogues, who, by means of advertiſements, cheat the multitude in a thouſand different ways; and although the people are daily inſtructed by frequent examples, which ought to baniſh their credulity, they are ſtill diſpoſed to believe every impoſtor.

Among theſe are the money-lenders, who wiſh to advance ſums on good ſecurities; and who, after they have got poſſeſſion of the notes, bonds, &c. inſtantly diſappear and leave the perſon 'duped to lament his folly. Others make an affecting recital of the melancholy ſituation of a widow burthened with a large family, or of an old gentleman who languiſhes in the utmoſt miſery, and whoſe name they are obliged to conceal, on account of his extraction: they, however, never fail, with the moſt ſcrupulous exactneſs, to mention the place where donations will be received.

The public papers uſually abound with offers of large ſums to thoſe perſons who have ſufficient intereſt with the great, to procure lucrative employments: to this tranſaction inviolable ſecrecy is always pledged. Many authors alſo inſert criticiſms in them on their works, and next day attack their own judgments under a feigned name. Their ſole aim is to make a noiſe, and to be known, and they often attain it.

Women of the town, under the maſk of the moſt ſcrupulous virtue, teſtify their wiſhes to procure a huſband of good character.

They never fail to add, that they are rich, young and handſome; and affirm that they want nothing with their future ſpouſe, but a ſmall fortune, or a little employment. Young men bred in the country

try, and others without experience, often fall into
the snare. On an interview, they find these bewitching creatures, who appear as mild and gentle
as innocence itself, know how to affect their compassion, by a touching recital of the persecutions of
their relations or guardians; and never fail to make
it appear clearly, that it would be the easiest thing
in the world to get possession of their fortune. This
story has the proper effect; the simpleton believes
every thing, and never finds, till too late, that he
has been grossly imposed upon.

There are also male advertisers, who make similar proposals; with this difference, however, that,
instead of offering to share a large fortune, they generally wish to meet a lady with one. If they are
not able to enumerate a catalogue of their personal
accomplishments, they are sure to boast of their good
sense, their excellent character; and in one word,
of their inclination to consult, on all occasions, the
happiness of their future wives. These latter sometimes succeed, but less frequently than the former.

Some people insert advertisements of this kind
merely from pastime. Under different signatures
they pretend to want husbands and wives, and
manage interviews between the persons who answer
them: this often gives occasion to the most comical
scenes.

But no men know better how to profit by the
newspapers than the stock-jobbers. They declare
war or peace at their pleasure, sign treaties of alli-
ance, and fabricate events, which they seem to sub-
stantiate with so much address, that they have all the
appearance of reality. By such arts, immense sums
are lost and won every day.

From the newspaperss which form a very lucrative branch of trade, the government have found
means to draw one hundred thousand pounds annually. Every paper pays three halfpence to the revenue

venue in ftamp-duty, and a tax of two fhillings and
fixpence is impofed on each advertifement.

All periodical publications are charged with a
certain impoft, and among thefe the pamphlets that
are daily printed and forgotten.

As I am now mentioning publications of this kind,
I fhall fay fomething of that celebrated paper called the
North Briton. The forty-fifth number of this gave rife
to a very fingular event; no publication, indeed, was
ever attended with fuch fingular confequences. It
occafioned a mifunderftanding betwixt the people
and the legiflative power of that puiffant empire,
which lafted more than ten years, and put the conftitution in the utmoft danger. It robbed the king
of the affections of his people, immortalized Wilkes,
the author, and eftablifhed minifterial influence for
ever.

As this circumftance, fo interefting for the philofopher, the politician, and every man of reflection,
is not well known in Germany, and the conduct of
Wilkes has been grofsly mifreprefented, I imagine
that it will not be improper here, to give a recital
of the whole, equally true and circumftantial.

The adminiftration of lord Bute, which commenced with the reign of the prefent king, and which
had for its firft-fruits the unpopular peace of 1762,
greatly difpleafed the nation. His Lordfhip was a
Scotfman; he difmiffed a great number of the
Englifh from their employments, to beftow them
on his countrymen; and this impolitic conduct
greatly added to the general difcontent. Wilkes
happened then to be a member of the Houfe of
Commons, in which he had fat two former parliaments. He poffeffed a found judgment, an enlightened mind, a profound knowledge of the rights
of the nation, a courage and a firmnefs that fitted
him for any enterprife; he was, however, deftitute
of one quality of the greateft importance in his fituation:

ation:- he was but a poor orator. After having dif-
fipated a confiderable fortune, he folicited a lucrative poft. Two forts of employment were the ob-
jeéts of his ambition; he wifhed to be a governor
of one of the American provinces, or ambaffador
to the Porte. He afks one of thefe from lord Bute:
that nobleman promifes to gratify his inclinations,
and difappoints him. This conduét irritated Wilkes:
as he wrote infinitely better than he fpoke, he feized
the pen, and cunningly profiting by the difcontent
of the people, attacked the minifter. This was almoft the fole intention of the periodical paper, entitled the North Briton. The fubjeét was ample,
and the imprudent conduét of lord Bute furnifhed
him with materials. That minifter burnt with revenge, and wanted nothing but a favourable opportunity to gratify it: one foon prefented itfelf.

The fpeech which the king makes to his parliament is always compofed by the minifter. Being
firft read and criticifed in the council of ftate, notwithftanding it is delivered by the fovereign, it may
be confidered as coming from the court party. His
majefty, when addreffing himfelf to both houfes on
the peace of Verfailles in 1762, made ufe of thefe
expreffions: " after having, in concert with my
" good brother the king of Pruffia, figned the *peace*
&c." All thofe who are the leaft acquainted with
the political hiftory of the times, muft recolleét in
what manner this peace was concerted betwixt them:
it is an anecdote well known in England; therefore Wilkes did not hefitate to obferve in one of
his periodical papers, that the affertion was a *falfe-
bood*. Lord Bute, under pretence that fuch an expreffion was a perfonal attack on the monarch, immediately caufed him to be feized, and imprifoned
in the Tower.

In this he followed the example of feveral of his
predeceffors, who before had exerted a fimilar
authority

authority; with this difference, however, that it was always in cafes of *high treafon*.

According to the *habeas corpus act*, the prifoner has a right to invefligate the procefs againft him, and fee if his confinement is conformable to the laws of the land. Wilkes accordingly claimed that privilege a few days after.

The Englifh nation was interefted in the event, becaufe the rights of every citizen were affected by it. Wilkes, the champion of the people, fupported by the firft and moft celebrated lawyers in the kingdom, prefents himfelf before his judges, accompanied by an innumerable multitude, who waited the iffue of this important affair with the greateft impatience. Judgment was given in his favour. He was declared innocent of the accufation; and the lords Egremont and Hallifax, who had figned the warrant, were declared to pay 5000l. fterling as damages.

They had gone fo far as to feize and examine his papers. Wilkes, therefore, the moment that he was releafed, repairs to Sir John Fielding, a celebrated juftice of the peace, to requeft from him a warrant to apprehend the two minifters; whom he treated as thieves, who had pillaged his dwelling-houfe. The magiftrate did not accede to this demand: however, the boldnefs of the proceeding did Mr. Wilkes a great deal of honour.

In the mean time fome of his papers gave his enemies, who were undoubtedly the moft powerful men in the kingdom, an opportunity to commence a new procefs againft him. Being unwilling to wait the event, he leaves England, and travels through France and Italy. His profecutors, profiting by his abfence, procure judgment againft him; and a majority of the Houfe of Commons being in the intereft of the court, he is expelled the parliament.

D   Being

Being foon after deftitute of money, and perfecuted by his foreign creditors, he finds himfelf conftrained to return to his native country. He accordingly repairs to London, in confequence of a bold plan which he had concerted ; and the prudence and firmnefs with which he accomplifhed it, were at laft crowned with the moft complete fuccefs. His firft ftep was to prefent himfelf before the court which had given judgment againft him : there he receives a fentence of imprifonment for two years in the king's bench. He fubmits to it, and goes to furrender himfelf: the populace however, try to prevent him, and he is obliged to conceal himfelf in a tavern. His defign was to remain there till the tumult was abated ; but this was in vain. The houfe was actually befieged ; and the mob, inftead of difperfing, became every moment more numerous. Having remained till night, Wilkes, who was determined to obey the laws, put a fcheme in execution which never had been practifed before. We hear every day of people difguifing themfelves to efcape out of prifon ; but, till then, I believe, no one ever difguifed himfelf to get into one. This was actually done by him ; and, in confequence of it, he arrived in the king's bench.

This prifon, fituated in St. George's Fields, was furrounded next day by a prodigious crowd. They intended to have demolifhed this enormous mafs from its very foundation, and thus deliver their favourite. This project was about to be executed, when Wilkes appears at a window, and, by means of prayers and entreaties, prevents them. The tumult was not, however, appeafed until the arrival of the military ; who, by the blood of fome of the ringleaders, put an end to the ftrange fcene. A young man of low extraction, called Allen, was killed on this occafion. His death, which in any other country would have fcarce been mentioned in a newfpaper, was treated as if it had been an affair of confequence.

consequence. The people became outrageous, moderate men murmured, the ministers trembled, and the king himself was displeased with the event.

In the mean time Wilkes lived very comfortably in prison. He received a number of visits daily; persons of the first rank and most distinguished merit went to see him, and offer their services.

His wants were supplied, and the society called the Bill of Rights paid all the debts which he had contracted in England, and which were very considerable.

He was, at the same time, elected knight of the shire for the county of Middlesex.

His confinement in 1770 was the signal for new troubles. The House of Commons, who looked on him as incapable of sitting in parliament on account of his expulsion, chose Colonel Luttrell in his place, as representative for the county of Middlesex, although that gentleman had but a few votes in his favour. This was looked upon as an attempt against the fundamental principles of the constitution; for all the legislative body united, and still less the House of Commons, have not power to reject a member chosen according to the proper forms.

Relying on the goodness of his cause, Wilkes defies the Commons, who were now abhorred by the whole nation, and treated by them in the most contemptuous manner. It would have been easy for him to have resumed his place in the house, and to have maintained himself there by the assistance of an hundred thousand of his adherents. Such an act of violence would have been attended with consequences entirely different from those of lord George Gordon's, whose party was composed entirely of the dregs of the people. Wilkes had, on

the

other hand, the best and wisest part of the nation in his favour; nay, even a third of that very parliament which he bullied. Some of his friends advised him to carry things to extremities; but this he would not consent to, and waited peaceably for a dissolution of parliament.

Notwithstanding the intrigues of the ministry, he was, during these transactions, elected an alderman of London, appointed one of the sheriffs of the county of Middlesex, and at last, in the year 1774, chosen lord mayor. His ambition was now fully satisfied, but the essential part of his scheme was still unaccomplished; he wished to possess wealth, and he attained it. In the year 1778, he was elected to the important and lucrative office of chamberlain of the city; an appointment that entirely satisfied all his wishes.

If a design wisely concerted, seconded by uncommon talents, by astonishing courage and firmness, and carried on to its completion with a perseverance that nothing could dishearten; if all these, I say, have a claim to our admiration, Wilkes surely is entitled to it.

Had he so pleased, he might have become the Catiline of his country: he abhorred the idea, and chose to be her benefactor.

On more than one occasion he has actually been so. During the lawless tumult occasioned by lord George Gordon, when the ministry trembled and remained inactive, and the magistrates durst not leave their houses, he was seen presenting himself to the tumultuous populace, and braving death itself to save the bank, which they were about to pillage. He made use of prayers, entreaties, and menaces by turns; he even went so far as to seize some of the ringleaders with his own hands. This behaviour, so courageous and so patriotic, restored him to the regard of his sovereign, fovereign, who, for twenty years, had vowed a mortal hatred againft him. He is at this very moment one of the moft active partizans of the minifter.

It was in the year 1772, when Wilkes was only an alderman, that Crofby, then lord mayor, had a fingular difpute with the Houfe of Commons, which, if detailed with fidelity, would better characterife the conftitution, the manners, and the ideas of the Englifh than whole volumes written on the fubject. Far from thinking that this anecdote compofed part of the hiftory of our own times, one would be tempted to imagine himfelf tranfported by the power of magic to fome country of romance, or carried back to that happy period when the fplendour of Rome and Greece fhone unrivalled in the world. This event, and indeed almoft every thing that concerns England, is only known in Germany by means of the newfpapers, and therefore muft be very little underftood.

A pamphlet having been publifhed, containing many reflections on the Houfe of Commons, they declared it a libel, and gave orders to the ferjeant at arms to feize the two printers who had publifhed it. This officer accordingly repairs to the city, where they happened to refide, with an intention to execute the commiffion. By his inftructions, he was not to attend the common forms, notwithftanding it is illegal to arreft any one in the city without having the warrant backed by the chief magiftrate.

One of the printers allows himfelf to be taken without the leaft refiftance. According to law, the prifoner muft be carried before a juftice of the peace, to fee whether the detention is legal; and this the officer of the Houfe of Commons complied with, notwithftanding his order was an emanation of the legiflative authority.

D 3

On his arrival at Guildhall, Wilkes and Oliver happened to be on the bench. On examining the warrant, these two aldermen, observing that Crosby's signature was not affixed, declare it to be informal, and release the printer.

The serjeant at arms, covered with confusion, departs to look after the other culprit, with whom he hopes to be more fortunate : for, as it was now dinner-time, he imagined that these two magistrates would depart ; and hoped, on his return, to find others more compliant.

Full of this idea, he goes to the other printer ; but he being better acquainted with the laws, insists on seeing the warrant ; and not finding it signed by the lord mayor, he immediately sends for a constable, secures the officer, and accompanies him to Guildhall, attended by a prodigious crowd. The aldermen being gone to dine with the lord mayor, the the prisoner is conducted to the mansion-house.

Crosby had the reputation of being a worthy man, but his knowledge was very superficial. It was only on account of his seniority and his wealth that he had been appointed to the high office which he then filled. His ambition was limited, and so was also his patriotism. His advanced age made him sigh after repose, and he had no wish for any thing else. The issue of this affair would, therefore, have been entirely different, if he had been allowed to proceed according to his own inclination : he was, however, obliged from circumstances to act in concert with his colleagues.

Wilkes and Oliver were the two most strenuous assertors of public liberty in the whole corporation of London. We have already given the character of the one : the other was a member of parliament, and equal to him in patriotism. Oliver was also a man of character, and had a noble and independent way of thinking.

Guided

Guided by these men, Crosby calls in the printer, hears his complaint, and orders the serjeant at arms to be carried to prison.

This act of authority occasioned a prodigious disturbance; and Crosby, Oliver, and Wilkes were summoned to appear before the House of Commons. The two first obey, and go in procession from the city, attended by several hundred carriages belonging to people of the first rank. Wilkes also accompanies them to the door; but, as he would not be permitted to appear as one of the members of Middlesex, he proceeds no further.

At their arrival, they are received with shouts of applause by a prodigious concurse of people, who surrounded the house, and mal-treated all those who were of the court party.

Lord North, who had been the most violent against the city magistrates, had procured two hundred of the guards to protect himself and his friends; but fearing that so small a number could not save him from an incensed populace, who threatened his destruction, he gets into a hackney coach, accompanied by a valet, and attempts to steal into the house in disguise.

This project, however, was unsuccessful; he is known, the horses are stopped, and he himself is dragged by the hair, and exposed to a thousand indignities.

The existence of this man, to whom England unfortunately gave birth, now hung suspended by a thread: but the destinies resolved that he should still live for the unhappiness of thousands of his equals. The soldiers having come to his assistance, and two of his creatures having generously shielded him with their own bodies, he was at last snatched from a certain death.—Having thus escaped the fate of the unhappy De Witt, he repairs to parliament, disfigured and almost unknown. He begins

with

with recounting his sad adventure, while his eyes stream with tears, in that hypocritical tone which had been so successful with Cromwell He beseeches Heaven to bear witness to his innocence, and the uprightness of his intentions ; which having no other end than the good of the nation, gave him a claim on the gratitude, rather than the curses of his fellow-citizens.

In this state of anxiety and grief, trembling lest the horrible scene, from which he had just escaped, should be renewed, he proposes to the accused member to repair, by an immediate apology, the irregularity of their conduct ; assuring them, that the house was disposed to accept a very slight one.

Oliver rejects this proposition with the utmost scorn ; adding, that to expect an apology from those who had supported the rights of their fellow-citizens, was the grossest insult ; and that he and his adherents ought rather to offer excuses to he whole nation for their mal-administration. Crosby being of the same opinion, they were, by a plurality of voices, sent to the Tower.

The Tower is not a horrible prison, like the Bastile ; it rather resembles a little town, abounding with tradesmen and artizans of every kind. A prodigious number of people reside there, and the apartments are very commodious. Crosby and Oliver, on their arrival, hired two little houses ; and the numerous visits of their friends scarcely allowed them to perceive that they were prisoners.

While confined here, extraordinary honours were conferred on them ; and it might be esteemed by both as the most happy epocha in their lives. Every ward in the city sent them deputations. These went in form, accompanied by an immense crowd of carriages, and in the name of the people of England, thanked them

for

for having courageously defended the rights of their
fellow-citizens, and sacrificed so generously their
own liberty for the public welfare. Besides this,
several cities, counties, and associations returned
them thanks; sent them their freedom and accompanied it with gifts. London in particular
presented them with two massy cups of gold, on
which the arms of the city were engraved.

It is impossible to recollect without admiration the fervour and patriotic enthusiasm which
prevailed every where during three weeks, at the
end of which time the parliament was proro-
gued.

On this occasion the magistrates of London,
clothed in their robes the sheriffs of the county
of Middlesex, the common-council, all the militia of the city, and an immense crowd of distinguished persons, repaired to the Tower, accompanied by drums, cymbals, and trumpets,
to receive the two prisoners. Being placed in
the state-coach, they were conducted to the Mansion-house in triumph, amidst the ringing of bells,
the firing of cannon, and every other demonstration
of joy. The windows were crowded with beauties, who waved their handkerchiefs and added
to the public triumph. The general enthusiasm
cannot be well described: I myself saw many
weep for joy, and realise the witty remark of
of lord Shaftesbury, who says, that enthusiasm
is epidemic, and, like yawning, affects every
body around.

Let the reader recollect, that all this was
transacted, not in the corner of a distant province, but in the midst of the residence of a
powerful monarch; that the ministers, whose
authority is very great, were the enemies and
the prosecutors of the two prisoners; and that
this was not a tumult or a revolt, but a public

act

- act which the laws, far from prohibiting, feemed rather to authorife.

I fhall never forget this memorable fcene;—with me it fhall always be facred. It is engraven in my mind in never-fading charaɛters, and can only be effaced with my exiftence.

———————

CHAPTER III.

The Fertility of England—Its Climate, Productions, and Induftry—Society of Arts—Duke of Bridge-water's Canal—Extraordinary Inventions—Wedgewood's Manufactures—Mrs. Abington—Beggars of Rank—Calas—Colonel Champigny—Societies of Rogues.

THE fouth of Great Britain is almoft an entire flat, and contains but very few mountains. If the the principality of Wales, and fome of the northern counties, be excepted, all that immenfe ifland refembles a garden, adorned with fine views and romantic profpects, which do not yield in any thing to thofe parts of Italy which are fo much extolled. The riches of the inhabitants; the neatnefs and cleanlinefs of their manner of living, which is difcoverable in the very cottages; the noble roads; and a fertile and well cultivated foil, form one *great whole*, which the moft phlegmatic obferver is forced to admire.

The greateft objection that can be urged againft England is the infalutrity of the air, and the indifpenfable cuftom of burning coals.

It

It is true that the climate is subject to frequent changes, but it is generally supportable both in the summer and winter. It is not bad health, but a love of variety and diſſipation, that drives ſo many rich Engliſhmen to the ſouth of France, either to ſquander their guineas there, or to economiſe in a country where every thing is ſold at a low price, after they have hurt their fortunes at home. As the reaſon of theſe journeys is not very flattering to their pride, they diſguiſe it under the pretence of the badneſs of their native air.

As to the Engliſh who have ſpent part of their lives in the Indies, and who have been of courſe uſed to a warmer ſun, it is very evident that they muſt feel, in a very lively manner, the difference on their return, and that the air of Provence will be more genial to them than that of England.

It was this circumſtance which obliged the celebrated lord Clive to ſpend two years of his life at Montpelier; where he hoped a long time, but in vain, to diſſipate thoſe hypochondriac humours with which he was tormented. He carried them back to England where they changed to a profound melancholy: which, after preying for ſome time on his body, at laſt became victorious, and conſtrained him, as it were, to deprive himſelf of exiſtence. Notwithſtanding the care of his family to conceal the manner of his death, all the world ſoon knew, that the vanquiſher and ſcourge of Aſia, hanged himſelf in his own bed-chamber.

What will fully evince, how little the climate and uſe of coal-fires are hurtful to the health of the Engliſh, is the great number of old men who may there be met with conſtantly. On reading the liſt of deaths, one readily perceives that this claſs of men is equal, if not more numerous in that than in any other country in Europe. How is it poſſible that we ſhould find ſo many aged people in London, where

the

the confumption of this kind of fuel is exceffive, if it were hu tful ? How comes it, that it does not affect the women, and that the complexion of the English is fuperior to that of all the other Europeans ?

The plague has ever been uncommon in England; and this is a high proof in favour of the goodnefs of the climate. To this may be added the healthy conflitutions of the natives, their vigour, intrepidity, and perpetual exertions. All the carpenters, black-fmith, farriers, miners, porters, and peafants are the moft robuft men in the world. Charles II. who had vifited a good part of Europe, was ufed to fay: "Notwithftanding all the complaints of the dif- "agreeablenefs and inconftancy of the climate of "my native country, it is neverthelefs certain, that "there is no part in Europe, where it is poffible to "be out of doors for fo many days in the year, or fo many hours in a day, as in England." They never experience inundations, fo hurtful in other countries; tempefts, earthquakes, and famine, are equally unknown to them.

The grafs in England is always of an unrivalled beauty, verdure, and extraordinary goodnefs. From hence proceeds the uncommon attachment of the Englifh to thofe fine lawns, which they fmooth and keep even by means of ftone rollers: they are fome-times fo very regular, that you may play at bowls on them with as much nicety as you could on a billiard table. This is a favourite diverfion, and is often en-joyed by people of the firft rank.

Every part of the country abounds with parks, which are adorned with the moft agreeable and ro-mantic landfcapes. Almoft at every ftep you meet with ally of fruit-trees, which conduct you to charming villages; the inhabitants of which are well fed and clothed, and in a ftate of plenty and a undance, fufficient to prove that theirs is the native country of riches, liberty, and improvement.

Neverthelefs

Nevertheless there is not in the whole island, either a society or an individual, whose business it is to animate this universal industry, or to bring agriculture, trade, or manufactures, to a greater degree of perfection. As no one is there limited in his rights, or disturbed in the possession of his property, all these advantages naturally accrue of themselves. To the same causes the flourishing state of Holland may be attributed. But however instructive the example of these two states may seem to be, one is nevertheless authorised to believe, from the conduct of almost all the sovereigns in Europe, that they have unanimously endeavoured to stifle that industry which in itself is so precious, and in its consequences so necessary to the grandeur of a state.

Some time since the minister, to augment the number of his dependants, formed the design of erecting a board to watch over the interests of trade. The project was carried into execution: but trade, so far from increasing, declined the moment that these counsellors of commerce began to give her lessons. Of this, authentic proofs were produced, and it was abolished in 1782. Mr. Gibbon, the English Tacitus, was a member of this institution.

The banks of the Thames, from Gravesend to London, are adorned with towns and villages; and the neighbourhood occupied by a prodigious number of builders, who are continually employed in the construction of ships of all dimensions, and of every kind. The river itself is covered with vessels, which are moored in rows, for several miles.

The great industry that reigns every where, forms the most agreeable spectacle. Several thousands live solely by their employments about the shipping. The coal-trade alone occupies an amazing number; the consumption to this article is inconceivable. I have seen a fleet of fifty sail arrive at once from Newcastle, and have been well assured that this is

not

at all extraordinary. The labourers who unload
these colliers receive nine shillings per day. The
coal-mines of Newcastle were not discovered till the
fifteenth century ; they are equally valuable as if
they produced gold. The trade of this mineral so necessary in Great Britain, is increasing, and has even been
doubled since the year 1700. It is easy to conceive
a proper idea of the wealth of that town, formerly
so little known, by observing that the revenues of the
corporation amount to nine thousand pounds a year.

An increase of buildings is visible in all the great
cities throughout England : in respect to London,
it is greatly disapproved, and not without reason.
This, however, does not immediately proceed from
itself, for the villages with which it is surrounded,
and which augment daily, by their additional popula-
tion, contribute greatly to its inhabitants.

The town of Stockton, which was but a hamlet a
few years since, now sends upwards of a hundred
and fifty. vessels every year to the metropolis. In
1778, six hundred thousand sheep belonged to Dor-
chester alone.

Commerce increases daily in Hull, Bristol, Plymouth, Liverpool, &c. it is the same with manufactures. Neither the revolution that has taken place
in regard to trade, nor the loss of the American colonies, has in the least decreased them. The city of
Exeter vended stuffs in the year 1779 to the amount
of a million sterling, a sum which almost seems
incredible.

Trade now flourishes in almost an equal proportion in Scotland. Edinburgh, Glasgow, Aberdeen,
and Elgin are full of excellent manufactures.

The Scots hitherto neglected the herring fishery ;
they left it entirely to the Dutch, who came annually to their coasts, and enjoyed, undisturbed, that
lucrative branch of commerce : they themselves
now participate in its advantanges. The town of

Inverneſs alone employs five hundred veſſels and three thouſand fiſhermen. Eight hundred ſhallops and ſix thouſand fiſhermen are employed in the river Forth, which this fiſh frequents during two months of the year, and procure a ſufficient quantity to fill forty thouſand barrels: one ſixth part is conſumed in the country ; the reſt is exported. This exportation produces annually twenty thouſand pounds ſterling. Several of the neighbouring towns alſo partake in the fiſhery ; Glaſgow itſelf ſhips three thouſand barrels every year for the foreign market.

It is the ſame in regard to the ſalmon. Aberdeen ſends a hundred quintals annually to London, and Yarmouth ninety.

Many naturaliſts are of opinion that in Hampſhire, where the air is pure and the climate warm, the vine and fig-tree might be cultivated to great advantage.

A letter is preſerved in the Philoſophical Tranſactions of the Royal Society, from Henry Barham to Sir Hans Sloane, written in the year 1719, in which he aſſerts that he had produced ſilk at Chelſea, which thoſe who were converſant on the ſubject, had declared to be equal to that of Piedmont.

It is well know that there were many vineyards formely in England. That old and celebrated record, called Doomſday-book, expreſsly ſays, that, before the Norman conqueſt, wine was made in the county of Eſſex.

It is but a few years ſince this intereſting production was diſcovered. It begins with the time of William the Conqueror, and contains a circumſtantial detail of the inventory which that monarch cauſed to be taken of all the produce of the kingdom ; and a liſt of all the manors, fiefs, rents, &c. This book is very difficult to decypher, being a mixture of French and bad German, written for the moſt
part

part in Gothic characters. In consequence of this there are but very few, even of the learned, who can read the manuscript. The English, for a long time, looked upon it as merely an hieroglyphic, of which they could only interpret some passages, till, on the arrival of Raspe in England, it happened to fall into his hands.

That illustrious and intelligent man, who had been for many years employed in the German libraries, was very capable of cutting this Gordian knot : of this he gave sufficient proofs. The government was eager to know its contents ; but as many of the first families in the kingdom imagined themselves in some shape interested in the translation, they did not think it prudent to entrust it to a foreigner. A learned Englishman was therefore preferred to Raspe, on whose assistance he greatly depended, on accepting this important and difficult commission : unhappily, however, they quarrelled, and Doomsbook was not translated.

The industry of the English has often received a new degree of energy from the assistance of my countrymen, the Germans. One of them called Spielman constructed, in the reign of Elizabeth, the first paper-mill. Gottfried Box, another, 1590, erected the first machine for the manufacturing of brass-wire, and afterwards another for copper-plates. Under the reign of the same queen a third built the first powder-mill. At this very day the best bookbinder in London, and an artist so famous in his trade, that his equal has never yet been found, is also a German.

My country was very near snatching from the English the honour of producing the best clockmaker, an art in which they so much excel, and of gaining the premium which the parliament had assigned in the time-piece which would best discover the longitude at sea. The sum allotted for this useful

ful difcovery was twenty thoufand pounds. A great number of the firft artifts in Europe, animated by the allurements of glory and of gain, became canditates for this reward; but an Englifhman, of the name of Harrifon, carried away both. It is, however, probable that a watch-maker of the name of Thiele de Breine would have fupplanted him, if this excellent artifan had carried his watch to London before the payment of the reward: for, in the opinion of the Englifh themfelves, his mechanifm was more ingenioufly comftructed, and much more likely than Harrifon's to obtain the end propofed.

It is incredible how much, and by how many different means, induftry is excited in England.

Without reckoning the ufual fums which parliament votes annually in bounties, new objects are continually craving their patronage. Several patriotic focieties, which labour with a zeal for the general good, worthy of admiration, follow their example.

The moft numerous one that has ever exifted in Europe, is the fociety for the encouragement of arts, manufactures, &c. It was founded in 1753, by William Shipley, and confifted, in 1784, of fix thoufand feven hundred members. The firft noblemen in the ration belong to this inftitution. Every member pays two guineas a year, and this fubfcription from a fum fufficient for the diftribution of a great many premiums, and thofe of a confiderable value.

Thefe rewards are always deftined to perfons who by original inventions have become ferviceable to mankind, or by an improvement of former difcoveries, have carried them to a higher degree of perfection.

Their meetings rarely confift of more than two hundred perfons; the reft very feldom attend, and content themfelves with contributing, by their pecuniary affiftance, to the noble defign of this ufeful eftablifhment establishment. It is not to be doubted that this is the sole motive, as no kind of honour nor any mark of distinction is attached to the members. The principle intention is to improve agriculture, and the arts, by keeping up a constant correspondence with persons of every rank and station, who project schemes likely to be attended with good consequences, or communicate experiments already made, whether unsuccessful or prosperous. Lord Romney has been for many years the president.

Another society has been formed in Brecknock-shire, a county situated in the principality of Wales. The object of this institution is agriculture in all its branches, the establishment of manufactures of linen cloth, and the improvement of woollens. They also attend to the reparation of the great roads, and the construction of new ones: in one word, their plan is to give to industry a greater degree of activity and extension.

It is to one man that England is indebted for her inland navigation. Till 1759 the project was not carried into execution; and all the rivers and streams in the island were soon after covered with boats. This benefactor to his country was the Duke of Bridgwater, who has immortalized himself by the construction of a canal, which would not disgrace a monarch. He was only twenty-one years of age, when he conceived this design, worthy of ancient Rome.

His artificial river unites the city of Liverpool with the populous town of Manchester. It is sometimes carried across immense rocks hollowed at top. Sometimes it suddenly vanishes, and makes a thousand turnings in a subterraneous passage eight English miles in length. After appearing all at once it seems suspended in the air, and crosses the Wevil by means of immense arches, in such a manner that one may even enjoy the picturesque sight of one

vessel

veffel navigating in the ftream below, and of another which croffes it, and feems to fail in the ele-
ment above.

An Englifhman of the name of Wedgewood has
built a whole village in Staffordfhire, which he
has called Etruria, a name well merited by its fuperb
works in the Etrufcan ftyle, which have become remarkable on account of the elegant forms into which
the various manufactures are fhaped. This perfon has
realifed an original idea, and acquired great wealth
and celebrity. He has chofen for his models every
thing that Italy and Greece has left moft perfect in
its kind, and which we ftill admire in Florence, Rome
and Naples. He poffeffes exact drawings of all the
ancient fculptures which have been preferved from
Gothic barbarity and the wafte of time, and copies
them with great exactnefs in his productions.

Of his vafes, &c. fome are gilded, others are
enamelled. He employs a great number of workmen, and has acquired a confiderable fortune.

It was in the year 1771 that Cox engaged in an
extraordinary enterprife. He knew that the princes
of Afia held our mechanical inventions in the higheft
eftimation; he was aware, however, that nothing
which was not adorned with gold, filver, and precious ftones, had any attraction for them. Every
thing of this kind which they have to ornament
their palaces, are clumfy and very badly executed.
His project, therefore, was to join the magic of
art to the impofing appearance of riches. A confiderable fortune added to a genius at once fubtle and
inventive, furnifhed him with the means.

The moft fkilful artifts in England and France,
fuch as jewellers, clock-makers, goldfmiths, &c.
were employed, and paid to exert their utmoft
fkill.

Every thing that they undertook was performed
with uncommon care and ingenuity, and he foon
beheld

beheld himself possessed of a number of mechanical inventions, unrivalled in point of excellence.

Cox was resolved to send this collection to Asia; he, however, kept it nine years in London, and shewed the whole by means of tickets, at half a guinea each. I myself have frequently seen it, and always with fresh admiration. Never was taste and grandeur, all the skill of mechanicks, and the magic of opticks, united in such a high degree of perfection. The eye met with nothing but gold, diamonds, and precious stones, which were shaped into the forms of a variety of animals, assumed their gestures, and seemed to be alive; birds of different kinds and of exquisite plumage sung the most ravishing notes; the swan of Europe swam in artificial rivers; the hare and partridges ran about in groves, planted by the hands of the most cunning workmen; while camels, elephants, and other productions of Asia, stalked around, and imitated nature with a scrupulous exactitude.

But the most romantic object in all this astonishing assemblage, was a castle six feet in height: it seemed to realise all the ideas which the imagination of the warmest poets, could conceive of a palace in fairy land.

This superb collection, in which the precious metals seemed to constitute the least valuable parts, cost more than a hundred thousand pounds. The present emperor of China received a similar one from Cox in 1759: it is placed by the side of his throne in the grand audience chamber at Pekin. That of which I speak was destined for the Great Mogul, but the enormous debts which the ingenious artist was obliged to contract, and of which the interest alone amounted to a great sum, unfortunately prevented him from completing his design. A part only was sent to the East, the rest was disposed of in London, by means of a lottery. Thus

the

the hope of forming a new branch of trade with Asia was defeated perhaps for ever. From this, not only England, but other countries might have drawn the greatest advantages.

Doctor Graham, a Scotchman by birth, in the year 1780, by means of his Celestial Bed, which cost him several thousand pounds, gave at once a proof of the *wealth* and the *cullibility* of the English. He called his house the *Temple* of *Health*, and acted as the high priest of that puissant goddess; in this capacity he affirmed that he joined the useful to the agreeable, and all the wonders of art to the precious secrets of his profession. Nothing, indeed, could be more superb than this temple; the electric fluid managed with uncommon skill, was darted around in beautiful irradiation; transparent glass of various colours chosen and placed with taste; valuable vases filled with the most exquisite aromatics, which awakened and softened the passions, and inspired the soul with a soft langour, were the first objects that presented themselves to the observation of the curious.

This modern Esculapius had undoubtedly founded his scheme on a perfect knowledge of the human heart; and the success that crowned his strange enterprise proved that he was not wrong in his calculation. Indeed it could not fail to succeed, for I really think that the sensual pleasures are carried as far, not to say farther, in London than in Paris.

Graham put an end to this farce about two years after it commenced, by selling his grand electrical apparatus, his instruments of musick, and, finally, his celestial bed.

Mrs. Abington, the celebrated actress, is engaged in a very singular occupation. As she possesses an exquisite taste, she is constantly employed in driving about the capital to give her advice

vice

vice concerning the modes and fashions of the day.
She is called in like a physician, and recompensed
as if she were an artist. There never is a marriage
or ball in which she is not consulted. A great
number of people of fashion treat her in the most
familiar manner, and as if she were their equal.
As she never appears on the stage but in the most
elegant dress, her taste is sure to be copied by all the
ladies who happen to be spectators. It is there that
this priestess of the fashions displays all her art,
being certain that she will be immediately copied
with the most trivial exactness.

In the same manner that the philosophical disci-
ples of antiquity imposed silence on the inconsiderate scholars, by observing, *our master has said thus*;
so it is sufficient for the beauties of London to observe *Mrs. Abington has worn such a thing*, to shut
the mouths of their fathers and their husbands. In
her contract with the manager of Drury-Lane in
the year 1781, it was agreed that the sum of five
hundred pounds sterling should be annually allowed
for her wardrobe; besides this she received eighteen
guineas every night that she acted, and a benefit at
the end of the season.

In a city such as London, where so many weak
people who happen to be affluent reside, it is not at
all-surprising that artful impostors should by means
of tricks and stratagems endeavour to avail themselves of the wealth of these fools.

Every thing is thought fair as long as the do not
transgress the laws; thus a number of quacks of
every kind exercise their various professions in peace
and security.

About twelve months since, a person appeared in
London who pretended to possess the secret of cutting the finger and toe nails in a manner so as to
render the hands and feet much more elegant and
beautiful *. Having

* This man advertised as a chiropedist.

Having this appealed to female vanity, the English ladies were enraptured with the fascinating idea of becoming more lovely, and this fellow being continually employed, was enabled to reside in an elegant house, and keep a fine carriage. He lived in this manner for two whole years, got a great deal of money and at the end of that time suddenly disappeared, leaving debts behind him to the amount of three thousand pounds.

Another trade practised in London is that of begging. It is indeed very uncommon to see an Englishman who is not one of the very lowest of the people asking for charity, although foreigners of good birth, and who appear to have received a certain degree of education, exercise that shameful profession among them, and subsist without much trouble. These do not stop people in the streets, where they would receive nothing but trifles, or at most a little silver. Being well dressed they get adttance into houses of people of distinction, shew proofs and documents, which for the most part are forged, and receive gold from the inhabitants, who are generally credulous and beneficient.

I knew an Italian, formerly in the theatre at St. Petersburgh, who, although he could neither read nor write, after he had procured another rogue to draw up a patent for him, gave himself out as a Russian colonel. Provided with this false diploma, he entered with inconceivable impudence into the first houses in London, would not be stopped by any servant, penetrated into the inner apartments, at last got sight of the master, and never quitted him without receiving a present.

It was in vain that the Russian minister discovered the roguery of this fellow; he could only inform a very small number of persons: the Italian still found out new benefactors, whom he imposed upon by means of his patent, and while he preserved

it

it with care, it would have been very difficult to
have punished him, After having practised similar
arts for three years, he left England with a confiderable sum of money, and is at this present moment at Dunkirk.

A Frenchman had a still better plan. He pretended to be the son of the unfortunate Calas, who,
as it is well known, lives in France, and is a physician. The general compassion for this unfortunate
family opened every door in London to him: he
received considerable presents, and departed with
great wealth.

This trade, so singularly lucrative in that country, had so many attractions for a M. de Champigny, formerly a colonel in the service of France,
and who arrived in London soon after the German
war, that he reduced it to a system, and followed
the profession with the most uncommon success.
He never went on foot, but (is it to be believed?)
in a brilliant equipage that belonged to him, and
very often the most elegant entertainments. As he
possessed a knowledge of the world, he knew how
to exercise his skill with so much success, that even
those persons who passed for misers, opened their
purses to him without any difficulty. To the few
who hesitated to make him those presents which he
requested, he presented a new history of England,
which he was about to write, and of which he
actually printed one or two volumes.

The generous and compassionate character of the
English, joined to the disgust so natural in man to
industry, occasions all the streets of London to be
crowded with beggars. These lazy wretches receive
three, four, and sometimes five shillings a day in
charity. They actually have their clubs in the
parish of St. Giles's, where they meet to carouse,
read the gazettes, and talk about politics. No one
dares to attend those assemblies unless he is a beggar
himself

himself, or introduced by one. A friend of mine who wished to see and converse with all descriptions of men, having one day put on a ragged coat, promised to reward a mendicant if he would conduct him thither. He was accordingly introduced, found a great deal of gaiety and ease, and nothing that bore the appearance of indigence, save the tatters that covered the members. One cast his crutches into a corner of the room ; one unbuckled his wooden leg ; another took off the plaister which concealed his eye ; all, in fine, discovered themselves in their own natural forms ; recounted the adventures of that day, and concerted the stratagems to be put in execution on the morrow.

The female beggars generally hire infants from those who are poorer than themselves, to rouse, by that means, the charity of the passengers. They pay various prices for these children, from sixpence to two shillings a day, according as they are more or less deformed. A child that is very crooked and distorted generally earns three shillings, and sometimes even more. I happened once to overhear the conversation of two women who were talking concerning their profession. One of them informed the other that she paid two shillings for the child in her arms : " What !" replies her companion, " are you a fool ? Two shillings for that charming " baby !—I would not give more for a monster."

In the same Parish the pick-pockets hold their meetings, and have an ordinary which they frequent, where they sell or exchange the handkerchiefs, snuff-boxes, and other articles which they have filched in the course of the day. In any other country these associations would be discovered, and the whole gang made prisoners : this is not, however, possible in London ; for as these rogues never act in a body, but each by himself, it is necessary that there should be proofs against every

E   individual,

individual, for the laws are fcrupuloufly obferved
in arrefting the moft defpicable wretch in the community. When any one of them is fufpected, his
perfon muft be fworn to; and his companions,
although well known, never run any rifk whatever.

This clafs of rogues, however, do not now affemble fo publickly as formerly. About thirty years
fince a houfe in St. Giles's became very celebrated as
the rendezvcus of this kind of thieves; at prefent it
is occupied by an honeft brewer. The knives and
forks were chained to the table, and the cloth nail-
ed to it. Not far from that place was alfo a fhop
famous for gin : over the door of which was the following infcription : " *Here you may get drunk for a
penny, dead drunk for two-pence, and have ftraw
for nothing.*"

This fingular liquor was fold in a cellar, which
was crowded day and night with a fpecies of beings
who rather refemble beafts than men. A ftatute
however, called the *Gin-act*, by impofing a high
duty on that liquid poifon, put an end to fuch horrid
diffolutenefs. It is neceffary I fhould remark here,
that the defcription I have juft given does not exhibit a picture of the capital during the prefent times,
and that I have only fpoken of an obfcure ftreet
which has been diftinguifhed for ages, by the poverty and the grofs and favage character of the wretches
who refide in it.

London ftill contains thofe pretended fortune-
tellers, who for the moderate fum of one fhilling,
augur a happy deftiny to the curious. Their
lodgings are ufually adorned with magical characters, and furnifhed with celeftial and terreftrial
globes. Their drefs is a green robe, a fur night-cap,
and a long beard tied under the chin. Thefe for
the moft part are young men, but by means of
this drefs, they affume the appearance of old age,
and

and pretend to be arrived from the Eaſt. That they may not be ſuppoſed to know a word of Engliſh, they make uſe of an interpreter, to give an air of truth to their impoſture, who explains the meaning of the oracle to the dupes, and ſhares the ſpoils with his maſter. Theſe fortune-tellers are always Engliſh or Iriſh, for as yet no foreigner has dared to make ſuch an attempt.

This kind of impoſition is ſeverely puniſhed, but neither ſo often nor ſo ſeverely as to aboliſh it entirely. As the public peace is not endangered by the practice; as no bad conſequences follow their ridiculous predictions; as fortune-tellers at bottom are only a kind of beggars; and as fools in all countries are determined to be deceived; from thence it proceeds that they do not proſecute theſe people with any degree of rigour, uuleſs they become too public, and make a prodigious noiſe.

Sometimes they carry their impudence to ſuch a length, that they advertiſe in the newſpapers, and inform the world of their abilities, their price, and their abode. If a magiſtrate ſhould go to the place appointed, they deny the whole, and affirm that ſome wag has done it to amuſe himſelf at their expence. On theſe occaſions they eaſily manage ſo as to hide their robe, cap, globes, and in a word, every indication of their profeſſion; ſo that not finding any proofs ſufficient to convict them, the officers of juſtice are obliged to retire, and the fortune-teller continues his trade in peace.

CHAPTER

CHAPTER IV.

THIRTY years ago it was difficult to aſcertain whether London or Paris was the larger city. Since, however, they have preſcribed certain bounds to the latter, which they are not allowed to exceed, and this wiſe regulation has not yet been adopted in the metropolis of England, which every day receives a new increaſe of buildings; it cannot now be doubted that the Engliſh have the misfortune to poſſeſs a capital infinitely more extenſive than the French. That which adds not a little to its magnitude, is the great number of large villages, which ſerve as country houſes; and which being incorporated as it were with the ſuburbs of the town, form with it a monſtrous aggregate, to which there are neither limits nor regulations. No leſs than forty-three thouſand new houſes were built, between 1762 and 1779.

Some enlightened patriots have attempted to ſtop this evil, which is continually increaſing. " It is madneſs," ſay they, " thus to *roof* all the county of Middleſex with tiles." The *ſagacious* North thought proper to impoſe a duty on bricks; but far from attaining the end propoſed, the *rage* for building ſeemed only to increaſe. The projectors were

not

not in the least frightened with this tax : being certain of always finding inhabitants, they only became anxious to make their houses more agreeable and commodious than formerly.

For these twenty-years past, an actual emigration has taken place from the eastern parts of London towards the western ; thousands have left the former, where they do not erect new buildings, for the latter, where the most fertile fields and most agreeable gardens are daily metamorphosed into houses and streets.

The city, especially the houses along the banks of the Thames, is composed of old ruins : the streets are narrow, obscure, and badly paved : it is the residence of the seamen, of the workmen employed in ship-building, and of a great part of the Jews who reside in London. The contrast betwixt that and the western parts of the metropolis is astonishing : the houses there are almost all new, and of an excellent construction ; the squares are magnificent ; the streets are built in straight lines, and perfectly well lighted : no city in Europe is better paved. If London were equally well built, no place in the whole world would be comparable to it.

It is a singular circumstance, and one that no traveller has ever remarked, that the western division of London, which is in extent more than half the capital, and which is entirely separated from the city, has not as yet received any name. When the citizens speak of any particular part of it, they content themselves with mentioning the name of the street ; and when they talk of the whole, they term it—*the other end of the town*. Foreigners and geographers do wrong in calling this prodigious assemblage of streets and squares Westminster : that district does not form a tenth of it ; all the rest is included in that of Middlesex.

E 3

As

As every thing in that country is singular, it is not in the least surprising that the capital should be placed in different counties, and each particular portion of it has a distinct jurisdiction.

The city, which is the smallest division of London, has its own magistrates; all the rest is governed by justices of the peace, which gives occasion to a remarkable difference in tne *police*. In the former it is more severe and exact; the love of order and industry is also more perceptible.

Two towns, a hundred leagues distant from each other, cannot have less resemblance than there is between the city and the other parts of London: the form of government; the regulations; the privileges; the taste and arrangement of the houses; the manner of living; every thing, in one word, renders this difference remarkable.

The citizens are represented in parliament by four members, whom they alone elect; the other inhabitants of the metropolis, according to the districts which they inhabit, vote for Middlesex, Surry, Kent, and Westminster.

During the fire in 1666, thirty thousand four hundred houses, eighty-seven churches, and twenty-six hospitals in the city were consumed by the flames. Of this terrible devastation no trace now remains; but as every person was anxious to rebuild his dwelling-house, necessity made them neglect to make the buildings either regular or convenient. From thence proceed the number of ill-formed masses of brick and mortar, dark and without taste; the crooked and narrow streets, and the obscure situation of the churches and other public edifices: faults which have been carefully avoided in the western parts of the capital.

The churches eastward of Temple Bar are heaped upon one another; they have all been rebuilt on their ancient foundations; and one would imagine,

from

from their number, that London was formerly compofed of chapels and convents. Weft of Temple Bar,
on the other hand, they are very few: the zeal to
lodge themfelve feems more to have influenced the
inhabitants, than the defire to erect places of worfhip
for the Deity: in fome parts, there are fix thoufand
houfes to one parifh church.

The fhops are open by eight o'clock every morning in the city; all is then in motion, every body is
at work; while on the other hand, at the *court end*
of the town, the ftreets are empty, the houfes fhut,
and even the very domeftics are afleep; the found
of coaches is not heard, and one feems to walk
about in a place that has been deferted. This difference, which extends to drinking and eating,
amufements, drefs, and manner of expreffion, occafions a kind of hatred between the inhabitants of
each. Thofe in the city charge the people who
live at the weft end of the town with luxury, idle-
nefs, effeminacy, and an attachment to French
fafhions; while the others fpeak of a citizen as a
dull, fat animal, who places all his merits in his
ftrong box.

But it is more efpecially when the lord mayor,
fheriffs and common council have an audience at St.
James's, to prefent a petition, or compliment his
majefty on fome great event, that the courtiers attempt to ridicule them. One may eafily imagine
that a fimple tradefman, totally unacquainted with
the modes and cuftoms of a court, will not be able
to acquit himfelf on fuch folemn occafions with the
eafe of a courtier, who has made *etiquette* his chief
and his only ftudy, and who looks upon it as the
moft interefting and the moft ufeful of all accom-
plifhments.

This antipathy is fo notorious, that it is mentioned in ballads, noticed on the ftage, and is not forgotten even in the Parliament itfelf. In Italy they
would

would arm themselves with poignards, and spill each others' blood on a similar occasion;—but so far from being attended with fatal consequences in England, it serves only to banish the *spleen* of the nation.

The English nobility generally live three quarters of the year in the country. This ancient custom of staying but a short time in the capital, is the reason why there are so few magnificent mansions in London. It is observed, however, that the metropolis having lately acquired more attractions, people of distinction now reside there longer than they were wont to do: however, they still look on their country seats as their principal habitations.

Many families who have twenty thousand a year, have but a few apartments in town, and, as they keep a prodigious train of servants, are of course confined in regard to room. In a short time this inconvenience will no longer exist, as a number of people of fashion are now building superb palaces.

It may be thought that this custom is encouraged by government; but although the chief design of all courts be, to draw around them the greater part of the nobility to add to their splendour, and take away from them the power of raising disturbances in the provinces; I am, however, of opinion, that nothing but the pleasures of the metropolis influence the English.

The nation already begins to be less attached to hunting, and to feel a greater passion for the fine arts, and every thing that can add to the pleasures of a sensual life. It is also certain, that the next generation of the nobility will reside, like those of France, entirely in the capital. When one considers that, since this custom has prevailed, those commotions which the great used formerly to foment, have altogether subsided; and that in England and Poland alone, where the nobility reside on their estates, disturbances of this kind have happened

in

in the prefent age ; it muft be allowed that luxury, againft which fo much declamation prevails, has been attended with at leaft fome good confequences.

This new inclination, by which the wealthy are induced to live in London, has given to projectors the idea of building large ftreets, and extenfive fquares, adorned with excellent houfes. Thefe houfes, which may be regarded as fo many palaces, are very lofty, exceedingly commodious, and have each of them two ftories under ground, to which fufficient light is communicated, by means of a forecourt. The fervants are lodged, and the kitchen, ftore-rooms, &c. are placed there, fo that the reft of the houfe is entirely at the difpofal of the mafter.

The builders have generally a leafe of ninety-nine years, and at the end of that term are obliged either to give up the premifes, or renew the agreement on paying a fine. The duke of Portland has eight thoufand buildings erected in this manner on his eftate in the neighbourhood of town.

It is to this cuftom that the want of folidity in the houfes, and the few mafter-pieces of architecture which we meet with in London, may be fairly attributed. If this reafon did not exift, rich individuals would glory in decorating the capital of their native country. However, the difadvantage is in a great meafure recompenfed by the commodioufnefs of the buildings.

Every houfe is abundantly fupplied with water, by means of pipes, which diftribute it to all the ftreets in London. This profufion is of the greateft ufe in cafe of fire, by placing the engines fo as to receive a conftant fupply, One need never be afraid of a fcarcity of this precious commodity ; for, not contented with making the Thames to run through all parts of the town, they have brought the New River from the county of Hertford for the

E 5   fame

same purpose. By means of engines at London-bridge they raise the river to a prodigious height, and then circulate it through wooden pipes.

They are careful in England not only to insure their houses and their shops, but even public buildings, such as churches, hospitals, and theatres. This precaution is not used in Paris, notwithstanding its boasted regulations are raised to the skies. Any one may also insure his goods and wardrobe ; nay, every thing but his ready money. This excellent establishment is, however, sometimes abused : more than one rogue has burnt his own house ; and as this kind of crime is very difficult to be proved, the office is generally obliged to pay the amount of the demand. Immediately after the fire, the assurers become entitled to their money, having first transmitted the amount of their losses, and attested the statement by an oath. Notwithstanding the number of houses annually consumed in London by the flames, a mere trifle is given for the risk : it is usually no more than in the proportion of half a crown for a hundred pounds.

No part of Europe exhibits such luxury and magnificence as the English display within the walls of their dwelling houses. The staircase, which is covered with the richest carpets, is supported by a balustrade of the finest India wood, curiously constructed, and lighted by lamps containing crystal vases. The landing-places are adorned with busts, pictures and medallions ; the wainscot and cielings of the apartments are covered with the finest varnish, and enriched with gold, bass-reliefs, and the most happy attempts in painting and sculpture. The chimneys are of Italian marble, on which flowers and figures, cut in the most exquisite stile, form the chief ornaments ; the locks of doors are of steel damasked with gold. Carpets which often cost three hundred pounds a-piece, and which one

scruples

fcruples to touch with his foot, cover all the rooms ; the richeft ftuffs from the looms of Afia are employ- ed as window curtains ; and the clocks and watches with which the apartments are furnifhed, aftonifh by their magnificence, and the ingenious complica- tion of their mechanifm.

'The Englifh have alfo introduced a new fpecies of fculpture ; this confifts in medallions of ivory, of which the workmanfhip is equally delicate and elegant. Thefe are placed upon black velvet co- vered with glafs, and contained in a frame of the richeft workmanfhip.

The prefent fafhion of adorning the capital by the magnificence and the luxury of their manfions, every day increafes among the great, and perhaps will at laft deftroy a cuftom, of which the lovers of painting and fculpture have fo long complained ; that of embellifhing their country-houfes with all the wonders of art, and which, thus entombed in the heart of a remote province, are for ever loft to the world. Where is the artift who has time and money fufficient to facrifice them in fearching for a production which he may not perhaps find ; or which, if he does meet with after a long and pain- ful fearch, he can only view in a tranfitory manner, without ftudying its beauties at his eafe ?

Exclufive of St. Pauls' cathedral and the col- legiate church of Weftminfter, London contains one hundred and two parifh-churches and fixty-nine chapels of the eftablifhed religion ; twenty-one belonging to the French proteftants ; eleven to the Germans, Dutch. and Swedes ; thirty-three to the anabaptifts and quakers ; twenty-fix to the inde- pendants : twenty-eight to the prefbyterians ; nine- teen to the catholics ; and three to the jews ; the number confecrated to the worfhip of the Divinity is three hundred and forty edifices. In this account I do not include twenty-one churches which do

not

not belong to any particular parish. The foregoing list was ascertained in 1779: I make this remark, because the anabaptists, quakers, &c. &c. augment, diminish, and often change the house where they assemble.

No city is adorned with such fine squares as London. They are all composed of noble and handsome houses: there are neither shops nor warehouses to be seen in them: in the centre there is usually a piece of ground laid out in a beautiful manner, which serves as an agreeable walk. Some are adorned with statues and obelisks. Markets, so common in other capitals, never disgrace them with their disgustful appearance. The squares in London offer such objects to the eye as announce the opulence and good taste of the inhabitants.: those who reside there, besides this, have the advantage of breathing a pure air, and are never disturbed by any noise.

The markets in the metropolis, which are very numerous, have certain fixed stations, where neither the buyers nor sellers need fear being run over by the wheels of carriages, or trampled upon by the hoofs of horses, being, by means of their situation, secured from such inconveniences. This regulation, which is the consequence of an excellent *police*, ought to be adopted in every great town.

Among the pecularities of London may be reckoned the pavement and the lamps. About twenty years since, that metropolis was the worst paved city in Europe; the evil was indeed felt, but the inhabitants did not then know how to remedy it. From almost every house an enormous *sign* was suspended, which darkened the streets, often fell down, and sometimes killed the passengers. Two acts of parliament appeared almost at the same time, and obviated these disadvantages; the signs disappeared, and the streets of London were covered with a pavement

ment unrivalled in its kind, and which cost four hundred pounds sterling.

By means of large foot ways of hewn stone, the passengers, without being incommoded by the horses and carriages, pass freely along. No coachman, under the penalty of twenty shillings, dares to drive upon this, or touch the *kirb stone*, even if he is obliged to wait whole hours. Considerable sums are appropriated towards the repairing of these excellent foot-ways ; a regulation at once singular and wise prevents the pavement from being hurt, as the carts, waggons, &c. are now obliged to make use of wheels with rims six inches in diameter. These, so far from hurting the streets, make them the more firm, and in a certain degree repair the damages which the chariots, coaches, and other light carriages have occasioned.

As the English are prodigal of their money and their time in favour of every public establishment, one may naturally expect to find that London is well lighted. Nothing, indeed, can be more superb. The lamps, which often consist of two, three, and sometimes four branches, are enclosed in crystal globes; and, being attached to iron supporters, are placed at a small distance from each other. They are lighted at sunset, both in winter and summer, as well when the moon shines as not. In Oxford-street alone, there are more lamps than in all Paris.

The great roads within seven or eight miles of town are also illuminated in the same manner ; and as they are very numerous, the effect is charming, more especially in the county of Surry, where they frequently cross each other obliquely, and at right angles. The highways are for the most part bordered with palisades and country houses ; little wooden boxes provided with bells, and containing watchmen armed with musquets, are also posted at every hundred paces.

A3

As all shops are open till ten o'clock at night, and exceedingly well lighted; this, together with the lamps in the streets, has a most astonishing effect. The prince of Monaco, after the demise of the late duke of York, who died in his territories, went to England on an invitation from the king. It being rather late when he arrived, his highness imagined that this brilliant illumination was made in honour to him, for he thought it impossible that the inhabitants could always support such an immense expence. The prince's mistake was soon divulged, and occasioned many pleasantries.

From what has been said above, it may be easily imagined that London contains many fine houses, and very few *palaces*. But notwithstanding, it is not customary among the English to give this appellation to Burlington, Northumberland and Somerset Houses, the latter of which is a superb edifice, and has lately been erected at the expence of the nation; it is, however, certain, that all these buildings are on every account worthy of being stiled so. This custom perhaps arises from that *spirit of equality*, which constitutes the chief pride of the nation. It is only the residence of sovereigns that they dignify with the name of a palace; every other edifice, however large and however superb, whether it belongs to the king's brother, or even the prince of Wales, is simply called a house.

The most noble works in architecture contained in London, are the churches, the bridges, the hospitals, and some other public edifices.

The cathedral of St. Paul's is not unworthy of the nation. Notwithstanding all its faults, it would be much more admired if the site, concealing its proper point of view from the spectator, did not at the same time hide all its beauties. It is generally known that it was built after the model of St. Peter's at Rome, and yet it only resembles it in its shape and
dome.

dome. The front towards Ludgate-hill is more fuperb, and has an effect infinitely more interesting
than St. Peter's: it wants, however, the admirable
fituation, the colonade, the *jet d'eau*, and the obe-
lifk of the latter.

There are a great number of engravings of the defign after which Sir Chriftopher Wren, the architect,
intended to have executed this building. His plan
was in the pureft Grecian ftyle; and if his advice
had been followed, London might now boaft the
glory of poffeffing the mafter-piece of modern architecture. The confent of the chapter of St. Paul's
being unfortunately neceffary on this occafion, they
rejected the idea, obferving at the fame time, " That
" fuch an edifice would rather refemble a Pagan
" temple than a Chriftian church."

There is no other example of a fingle architect
having begun and executed a building of fuch an aftonifhing immenfity. It was the labour of thirty-
feven years, and coft a million two hundred thoufand
pounds fterling.

Divine fervice is celebrated in only a fmall part
of it; all the reft is empty, and without any ornament, which has a very difagreeable effect. It is at
laft perceived how much this fuperb edifice fuffers by
its fad and doleful vacuity; for which reafon they
have for fome time paft formed the defign of furnifh-
ing it with monuments to the memory of illuftrious
Englifhmen. In confequence of this project, the
king was petitioned by the common council of
London, in the year 1778, to permit the monument to be placed there, which the parliament had
voted to the memory of lord Chatham. The
minifter, who wifhed as much as poffible to detract
from the reputation of that great ftatefman, did
not choofe to acquiefce in the demand; the funeral
trophies were therefore banifhed into one of the
moft obfcure corners of Weftminfter abbey, where
the

the effect is entirely loft.. The fculpture has alfo been confided to an artift who is but little known. If the minifter had acceded to the propofition of the citizens, St. Paul's would have been infenfibly filled with the nobleft memorials of national glory.

The church or abbey of Weftminfter is, perhaps the moft beautiful fpecimen of Gothic architecture now in exiftence. The grandeur of its columns, the boldnefs of its arches, its immenfe extent, its ornaments and their diftribution, taken altogether, make this a moft extraordinary edifice. It was formerly a convent of Benedictines; Cromwell converted it into a ftable for his cavalry. In no part of the world is fuch a multitude of fuperb monuments to be met with; for, notwithftanding the prodigious fpace within the walls, in a few years there will not be room for any more.

This is the burial-place of the Kings of England, and of many celebrated men, to whom either their friends or the nation at large have erected memorials. If any place is capable of infpiring holy awe and religious terror, it is this. This fpot is alfo facred to men of letters and the moft famous poets; here the man of genius elevated and inflamed at the fight, beholds the moft celebrated names of which the world can boaft. It is here too that the monuments of the ftatefman, the general, the admiral, the philofopher, the poet, the man of learning, and the artift, touch one another.

The tomb of Newton is finely executed, and placed in an excellent fituation; on the bafe you read the following fentence: " Mortals, rejoice that " you once poffeffed this ornament of human " nature!" The infcription, which is in the Latin language, was preferred to the Englifh epitaph, written by Pope, which, although exaggerated, is noble and poetical.

Nature, and Nature's laws, lay hid in night;
God faid—Let Newton be! and all was light!

There are alfo many foreigners of diftinguifhed
merit buried here. The tombs of St. Evremond
and Handel are truly admirable; that of Handel in
particular is reckoned by the conroifleurs to be the
moft beautiful and ingenious one in the whole abbey.
The Englifh never efteemed any ftranger fo much
as him; it is not therefore aftonifhing that they
fhould raife fuch a magnificent tribute to his memory. The idea is fublime: Handel, awakened by
a trumpet blown by an angel, ftarts from his tomb:
a fentiment of religious terror is not what agitates
his foul at that moment: the founds of the tru mpet
fix all his attention; his arms, which he elevates,
his ear, with which he liftens, every feature in his
countenance feems to indicate, that, entranced in
this celeftial harmcny, his foul is unable to attend to
any thing elfe.

The infcription beneath the buft of Shakefpeare,
is taken from a fine paffage in one of his dramatic
pieces called " The Tempeft."

The cloud-capt towers, the gorgeous palaces,
The folemn temples, the great globe itfelf,
Yea, all which it inherits, fhall diffolve;
And, like the bafelefs fabric of a vifion,
Leaves not a wreck behind.

Gay fo celebrated on account of his Fables, has
the following lines on his tomb:

Life is a jeft, and all things fhew it;
I thought fo once, but now I know it.

Thefe monuments, erected to the *manes* of great
men, and which have eternized the very artifts employed

ployed in them, form a spectacle equally impressive
and magnificent. England is undoubtedly the
country in Europe were learning is most nobly recompensed: it is this sentiment which has been ex-
pressed with so much truth and propriety by Engel
on the tomb of Lessing.

Wenn er ein Teut soher nicht, wenn er ein Britte waere,
So schlosse seinen sarg die Gruft der Koenge ein.
So wurd ein Volk, gefuhlvoll fur die Ehre,
Ihm œffentlich ein ewig Denkmal weihn.

" If he had been an Englishman, instead of a
" German, his body would have been entombed
" among kings. A nation to whom honour is so
" dear, would have erected a monument to his
" memory at the public expence, and rendered his
" name immortal!"

Westminster abbey also contains the bodies of
many sovereigns; among others are the monuments
of Henry VII. and Henry VIII. Their successors
have not been equally honoured, Elizabeth herself
has only a simple epitaph. Instead of sculpture,
they have of late adopted the singular and childish
custom of placing a portrait in wax over the grave,
which becomes hideous at the end of a few years.

In the reign of queen Anne the parliament granted four thousand pounds sterling for the repairing of
this church.

This is the place to recount a singular anecdote,
to which the best English historians, although they
were too prudent to declare it on account of the
honour of the nation, are yet nevertheless said to
have given credit.

If we are to believe tradition, the body of the unfortunate Charles I. was immediately after decollati-
on buried in the chapel of Windsor castle; it is still
said to remain in a vault under the choir, of which
no one either does know, or at least chooses to own

the

the situation. This strange ignorance of such a remarkable circumstance, and which leaves so much to supposition, is an argument in favour of what I am about to relate.

It is asserted, that some royalists conveyed in the most secret manner the remains of their sovereign from Windsor to Westminster abbey. On the restoration of Charles II. the supposed body of Cromwell was dug up, dragged through the streets, and exposed on a gallows. Now it is pretended that, either through a mistake, or a concerted design, this was actually the corpse of Charles I. which experienced this ignominious usage ; for when, in the presence of an innumerable crowd of spectators, the executioner was about to cut off the head, to his utter astonishment, he found the ceremony had been already performed.

The more modern churches in London are built with a considerable share of taste: but I shall only mention St. Martin's, the front of which is an imitation of the Pantheon at Rome. The connoisseurs, however, are much disgusted to see in all of them steeples and belfries, instead of domes, which are so much more majestic, A metropolis possessed of such immense riches, and which boasts of, perhaps, two of the best architects in Europe *, ought to excel in this species of buildings.

Adam has erected towards the Thames a pile of buildings, called the Adelphi, which, on account of their convenience and situation, may be quoted as models. All the houses are built on arches, whose grandeur and solidity deserve to be compared to those magnificent common sewers which at this very day are accounted among the wonders of ancient Rome.

Many of the English, with great propriety, imagine that, if the present king had a taste for architecture,

---

* Mr. Adams and Sir William Chambers.

chitecture, and would use his powerful influence in raifing palaces and other public buildings worthy of the nation, London would actually become the moft fuperb city in Europe.

It is extremely probable that, if the unfortunate American war had not taken place, and the flourifhing trade of thefe proud iflanders had continued, in twenty years time their capital would have excited the jealoufy of all the furrounding nations.

The Manfion-houfe, where the chief magiftrate of the city refides during his mayoralty, ought alfo to be mentioned. It was built about half a century ago, at a period when the Englifh were not initiated in the fine arts. The common council being affembled on purpofe to examine the plans laid before them for this edifice, a nobleman who had been in Italy fent them a defign of Palladio's, which he had brought with him from that country; and which as they were determined to fpare no expence, was by its elegance and grandeur peculiarly adapted for the purpofe.

Thefe refpectable citizens, however, were entirely unacquainted with Palladio; they defired to know who he was, and wanted very much to fee and converfe with him. After a long debate, an alderman obferved, that Palladio was a foreigner who had been dead for fome years, and that it would be exceedingly ridiculous to execute the plan of a ftranger, when London produced fo many excellent architects.

After this he propofed a fhip-carpenter, who was immediately accepted without any difficulty.

This man accordingly planned and executed the building, as may be eafily feen at the firft glance; for the front exactly refembles the *ftern of a man of war*. The apartments are obfcure and badly diftributed, and the ftairs, which look like *ladders*, are very ill contrived. It is in this edifice, which taken altogether has nothing abfolutely difagreeable in its

appearance

appearance, that the lord mayor is obliged to refide, notwithftanding he may have a houfe of his own in the neighbourhood.

The beauty and grandeur of the three principal bridges acrofs the Thames, are a high proof of the wealth of the nation, and of its paffion for great enterprifes. I fhould blufh to compare the *Pont Neuf* and *Pont Royal* at Paris to thofe of Weftminfter and Blackfriars. An Englifhman is proud, but he is not a boafter; we therefore hear but little of thefe mafter-pieces of architecture, which by their grandeur, magnificence, and conveniency, are the firft works of this kind that are to be found in Europe, I will not even except the Rialto at Venice; for the un-polifhed blocks of marble with which it is compofed, have nothing magnificent in their appearance. Even the fingle arch of which it confifts, and which is fo famous on account of its grandeur and extent, has been rivalled in great Great Britain by a bridge acrofs the Don in Ayrfhire, the two extremities of which are placed on the oppofite banks of the river, and are 90 feet diftant from each other. The fpan of the Rialto is exactly of the fame dimenfions.

The new bridges at London are equally grand and commodious. That of Weftminfter is 1223 feet long, and 44 broad. It is extremely well paved; the fides are adorned with ftone baluftrades; the foot-paths are broad; the lamps are numerous, and the alcoves, placed at proper diftances, fhelter the paffengers from the rain. It has fifteen arches; the centre one of which is 66 feet in width; they are all adorn-ed with columns, and remarkably well vaulted.

This immenfe pile, which was twelve years in building, coft one hundred and fifty thoufand pounds.

The prodigious expence did not, however, pre-vent them from immediately laying the foundation of another, called Blackfriars, which is placed in the
centre

centre of the city, and joins it to the county of Surry.
It is still more elegant and magnificent than that of
Westminster. Its arches are adorned with columns
of the Ionic order, and placed two and two; their
bases touch the river, and have a fine effect. This
bridge was entirely constructed at the expence of
the citizens, and cost one hundred and sixty
thousand pounds, which was repaid by means of a
toll on carriages, horses, and foot passengers.

Some years since another was projected, betwixt
the two new ones: the execution, however, of
this has been deferred.

Notwithstanding London bridge is a very good
one, yet it is nothing comparable to the others. The
solidity of it, however (for it was built more than
800 years since), gives us a favourable idea of the
ancient manner of building. Its arches are low,
and very narrow: circumstances which, together
with the rapidity of the stream, occasion many ac-
cidents.

Formerly this bridge was covered with houses,
like *Notre Dame* at Paris.

Near to this stands a column of the Doric order,
commonly called the *Monument*; it was built to
perpetuate the memory of the fire by which London suffered so severely in the year 1666. Being
erected in the very place where the conflagration
began, all its beauty is lost by the badness of its
situation. It is two hundred feet perpendicular, and
consequently exceeds in height that of Trajan at
Rome; it has like it a winding stair-case in the inside. The sum appropriated to its erection was
thirty thousand pounds sterling.

As its fall is continually apprehended, and would
be attended with the most fatal consequences, it has
been often proposed to remove this immense quarry
of stone.

The

The Royal Exchange and the Bank ought not to be forgotten. The exchange is not the largeſt, but it is certainly certainly the moſt magnificent in the world. It is decorated with the ſtatues of the kings of Great Britain, and ſurrounded by a prodigious number of coffee-houſes, where the merchants tranſact their buſineſs. Its ſituation is extremely convenient, being only a few ſteps from the Poſt-office, the Manſion-houſe, Guildhall, the India-houſe, &c. &c. &c.

Although the bank is only one ſtory high, it is neverthleſs a fine building. Moſt of the apartments are lighted from the top, and the ſtoves are con-trived with ſo much art, that neither the door nor the tunnel can be perceived: each of theſe coſt a hundred pounds ſterling. As the bank is the pro-perty of the nation, all the offices in this immenſe edifice are open to every one; in the outer hall, there are tables on which pens, ink, &c. are placed for even the loweſt of the populace, although they may have no buſineſs there. However trivial theſe little circumſtances may appear to ſome people, I cannot but admire even in them that republican ſpirit which animates the whole nation.

The ſhops and warehouſes, which join each other, and ſometimes extend for a whole mile without in-terruption, ſtrike a foreigner with ſurpriſe. The part towards the ſtreet generally conſiſts of a bow-window and a glaſs door, through which every ar-ticle that is elegant and faſhionable may be ſeen, arranged in the utmoſt ſymmetry.

Mathematical inſtruments, and every thing curi-ous in that ſcience; which for rarity and perfection are not to be ſurpaſſed in the palaces of princes, appear in abundance. Nothing can be more ſuperb than the ſilver-ſmiths' ſhops. In looking at the pro-digious quantity of plate piled up and expoſed there, one can only form a proper idea of the riches of the nation.

nation. The greateſt ſhops in *St. Honore'* at Paris, appear contemptible when compared with thoſe in London. I have ſeen in Cheapſide (and it is a well known fact) a warehouſe of this kind, the contents of which were eſtimated at a hundred thouſand pounds ſterling.

The print-ſhops are actually ſo many galleries of painting. To the number of privileges enjoyed by theſe iſlanders may be added that of publiſhing *caricatures,* which ridicule the occurrences of the times.

The French compoſe ſongs; the Dutch, of a duller caſt, ſtrike medals; but the Engliſh have choſen *engravings* as the moſt proper vehicle for their ſatire. In 1784, when Mr. Fox carried every thing before him in the Houſe of Commons, he was repreſented ſitting at a mirror which reflected the picture of Oliver Cromwell.

The government of the city is an exact copy in miniature of that of the whole kingdom. Like the latter, it is divided into three diſtinct branches; the lord mayor repreſents the king; the court of aldermen the houſe of Peers, and the common council the Houſe of Commons. The latter are choſen by the *livery,* who form a body of nine thouſand citizens. There are no emoluments attached to the rank of alderman; it is the honour, the influence, and the hope of becoming the chief magiſtrate, which makes that ſituation deſirable. However if the office of alderman is not lucrative, no expence is entailed on the execution of it:—but that of a ſheriff often amounts to two or three thouſand pounds ſterling in a ſingle year.

When Wilkes was appointed to this office, his friends ſubſcribed the neceſſary ſums. This being the firſt ſtep towards the mayoralty, the court employed every artifice to prevent him, but in vain. As the influence of the miniſter is very trifling in the corporation,

corporation, it so happens that the citizens of London are not very much in favour at St. James's: they, however, console themselves with the best grace in the world. They repeat with great pleasure a witty expression made use of by one of their body, in the reign of Charles II. That monarch being greatly discontented with the citizens, who would not consent to *lend* him certain sums to support his foolish dissipation, one day menaced a deputation who presented him an address, with the threat of leaving London and keeping his court at Oxford. An alderman on this occasion, turning towards a courtier, observed, " That the king " seemed to be in a great passion." " I hope, however," adds he, " that when his majesty re- " moves, he will not carry the river Thames along " with him." This sally had its proper effect, and no English monarch has ever since thought proper to express a similar intention.

No person can become a liveryman of London without being admitted into one of the twenty-six companies, of which that body consists. A member whose name is registered in any of these may aspire to the first employment in the capital, notwithstanding he may be one of the very dregs of the people; such as a taylor, a blacksmith, &c. &c. When princes and people of quality are presented with the freedom of the city of London, they are always requested to name their *trade*; and it is generally that of the lord mayor that is fixed upon. The present king of Denmark is a member of the goldsmiths' company.

The lord mayor sits every day at the mansion-house to distribute justice, which he does without *appeal* in trifling disputes; in matters of greater consequence the culprit is sent to prison, and takes his trial in the usual manner.

F

If

If the chief magistrate for a moment should depart from the line of conduct prescribed to him by the laws, he is obliged to submit to justice like one of the meanest citizens.

As there are no justices of the peace in the city, the aldermen supply their place, and settle petty differences. Like all other magistrates, they are obliged to release a prisoner on giving bail, except in the cases of high-treason and felony.

The office of lord mayor is not only very honorable, but has also a considerable revenue annexed to it. The citizens look upon him as their *king*. The number of his attendants, his equipages, and his rich liveries, give a certain degree of splendour to his dignity. He is addressed by the title of " My Lord," even by the sovereign. A prodigious number of privileges are attached to his office. The military cannot enter the city without his permission, nor can any seaman be impressed there, unless he backs the warrant. He is also conservator of the Thames.

The principal part of his revenue proceeds from the sale of places that become vacant during his mayoralty. It is always customary, on entering upon his charge, to give a great entertainment which concludes with a ball: all the nobility are invited on the occasion; very few, however, attend.

It is very uncommon to see the same person twice lord mayor. William Beckford, however, who to uncommon knowledge and great patriotism united a revenue of thirty thousand a year, was for the second time invested with this dignity in 1769. He was consequently in that office in 1770, the time when the city, and a great number of the English counties, petitio. d the sovereign to call a new parliament; for that had, by its conduct in regard to Wilkes, entirely lost the favour of the public:

but

but the king who thought it his interest to continue it, constantly refused the request. The city of London, however, reiterated their complaints; and the lord mayor, the sheriffs, and common council were continually going to St. James's, where his majesty, according to custom, received them on the throne; the answer, however, was uniformly the same, viz. " That the king was content with " his parliament; but, as he always should esteem " it a pleasure to attend to the solicitations of his " people, that he would consider of their petition, " &c. &c.

Beckford, who was disgusted at being obliged, on account of his situation, to act the first character in this farce, secretly resolved to treat the affair in a more serious manner.

In consequence of this, he repairs with a numerous train to court, reads the petition, and receives the usual reply. It is then the custom, after kissing his majesty's hand, to retire; but Beckford, who had not gone there on account of a ceremony so little conformable to the genius of a free people, turned towards the king, and addressed him again in a speech delivered with the most profound respect, but at the same time with the most undaunted firmness, beseeching his majesty " not to treat the petiti- " on of the first city in his kingdom with so much " indifference, but to yield to the continual solicita- " tions of his people."

This address was not only unexpected, but even without example. I myself was one of the spectators, and I confess that I never in my whole life have been witness to such an extraordinary affair. The confusion and dismay of the courtiers were perceptible in their countenances, while the citizens shewed in the most unequivocal manner, that the courage of their chief magistrate gave them the highest satisfaction.

In

In the mean time Mr. Beckford stood before them, and with the utmost tranquillity expected the royal answer. As the king, however, was not *prepared*, a profound silence reigned for some minutes in the audience chamber, during which the spectators appeared mute and stupified. At last the lord mayor, thinking it time to put an end to such a strange scene, bowed and departed.

One may easily imagine how much they were disgusted with this conduct at St. James's, where they termed it impudent, and threatened to commit his Lordship to the Tower: in the city, however, he was presented with the thanks of the corporation, which were accompanied with the most flattering marks of regard and esteem.

Being obliged eight days afterwards to return to St. James's, to congratulate his majesty on the safe delivery of the queen, the lord chamberlain, after having mentioned his former behaviour, informed him at the same time, that a repetition of such a conduct would occasion the city of London to be deprived of the privilege of presenting their petitions to the king *while sitting on the throne*.

Beckford on this requested that the declaration might be given him in writing; and, on the refusal of the chamberlain, observed, that he should consider such a menace as if it had not been uttered.

This great patriot happening to die a few months afterwards, the city of London erected a monument to his memory in Guildhall. It is of white marble, and as large as the life. He is dressed in his robes; stands in the same position as when replying to his majesty's answer; and, instead of an inscription, the speech itself is engraven on the pedestal.

It is not at all uncommon to see an orator turn towards this statue, invoke the *manes* of Beckford, and conjure his fellow-citizens by the memory of this great man, never to lose sight of the public welfare.

welfare. It is in this manner that those illustrious islanders so gloriously imitate the ancient Romans, and prove by their actions how advantageous patriotism is to a nation, notwithstanding it may sometimes be carried to a blameable excess.

CHAPTER V.

The State of Religion in England—Toleration—The Catholics—The Clergy—The Puritans—The Methodists—Whitfield—Sunday—Anniversary of the Martyrdom of Charles I.—Quakers—Anabaptists: Deism—The Reverend Mr. Williams—Suicide—Hon. Mr. Damer—Lord Clive—The Jews—Doctor Falkon—The Philosopher's Stone—Linguet.

VOLTAIRE observes that, if there was only one religion in England, despotism would infallibly ensue: —if there were but two, adds he, they would cut one another's throats; but as such a number of sects are there tolerated, who worship the Supreme Being in so many different manners, a *holy enthusiasm* never troubles their minds, and they live in quiet and tranquillity. This remark is undoubtedly just; and the tumult in 1780, in which the name of the protestant religion was made use of as a pretence, proves nothing to the contrary.

The legislative power has reduced the principles of toleration to a system which seems to have attained the highest degree of perfection; and it ought to be remarked to the honour of the English parliament, that at the moment when they were surrounded by a furious multitude, and the life of every member was in danger, no one proposed the repeal of the

bill

bill in favour of the Roman Catholics, which had occasioned the tumult.

If the tenets of the established faith were alone permitted, the people would soon groan under the pressure of slavery; for the king is head of the church, and in that capacity his power is unlimited.

Persecution, a practice which the christians have borrowed from the Jews, and which they have made use of against them, will never, in all probability, take root in England. The prodigious number of dissenters; the liberty with which mankind are there allowed to think and to act as they please ; their intercourse with foreign nations, which is the source of their riches ; and a thousand other considerations, all tend to establish that toleration to which the kingdom owes its grandeur, its opulence, and its prosperity.

It may not be improper to quote here a celebrated saying of Lord Chesterfield's to a monk at Rome. The holy zealot having assured him that he was about to make a voyage to England, with the sole view of converting the inhabitants to the catholic faith, and *that be was ready to suffer every thing for the sake of religion:* " You will be too late, " my good father," replies the earl: " it is in vain " that you are solicitous to obtain the crown of " martyrdom; alas! my ungrateful countrymen " bestow it now no more."

To obtain any employment under the government, it is necessary to take the oaths of supremacy and allegiance ; but as the catholics either cannot or will not take them, they are deprived of a great many advantages, and excluded from a number of offices, to which their birth and merits fully entitle them.

The first and most ancient family in England is in this predicament : it is that of Howard, of which the duke of Norfolk is the head; to this title the

office

office of hereditary marſhal of England is attached;
his religion, however, not only precludes him from
executing the duties of this high employment in
perſon, but alſo from taking his ſeat in the Houſe of
Peers.*

The catholics in England have their biſhops as
well as the proteſtant: theſe commonly reſide in
London, and live on eleemoſynary contributions.
Among theſe *titular* prelates there is an archbiſhop
of Canterbury, who is their head. In the year
1778 there were forty th uſand members of the
church of Rome in the capital; I doubt whether
there are at preſent ſo many in all the other parts
of the kingdom, as the chapels of the foreign miniſters attract prodigious numbers to the metropolis.
There are a great many, however, in Lancaſhire,
Staffordſhire, and Suſſex.

Notwithſtanding the clergy of the church of
England have large incomes, and its dignitaries live
in great magnificence, they are but very little reſpected by the people. The reaſon is evident.—
The various ſects that prevail in that iſland, weaken
the intereſts of religion in general, and inſpire but
little eſteem for theſe eccleſiaſtics, who live, for
the moſt part, according to their own caprice. The
exceſſes alſo, and the depredations they commit,
leſſen the reſpect that their ſacred function ought to
inſpire. Soon after the execution of Dr. Dodd for
forgery, another prieſt was puniſhed for debauching
young girls from ten to twelve years of age, whom
he had been employed to inſtruct in the principles
of morality and religion.

It is common to ſee clergymen fight duels;—I
ſhall ſay nothing of their drunkenneſs, and a thouſand other ſcandalous vices which they practiſe with-

out

---

* Since our author wrote, lord Surry, now a member of
the church of England, has ſucceeded to the dukedom of
Norfolk.

out shame. They are often imprisoned for debt; and it is only twenty years since, that they used to administer one of the most aweful ceremonies of religion, for a mere trifle.

They do not now celebrate clandestine marriages: formerly it was not necessary to run to Scotland to marry against the will of parents and guardians; a number of wretches were ready at all times of the day to bestow the nuptial benediction for the sum of two shillings. When one of them had pawned his gown—a circumstance not at all uncommon—he used to officiate in a brown or grey coat, and tie the *happy pair* as firmly together as a prelate clothed in his pontifical vestments, and administering the ceremony at the altar of his cathedral.

The church of England is governed by two archbishops and twenty-four bishops. The archbishop of Canterbury, who is the chief, is at the same time primate of England, and ranks next to the princes of the blood. He has twenty-one bishops under him; the remaining three are suffragans of the archbishop of York. All these prelates sit in the House of Peers, and are commonly devoted to the interests of the court. It is very uncommon to see them take part in the political debates, even if they are eloquent, for fear of exposing their dignity, which the peers in opposition would not, perhaps, have the modesty to respect.

As the clergy in all ages, and among all people, could never brook contradiction; and as this prerogative, which they arrogate to themselves, is not allowed in England, they have very wisely resolved to remain silent, and be altogether passive in parliament.

In the ages of barbarity and ignorance a law was enacted in favour of the church, equally singular and ridiculous; and as it formed one of the privileges

leges of a numerous and powerful body it would be very difficult, even now, to repeal it. At the time when the civil and ecclefiaftical ftates formed two feparate and diftinct bodies, and when none but the priefthood had any knowledge of learning, if a culprit was able to decypher a few of the Gothic characters in which the Bible was then written, he was allowed to efcape from punifhment.

As every one is able to read at this enlightened period, the penal ftatutes have now always a claufe, excluding the benefit of clergy.

The principles of toleration adopted by the Eng-lifh, account for the little zeal difplayed by them in making profelytes to their religion.

Scarce a fingle miffionary is to be met with in all their immenfe territories in Afia. There are only a few methodift, and fome anabaptifts, led thither by enthufiafm.

The laws oblige every fhip navigated by a hun-dred men to carry a clergyman with them; this is ftrictly obferved in all the king's fhips; the Eaft India company, however, regarding the church as a very unprofitable part of a cargo, take only ninety-nine men on board, and thus evade the ftatute. That opulent body never trouble themfelves about religion; for throughout all Bengal there is neither church nor chapel.

The Puritans are properly nothing elfe but Cal-vinifts; for all their ceremonies and principles are founded on the doctrines of that reformer. The French proteftants, however, do not join in their communion, but as in Gemany, follow their own liturgy, and perform divine fervice to this day in the French language. Their countrymen are ready to conclude from thence, that to reftore fo many thoufands to their native foil, the free exercife of their religion is only wanting. I doubt, however, whether fuch a toleration would make any im-

preffion

preffion on the *refugees* in England or Holland, and far lefs on thofe who refide in Germany.

'I he methodifts form a very numerous body: Whitfield was their founder. He was a man of profound knowledge and inflexible virtue, and has only died a few years fince. It was cuftomary with him to preach in the moft frequented ftreets and fquares in London. His intention was to reform and purify the morals of his fellow-citizens. The novelty of his fermons, and the place where he delivered them, always procured him a numerous auditory. The clergy were alarmed, and all the pulpits refounded with imprecations againft this man, who was defcribed as at once a fool and a fanatic. From that moment the people began to perfecute this zealous reformer, wherever he had the courage to appear. To outrage he oppofed fweetnefs of temper and invincible patience ; and, by means of this fage conduct, multiplied the number of his adherents. People of diftinction, who vifited him from curiofity, often became his difciples.

His fobriety and difcretion were very remarkable : his honefty alfo was unimpeachable; for he diftributed, with a fcrupulous exactnefs, the *alms* that were confided to his care. At length, being incapable of adminiftering the duties of his miffion to fuch immenfe crowds as attended him daily, he called in the affiftance of fome of his friends, and particularly of the celebrated Mr. Wefley. Soon after he built a church in the neighbourhood of Moorfields, called the Tabernacle, which is ftill held in high eftimation by his followers; many of whom have erected houfes in the neighbourhood.

Whitfield went four times to America to preach this doctrine, and was amply rewarded for his zeal. If ever the chief of a fect merited the efteem of a philofopher, it is without contradiction this fingular man. Without being impelled by ambition, or

avarice,

avarice, to carry on his projected reformation, he remained till his laſt moment faithful to his *aim*; which was, to make mankind better by means of a purer ſyſtem of morals.

It is eaſy to perceive from the *phlegm* with which the Engliſh perform the duties of their religion, that they are very little impreſſed by a ſenſe of its awfulneſs. Even in a collegiate church, when they are *chaunting* in full choir, the cold, inanimate, and ſometimes irreverent manner in which they acquit themſelves, ſhocks the feelings of a ſtranger.

The clergy and the laity who wiſh to paſs for good chriſtians, ſeem to think, that abſtaining from all works and worldly affairs on a Sunday entitles them to ſuch denomination. This Judaical and popular cuſtom is ſupported by a ſtatute which was enacted when puritaniſm was in full vigour, and which has not a little contributed to that gloomy taciturnity which forms ſuch a conſpicuous feature in an Engliſhman's character.

The above law prohibits the amuſements of muſic and dancing on the only day when the tradeſman or mechanic has time to divert himſelf.

We cannot but deplore the weakneſs of human nature on beholding great and enlightened men becoming the zealous partizans of ridiculous and even pernicious cuſtoms. The learned Dr. Johnſon was ſo attached to this in particular, that, on his deathbed, he conjured Sir Joſhua Reynolds to grant him one requeſt:—The Engliſh Apelles promiſed his aſſent—and found it to be—" That he would not paint *on a Sunday.*"

The pulpit is often made uſe of in the capital to inſinuate and propagate political principles. The court party generally make uſe of this method, which is notwithſtanding always hurtful to their intereſts. The clergy on ſuch occaſions are invariably led by the hope of preferment: no one, however

ever

ever, is *duped* by their conduct. When they confine themselves to subjects in which politics are not concerned, they are for the most part heard with attention.

Soon after the earthquake at Lisbon, they declaimed against masquerades, and occasioned the abolition of that species of amusement for many years.

By proving that *inoculation* was an useful and a necessary operation, they brought it into fashion: they even went so far as to interest the conscience of parents, and make it appear a duty.

All *fasts* are appointed by the king, as head of the church. Those days are not so solemn as Sundays: they are, however, literally *penitentiary* to the poor, who by means of them are prevented from procuring food for their wives and children.

The anniversary of the unfortunate Charles I. which is celebrated on the 30th of January, has now degenerated into a *mere farce*. Wilkes once asserted in the House of Commons, that this day was the most glorious in the annals of his country!

I beg leave to observe here, that the opinions concerning any monarch of modern times have never been so contradictory, as in respect to that sovereign. Among many, he passes as a state criminal who merited his fate: the greater number, however, revere him as a saint who was the innocent victim of a party composed of fanatical and ambitious men.

The famous Hume has not a little contributed, in his History of England, to propagate this latter opinion. The end he proposed was undoubtedly to sacrifice the public confidence, of which every historian ought to be ambitious, on the altar of riches and preferment. At the reign of Elizabeth he leaves the right road, and ceases to follow the track

of

of truth. Thofe who wifh to inveftigate the hiftory of that country under the government of the houfe of Stuart, can follow no better guide than Rapin de Thoyras; an impartial writer, who has proved all his affertions by authentic documents, and by that means acquired and maintained an extraordinary degree of reputation in England.

But if we will fuppofe for a moment that the innocence of Charles is only imaginary, it muft be allowed that a free people, who have eftablifhed certain principles of their own concerning the laws and the rights of human nature, are alone capable of judging whether, in fuch a' cafe, a head encircled by a royal diadem merits the hatchet of an executioner. The philofopher of onother country can only think in his clofet on this tragical and memorable event.

I now return to my fubject. The Quakers in England, twenty years ago, amounted to fixty thoufand: they are not fo numerous at prefent. The young men, in whom religious fervour is not fo ardent as formerly, abjure a faith which excludes them from all employments and dignities. The young women, too, are by it limited in their ambition, with regard to marriage; and their vanity is not a litte mortified, with refpect to drefs, which is fo natural to their age and fex. As they cannot ufe fancy colours, nor wear powder, feathers, ribbands, nor jewels, they ufually wear the deareft ftuffs: this does not, however, compenfate for what they lofe in regard to other parts of their apparel.

The coats of the men are generally without buttons and without plaits; the hats are alfo large and round: many, however, neglect all this, and appear like other people. The moft zealous of the fect are thofe only who ftill preferve an outward diftinction: their averfion to oaths and criminal profecutions is a characteriftic common to all.

The

The legiflative power has been exceedingly indulgent towards them. Their folemn affirmation is
admitted in every cafe where the life and liberty of
the fubjeƈt is not interefted. One never fees a
quaker the profecutor in a criminal aƈtion. Their
averfion to war is fo great, that, during the invafion
of the favages of Pennfylvania in 1775, they allowed
their country to be ravaged, and their fellow-citizens to be maffacred, without choofing to revenge
them. They remained deaf to all their calamities
and misfortunes; and it was not till defpair had
taken poffeffion of their fouls, and the dead bodies
of their flaughtered brethren had been expofed before the ftate-houfe at Philadelphia, that the
quakers had confented to take up arms.

The anabaptifts decreafe in numbers, and for the
very fame reafon as the quakers. They do not
affeƈt to diftinguifh themfelves from the reft of mankind by the originality of their drefs, manners, or
language.

It is at Chelfea, a village beautifully fituated on
the banks of the Thames, where their principal
place of worfhip is, they have alfo feveral others in
London.

Notwithftanding the prodigious number of different perfuafions in England, *deifm* makes a rapid
progrefs. The reverend Mr. Williams, in the
year 1776, formed the refolution of eftablifhing a
new feƈt. In confequence of this, he hired a chapel
in the metropolis, and procured a great number of
fubfcribers. This hardy attempt made much noife.
Two letters, one from the late king of Pruffia, and
the other written by Voltaire to this clergyman, in
which thefe two great men beftowed many praifes
on his undertaking, helped to make the attempt ftill
more remarkable. As this projeƈtor joined fome
talents to a great knowledge of the world he put in
praƈtice every fcheme to eftablifh his enterprife.

One

One might then fee a circumftance before unexampled in the annals of mankind : a numerous affembly compofed of people of all religions united under one head, laying afide all manner of myfteries and ceremonies, and adoring the God cf the univerfe in concert. The fervice had fomething in it very engaging on account of its fimplicity ; but its famenefs was not fufficiently fafcinating to mankind in general. To the *deift* it was, however, too ceremonious; becaufe it is very difficult to perfuade him of the utility of any form of worfhip whatever.

In fine, the fcheme failed. Thefe meetings have not been held thefe fome years paft ; and the chapel is now become a conventicle for methodifts. Williams has publifhed his liturgy. It is an excellent work ; has had much fuccefs, and is ftill read with pleafure.

/ Deifm is in a great degree the caufe of fuicide—a crime at prefent fo common in England. The Englifh have actually a form of prayer, in which they befeech God to banifh from the hearts of his fervants fuch a frightful temptation! j

The crime, however, is as frequently committed at Paris as in London ; a circumftance which proves very forcibly to me, that this epidemical diforder proceeds lefs from the climate and the ufe of feacoal fires, than we imagine on the continent. The Englifh view it as a difeafe of the foul, which, far far from deferving reproach, ought rather to excite compaffion. The punifhment, which, to the difgrace of reafon, is ftill in many countries attached to felf-murder, never reftrains defpair, which mocks it, but falls wholly on innocent and afflicted families.

This malady (for I can call it no other) often gives occafion to the moft fingular fcenes. I one day beheld an ill-dreffed man, with a countenance diftorted by a thoufand paffions, who walked backwards

and

and forwards on the baluſtrade of Blackfriars-bridge,
and ſeemed to be in the profoundeſt reverie. The
danger that he was expoſed to, ſoon made him remarked, and occaſioned great inquietude to the paſ-
ſengers. One perſon having urged him to deſcend,
he made no anſwer: at length ſome of the ſpectators becoming more preſſing in their entreaties, he
aſked one of them if he would do him a favour. On
being anſwered in the affirmative, he beſought him
to find out a certain perſon, whoſe dwelling he deſ-
cribed with the utmoſt exactneſs, and recount to him
what he had ſeen.——With theſe words he leapt into
the Thames.

The conduct of the honourable Mr. Damer,
only ſon to lord Milton, was ſtill more extraordinary, and gave riſe to a thouſand melancholy reflections. Young, handſome, tenderly beloved by
his father, nearly adored by the ladies, and with all
the honours and dignities of the ſtate within his
reach, he conceived a ſudden diſguſt to life.

Having repaired to a bagnio, he commanded
twelve of the moſt handſome women of the town to
be brought to him, and gave orders that they ſhould
be ſupplied with all manner of delicacies. Having
afterwards bolted the door, he made them undreſs
one another, and, when naked, requeſted them to
amuſe him with the moſt voluptuous attitudes.
About an hour afterwards he diſmiſſed them, loaded
with preſents, and then, drawing a piſtol from his
pocket, immediately put an end to his exiſtence.
This happened in the year 1776.

It is mortifying to reflect that this hatred to exiſtence ſhould have taken poſſeſſion of the mind of ſo
great man as lord Clive, who alſo terminated his
glorious career with his own hand. It is neither his
rank nor his immenſe riches, but his great abilities
and his extraordinary exploits in Aſia, which make
him appear great in my eyes. I am convinced that
this

this nobleman, as a general and statesman, would
have been equally eminent. in Europe as in Afia.
Let it be remembered, however, that I fpeak of
nothing but his talents, as I am very careful of faying much about his private character. If the
clamours of plundered and oppreffed Indians and
Europeans had never reached from the borders of
the Ganges to the banks of the Thames, his immenfe riches alone would have attefted his infatiable
avarice. All his treafures, however, could not prevent a profecution againft him, which expofed his
character to obloquy, and his conduct to obfervation; and which, by infenfibly augmenting the
melancholy that had long preyed upon his mind,
precipitated that fatal refolution which delivered
mankind from the fcourge of Afia.

———————

The Jews are allowed in England, as well as in
Holland, the free exercife of their religion; their
numbers and their riches are therefore continually
augmenting. One is aftonifhed at the prodigious
difference between the Portuguefe and German
Jews eftablifhed in that ifland. Drefs, language,
manners, cleanlinefs, are all in favour of the former;
who indeed can fcarce be diftinguifhed from Chrifti-
ans. This extends even to their prejudices and
their public worfhip: the features peculiar to the
whole race are the only peculiarity that they have in
common.

The famous Toland, in the year 1715, recommended the naturalization of this people; a circumftance that actually took place in 1752, by means
of an act of parliament. However, the general
difcontent of the nation, occafioned by the German
Jews (a clafs of men who may be looked upon as
the very refufe of human nature) obliged the
legiflature

legiſlature to repeal it in the courſe of the following year.

All the children of Iſrael, who are obliged to quit Holland and Germany, take refuge in England, where they live by roguery: if they themſelves do not ſteal, they at leaſt help to conceal and to diſpoſe of the plunder. They are therefore ſo much hated in England, that the honeſty of their Portugueſe brethren cannot weaken the unfavourable impreſſion which ſuch a band of robbers has occaſioned.

There is a perſon of this nation called Cain Chenul Falk, but better known by the name of Doctor Falcon, who for thirty years has been famous for his cabaliſtical diſcoveries. He lives in a large houſe; is attended by a ſmall number of domeſticks; is engaged in no manner of buſineſs; and gives away a great deal of money to the poor. When he goes out, which is indeed but ſeldom, he is always clothed in a long robe, which agrees very well with his flowing beard, and noble figure. He is now in the 70th year of his age. I ſhall not here recount the wonderful and incredible ſtories told of this old man. It is moſt probable that he is a very great chymiſt; and that he has, in that occult ſcience, made ſome extraordinary diſcoveries, which he does not chooſe to communicate. A certain prince, who was very zealous in his ſearch after the philoſopher's ſtone, ſome years ago wiſhed to pay him a viſit, Falkon, however, could not be prevailed upon to grant him an interview.

It may be eaſily imagined that, in a city like London, there are a great number of weak people who may be eaſily impoſed upon. As the Engliſh have a high opinion of the German alchymiſts, the projectors of that country often pretend to have found out the art of making gold, and dupe them of their guineas by means of this ſtale trick.

Magic

Magic, contented with exercifing its defpotifm within the ten circles of High Germany, has not as yet, by a bold flight, attempted to crofs the ocean. If this filly and ridiculous paffion were ever to take root in England, its effects would be very uncommon in that country, where every thing is in extremes.

In the year 1777, Linguet went to London with the profeffed intention of reforming the national character : he had, however, unfortunately neglected to learn the language.

This Frenchman was always fond of paradoxes.

His pride was flattered to fee certain objects in a different light from the reft of mankind ; he had, in his own country, written a panegyric on the virtues of a Tiberius and a Nero—two monfters, who were a difgrace to human nature. He affirms, " That " England never produced any one great man ; " that its boafted conftitution does not preferve " liberty to the fubject ; that the inhabitants are " not induftrious ; that their navy is contemptible ; " that their failors are both ignorant and cowardly ; " and, laftly, that Garrick was a bad actor."

Under pretence that he was afraid of being perfecuted by the Englifh government, this fingular man fuddenly difappeared, and returned to his ungrateful countrymen, who recompenfed his patriotifm with a lodging in the Baftile.

CHAPTER

CHAPTER VI.

Public Spirit—National Characteristics—Hospitals—
General Wolfe—The Duke de Nivernois—Genero-
sity of the English Ladies—Maria Theresa—Lord
Tyrconnel—Lord Chatham.

ONE of the most distinguished characteristics of
the English is their *public spirit*; a virtue unknown
in any other country, and which no other language
than theirs is able to express. This passion consists
in the active zeal of every individual, to co-operate
towards the general good: the very lowest of the
people possess it in a very extraordinary degree.

During the American war, many common sailors
refused the bounty that was offered by parliament, and entered into the navy from mere attachment to their country. I have known several poor
people, who, at a general election, have remained
deaf to the most lucrative offers, and reserved their
voices for those who, by their patriotism and their
talents, were most capable of serving the state.

The great number of public foundations, every
where to be met with, prove in an eminent degree
the warmth of this national virtue. Without mentioning either the naval hospital of Grenwich, or
the military establishment at Chelsea, which rival
royal palaces in magnificence, London contains a
prodigious number of public edifices which are
regulated with astonishing order. St. Bartholomew's
hospital alone can admit 5000 patients at one time.
Bedlam, which is appropriated to the cure of madness, is celebrated for its conveniencies, and the
attention which is paid to the unfortunate wretches

who

who happen to be afflicted with that terrible malady. At the gate are two statues, executed by an English artist, of the name of * Cibber, which may be reckoned among the few excellent specimens of sculpture which England has produced. One of these represents a wretch absorbed in the most profound melancholy; the other a desperate maniac loaded with chains. These two figures are executed with so much expression, that they may dispute the palm with thee first performances in Westminster-abbey.

In regard to works of national munificence, and public utility, the court party and the opposition constantly unite. Even in places of diversion, the English endeavour to excite patriotism. The most brilliant actions of some of the most famous of their generals are represented in tbe saloon at Vauxhall. It is thus that the memory of Clive, a Boscawen, and an Amherst are immortalized; and that their fellow-citizens are inflamed, even in the very lap of pleasure, with the noble emulation of rivalling their virtues.

The source of this lively interest, which every Englishman evinces in the affairs of his country, proceeds from the idea that the very meanest subject is benefitted by the prosperity of the commonwealth. This gives rise to the most singular customs. After a victory, they compliment each other. The glory of a state, of which every individual is a member, sometimes affects them in such a manner, that I have seen persons remarkable for their phlegm, congratulate one another with the utmost transports of joy.

It is not till become venerable by age, that the human eye, which observes every thing too near it in a bad light, is at length accustomed to see things in their true point of view. We regard with an

attachment

* Father to Colley Cibber.

attachment bordering on enthufiafm, the actions
of the great men of antiquity, and pay but a cold
admiration to the fame actions, when performed
by our contemporaries. Of this the name of general
Wolfe is a striking example.

Thofe who are acquainted with the events of the
war before the laft, muft recollect that this great
man perifhed before Quebec in the arms of victory; but few, perhaps, know that to him alone
the glory of conquering Canada belongs.

Both the navy and army were agreed on the propriety of raifing the fiege of Quebec, which was
deemed impregnable. Wolfe alone thought otherwife, and he was triumphant. In the midft of the
action, having received a mortal wound, he immediately fainted, and was carried out of the field of
battle. In the mean time the enemy's line being
broken, fome of the foldiers employed in attending
him called out, " They fly." Thefe words, as it
were, penetrating to his very foul, recall him to
life ; he opens his eyes, and afks with great eagernefs, " Who fly ?"—" The French." " Then
" God be praifed !" he replied,—and immediately
expired.

Epaminandos in the fame manner died invoking
the gods for victory with his laft breath.

The duke of Nivernois, who went into England
in the year 1762, in quality of ambaffador extraordinary from the court of Verfailles, to fign the
peace betwixt England and France, experienced
the effects of the national fpirit in a very uncommon
manner. The firft night after his arrival, having
flept at Canterbury, the mafter of the Inn thought
that he ought not to let flip fuch a good occafion
of making a long bill. " A nobleman," fays he,
" of fo elevated a rank, charged with the reconci-
" liation of two great nations after a bloody war,
" will not fignalize his entry into the kingdom by a
                                                " difpute

" difpute with a tavern-keeper about a reckoning."
He accordingly demanded fifty guineas next morning for a night's lodging. The impudence of the
charge aftonifhed his grace; who paid it, however,
without hefitation, continued his journey, and foon
forgot the petty impofition, leaving the inn-keeper
in raptures; who, thinking that the whole affair was
à fecret, plumed himfelf upon his management.

The inhabitants of Canterbury, however, happening to hear of the circumftance, notwithftanding their
natural antipathy to the French, were feized with indignation, and thought that the national honour was
concerned in the punifhment of it. In confequence of
this, the firft people in that city affembled together,
and befought the duke to bring the delinquent to
juftice. The ambaffador thanked them for their
intentions, but would not hear of a profecution.
Thefe gentlemen, therefore, refolved to punifh him
themfelves. The inn, kept by this fellow, was the
largeft and beft frequented in the whole town; the
refort to it was prodigious; the neighbouring gentlemen held their clubs and affemblies in that place.
On being informed of this circumftance, they all
with one accord determined never to enter the houfe
any more. The landlord put every fcheme in practice to bring back his cuftomers; but they were
deaf to his prayers and entreaties. In this fituation
he was affailed by his creditors, and in a few
months experienced all the horrors of poverty. He
died fome years afterwards in London, where he
had refided in the fituation of a waiter.

Such circumftances of national fpirit are not uncommon in England: they are, however, related to
as in Germany in fuch fantaftical manner, that,
inftead of exciting fentiments of admiration, they
only occafion us to fmile.

The generous refolution of the Englifh ladies in
1742, is an anecdote extremely well known. The
misfortunes

misfortunes of Maria Therefa affected them so deeply, that they unanimoufly refolved to difpofe of their jewels, and fend her Imperial Majefty the produce of them, to help her to carry on the war againft her enemies. They accordingly opened a fubfcription. The old duchefs of Marlborough gave 20,000l. and the fum total amounted in a few days to 100,000l. fterling. The emprefs, however, refufed the offer, and in a moft affecting letter, after returning her thanks for their generous intentions, obferved, that it was the affiftance of the whole nation, and not that of individuals, that her majefty could accept of.

If this magnanimous conduct of a few women who knew nothing of Maria Therefa, but her misfortunes, had happened fome centuries ago, it would at this day be the object of our admiration and aftonifhment: it made the moft lively impreffion on the mind of the emprefs queen.

Strangers, and more particularly the French, are pleafed to ridicule the intereft which the Englifh take in regard to political tranfactions; this *tafte* appears to them extremely foolifh.

Lord Tyrconnel, a nobleman of Irifh extraction, but who, being born and educated in France, had of courfe adopted their manners, their fafhions, and their maxims, when he was thirty years of age vifited England for the firft time. As he underftood the language extremely well, he was obliged to hear political difcuffions wherever he went; fo that his averfion to this fubject foon amounted to an infurmountable difguft. At laft, refolved to divert himfelf without being eternally plagued about ftate affairs, he repairs to a bagnio, and invites fome females to fup with him: he had, however, fcarcely taken his place at table when thefe female politicians began alfo to difcufs parliamentary queftions. His lordfhip in vain attempted to give another turn

to

to the converfation;—it had too many charms for thefe nymphs to be dropped fo eafily; they always returned to the fubject, till at laft this Frenchified Irifhman, lofing all patience, left them in a paffion, and next day returned to France.

It is feldom or never that an Englifhman unites the character of a minifter with that of a patriot. The prodigious power, and the facility with which they are enabled to amafs aftonifhing riches, generally make the minifters forget thofe principles, which by giving them popularity, raifed them to eminence.

Would it be imagined that in a kingdom where the power of the fovereign is reftrained, that of his minifters fhould be more extenfive than in moft defpotic governments? This is, however, the cafe in England, where the king, according to the principles of the conftitution, can do no *wrong*, and where thofe whom he employs are obliged to be anfwerable for every thing. They not only influence parliament; the honours, the dignities, the very treafure of the nation are confided to their care;—in fine, they difpofe of every thing. It is fingular enough to fee a fimple efquire making dukes and earls at his pleafure, beftowing ribbands which he himfelf does not poffefs, and giving away employments which are at once lucrative and certain, while the duration of his own power depends entirely on the king's pleafure.

Of all the ftatefmen whom England has produced, no one was ever fo zealous a patriot as the immortal Chatham, who joined to extraordinary talents the pureft attachment to his country. Never was any Englifh minifter fo much honoured with the public confidence; and never was there fuch a happy concord between the king, the parliament, and the people, as under his adminiftration. Alas, it was too fhort for the welfare of England!

G   It

It is thought that, if he had remained two years longer in office, the American war would never have happened, and the flourishing situation in which his country found herself in the year 1762, would have been nothing more than a presage of that glory to which she would have afterwards arrived.

During his administration, all the power of the state appeared to be wholly centered in him, for his associates in the government seemed only so many subalterns acting under his directions. By his means Great Britain, with a degree of felicity unexampled before among any of the European nations, was triumphant in the course of one * year, in the four quarters of the globe.

France never had so dangerous an enemy :—it was a principle with him to humble that formidable power.

He was not fond of a court;—during the time of peace, he could scarce hide his aversion to it, as he was persuaded that it was impossible to be at the same time the favourite of the sovereign and the friend of the people.

Notwithstanding his infirmities, he *never failed*, even towards the latter end of his life, to pay the most exact attention to his parliamentary duties: wrapped up in flannels, and supported by crutches, his voice was a terror to the ministry. He may be truly said to have died in the service of his country; having been seized with a mortal distemper in the midst of a speech in the House of Peers, in which he asserted its dearest interests.

At the very last moment of his life, his mind was occupied by the cares of patriotism. Lord Camden was present at his dissolution. This nobleman was the intimate friend of the hero; his integrity, his abilities, and an uniformity in principles had con-
ciliated

* 1759.

ciliated his efteem and rendered him worthy of it.
Socrates at his laft hour philofophifed with his
friends; and thefe two great men converfed about
ftate affairs at the very brink of eternity. At length
perceiving his death to approach, the noble patriot,
after locking his friend's hands in his own, exclaimed " My dear Camden, fave my country!"
The beft proof that can be given of the virtue of
this great man, is the confideration, that he was
for many years prime minifter of Great Britain
without either becoming more rich, or more haughty, than while a private gentleman.

After his deceafe, the greateft honours were paid
to his memory, the expences of his funeral dif-
charged by the public, and a large penfion affigned
to his family. His body was accompanied to the
grave by moft of thofe who, on account of their
birth, their rank, and above all their talents, might
be reckoned the greateft men in the ftate. It was
not a flight lofs that they deplored —every one was
deeply afflicted; even the fpectators were in tears.
Colonel Barre, a celebrated orator, and who in
Lord Chatham's life-time had often oppofed his
meafures, amidft the emotions of his grief, fnatching
the banner of the deceafed earl from one of his
domeftics, carried it with his own hand into the
church. When the corpfe was laid in the grave,
the marquis of Landfdowne exclaimed, " The fun
" of England is now fet for ever."

CHAPTER

CHAPTER VII.

Commerce of the English—The Peace of 1762—The Duke of Bedford—Duc de Choiseul—The Merchants—Sir George Colbrooke—Bank of England.

ALTHOUGH the principal natural productions exported from England are only tin and coal, yet the inhabitants are the first commercial nation in the world. It is to an excellent constitution, wise laws, and an active and indefatigable genius, that this eminent advantage is to be attributed.

It is natural that the last of these qualities, joined to enterprise and prudence, should extend its trade, and add daily to its riches, From this also proceeds that spirit of conquest which the English of the present age, and the Carthaginians of old, have interwoven in their commercial system. This has never been the case with the Dutch; their acquisitions were entirely the effect of a happy conjuncture of circumstances at a period when, with arms in their hands, they were obliged to defend their liberties—nay, I may add their lives.

Since the time of Cromwell, the real or pretended reason for all their wars was commerce alone. They never have acceded to any treaty of peace since the protectorate of that great man, (except the unfortunate one of 1783), which did not procure them some incontestable advantages in favour of their trade. All their statesmen, however differently they may have thought in respect to other

matters,

matters, have agreed unanimoufly in this great national principle; even in the moft critical fituations this was never forgotten: the reafon is indeed apparent; it alone could make their adminiftration popular, cover their blunders, and acquire them reputation.

If we are to believe the chevalier d'Eon, the late duke of Bedford was one of thofe infamous minifters, who from venal motives betrayed their country to France, by the peace of 1762. There can be but little doubt concerning the juftice of this accufation, as it came from a perfon who was at that very time *charge de'affaires*, and minifter plenipotentiary from the court of Verfailles; and who confequently had good opportunities of knowing the fact, and indeed offered to give the moft convincing proofs of it.

This nobleman, although he made no difficulty in felling his country for gold, was neverthelefs capable of an action feemingly very great, but which had its fource in fear; for although an Englifh minifter fhould defpife both the king and the parliament, he dare not brave the fury of the people. This dread of the people is a new proof of the excellence of their conftitution. A courtier may be furrounded with honours, and invefted with dignities; but an open and upright conduct alone can give him reputation and conciliate the favour of his fellow-citizens.

The duke of Bedford, the richeft fubject in England, was fent in the year 1762 to Paris, in quality of Ambaffador, to fign the peace. He was oppofed to the duke de Choifeul, and this univerfal genius was evidently fuperior to him in regard to talents. The preliminary articles having been figned, were foon known in Paris, and the next morning an Englifh Jew requefted an audience of the duke of Bedford. This man, who had been

G 3   for

for many years in Afia, made his grace fenfible, that, from an ignorance of the trade and even the geography of that country, he had committed fuch grofs faults that the Eaft India company would lofe feveral thoufand pounds fterling yearly by his means, and that the treaty itfelf would be the occafion of new quarrels between the two nations.

The ambaffador faw that the Jew was in the right, and refolved inftantly to repair his fault. Having procured the new articles in writing, he immediately departed for Verfailles, and befought the duke to have them acceded to. " I did not " think," obferved Choifeul, " that I had been " negociating with a novice in politics, but with " the minifter of a powerful nation, who knew the " validity of a treaty figned with his own hand." The duke of Bedford replied to this with all the boldnefs and noble franknefs of a true Englifhman. " You " are in the right—I am but a novice, and not an " experienced minifter. I have erred through " ignorance; but I fhall not by a bafe treafon " aggravate the fault which I have committed, for " to be filent in a cafe of this importance would be " actually to merit the name of a traitor. Choofe " therefore for yourfelf—either confent to make " the propofed alteration which I have mentioned " to you, or I fhall inftantly depart and lay my " head at the mercy of the Englifh parliament."

A peace was then abfolutely neceffary for France: the duke de Choifeul agreed to fome of the propofitions; and, if we may believe report, the negociation was haftened by a prefent.

The profeffion of commerce is highly efteemed in England, and is honoured and confidered as the fource of all the wealth of the ftate. A merchant may become a juftice of the peace, or a member of parliament; in fine, he may afpire to the firft dignities.

nities, provided his talents correfpond with his ambition.

Even tradefmen are hel'd in fome degree of
refpect, and indeed feem entitled to it both by their
behaviour and their riches. Some of them are exceedingly affluent. I myfelf know that the late duke
of Newcaftle owed his butcher no lefs than 11,000l.
at one time.

The love of convenience, to which the Englifh
are fo much attached, makes them confide their
cafh to the care of a banker. Not only merchants,
but alfo wealthy people in private life, and fometimes even the public offices, depofit their money in
this manner. There were forty eight banking houfes
in the metropolis in the year 1784.

The eminent merchants alfo open accounts with
the bank of England, which receives more than
half the ready money in the kingdom, and in return
circulates its own paper.

None but very rich people ever become bankers ;
of thefe two, three, or four, generally affociate together, and depofit a large fum of money to anfwer
the neceffary demands. The duke of Marlborough
generally keeps 15, or 20,000l. in the hands of
Child ; Drummond often has 100,000l. fterling
belonging to the Admiralty and War-office.

About twelve years fince Sir George Colbrooke
exhibited a wonderful example of that thirft after
wealth, with which fome men are fo unfortunately
curfed. This gentleman was a member of parliament, the firft banker in London, and for many
years chairman of the Eaft India Company. He
gave great entertainments kept a numerous retinue
of fervants, and could command any fum of money.
Would it be imagined that fuch a man could ever
be ruined by a fpeculation upon alum? It is actually
a fact, that having attempted to monopolife this article, and by that means acquire a new acceffion to

his

his immense fortune, he failed in his project, and became bankrupt. His poverty was at length so great that he was obliged to solicit support from that very company whose affairs he had formerly directed with unbounded sway.

Having obtained with some difficulty an annuity of two hundred per annum, he went to France, and lived for many years at Boulogne.

On the commencement of the war, in the year 1778, the court of France, who had given orders for the departure of all the English from that kingdom, were so affected with his catastrophe, that an exception was made in favour of him and his family.

The order and regularity which prevail in the bank of England are truly admirable. It is reckoned that the notes lost annually by shipwreck, fire and other accidents, pay all the expences of this great establishment. The duke de Choiseul once attempted to ruin its credit ; for some days there was a continual demand upon it, and the directors taking fright, began to pay in silver, which was counted out very slowly by the clerks. The emissaries of France every where prognosticated its downfal ; all England was alarmed : it was saved, however, by the public spirit of the merchants, the principal of whom associated together, and agreed to take its notes in payments.

The East India company keep their money in the bank of England, and have been known on the arrival of a fleet, to give a draft of 160,000l. sterling for the duties, on a small slip of paper.

Some years since a Hertfordshire farmer applied to one of the clerks of the bank for the loan of 800l. for a few days, on a note of 10,000l. which he held in his hand, and offered to deposit with him. The clerk refused him, observing that such a thing was unusual, at the same time offering either to pay him

him the whole amount in cafh, or exchánge it for lef-
fer notes. This, however, would not fatisfy the farmer, who ftill perfeyered.—What would have been
done to a peafant in fuch a cafe, either in France or
Germany! He would have been beat by the domeftics, and then pufhed into the ftreet.

He may thank his ftars for having been born in
England. Inftead of fuch treatment, at his own
requeft he was waited upon by Mr. Payne, one of
the directors, who inftantly lent him the money required.

Having returned, according to his promife, at
the end of eight days, and punctually repaid the
fum which he had borrowed, on being afked, why
he had fuch an attachment to that particular note,
he frankly replied, " Becaufe I have the fellow of
" it at home."

Notwithftanding it is extremely difficult to coun-
terfeit a bank-note, more efpecially on account of
the water-mark, which is imprinted on the paper
while making, yet the allurements arifing from fuccefs have induced many to make the attempt. In
the year 1776, a great number were iffued, in
which the original was imitated with wonderful art.
The fraud was not difcovered until notes to the
amount of thirty-fix thoufand pounds fterling had
been circulated among the public.

After prodigious trouble and expence, the bank
at laft difcovered, feized, and imprifoned the ingenious culprit.

This circumftance gave occafion to an event,
which puts human nature to the blufh ; it is, indeed, fo diabolically atrocious, that one would readily believe it to be an anecdote borrowed from the
annals of the infernal regions.

The perfon who had committed the forgery was
of the name of Morton ; he was a young man of a
reputable family, and as foon as apprehended was

G 5   carried

to gaol, and being put in irons, languished amidst
all the horrors naturally inspired by a criminal profecution.

The governors of the bank were exceedingly re-
joiced, as they hoped, in the course of the tryal,
to discover the whole of this mysterious affair,
which levelled at the very source of their credit.

It was on this idea that a pretended friend of Morton's founded his infernal project. This person
whose name was D—, repairs to the prison, informs
the young man how much he was affected with his
unhappy destiny, and assures him that he is disposed
to attempt every stratagem to snatch him from ine-
vitable destruction.

A friend in such a situation is always welcome.
The prisoner, who expected nothing else than an
infamous and speedy death, thinks that he sees his
guardian angel before him, and puts his destiny entirely
in the power of the traitor, who in a short time, by
means of money and ingenuity, accomplishes his
escape from the dungeon where he was confined.

Every thing being prepared for flight, Morton
next morning has the inexpressible satisfaction of
seeing himself at liberty. and in the dominions of
France. He changes his name, takes the road to
Flanders, and arriving at Bruges, resolves to reside
there.

D—, in the mean time had not lost sight of his
plan. He proposes to the bank, who were greatly
embarrassed at the escape of Morton, to deliver him
into their hands on condition of receiving the sum of
5000l. as a reward.

The governors thought that this was too high a
premium, and perhaps imagined, with great justice,
that a man who offered to betray his friend for five
thousand pounds, would find no great reluctance in
committing the same villiany for one thousand ; and
he

he feeing that he could obtain no more, at length gave his confent.

In the mean time that paffion which the Englifh entertain for their native country preyed fo violently on the mind of Morton, that all his wifhes pointed folely towards England.

Four months were already elapfed, and he was ftill at Bruges; from hence he had kept up a conftant correfpondence with D—, who from time to time had fent him fome trifling fupplies of money, when he received the joyous news that he might now go back to England in fafety; as his family had fucceeded in the negociation with the bank, for that purpofe. Thus what neither the fignature of all the governors, nor the very word of the fovereign himfelf could have accomplifhed, was inftantly effected by a fimple letter from his perfidious correfpondent.

Full of a blind confidence in his deliverer and benefactor, who had defired him to return immediately, he arrives in London, and is arrefted; the profecution is immediately commenced, D— receives the reward of his treachery, and Morton was executed in a few days after.

CHAPTER

CHAPTER VIII.

Public Executions; Earl Ferrers—Alderman Sayre—
The celebrated Chevalier d'Eon—Monf. de Mo-
rande—Dr. Dodd—An Anecdote—Barbarous Pu-
niſhment in Scotland—Singular Law with regard
to women—Prohibitions againſt Swearing—Hunt-
ing of Animals—The Lord Chancellor—Free Ma-
ſons—Strict Obſervation of the Letter of the
Law.

ENGLISH Liberty would actually be what it
appears to the ignorant, a mere chimera, if the
laws of that country did not act with the ſame vigour againſt the nobility as the people.

An infraction of them, whether it is in regard to
property or life, is puniſhed without any reſpect
to the rank or fortune of the culprit : and although
ro bounds are ſet by the conſtitution to the mercy
of the king, yet he never protects thoſe criminals
who ſurrounded with titles and dignities imagine
that they are thereby ſheltered from the puniſhment
which the law denounces againſt their actions. It
is indeed certain that in England, as in all other
countries, a thouſand machines may be put in motion, and a multitude of intrigues practiſed to blind
the eyes of the monarch, and procure pardon for
criminals of diſtinction ; this is a cuſtom which
neither the ſovereign nor the legiſlature can aboliſh
without overturning the conſtitution.

I ſhall produce ſome examples of this impartiality
from the hiſtory of our own times, a method which
I intend

I intend to purfue as often as poffible in the courfe of this work, and which is undoubtedly more entertaining and inftructive, than long and fatiguing arguments. Among other advantages it will enable the reader to fupply my incapacity by allowing him to form his own judgment on facts, for the authenticity of which I pledge myfelf.

Every body knows that after the battle of Culloden many noblemen were executed for their attachment to the houfe of Stuart: but for more than a century before that no peer of the realm had been condemned to death for any other crime than treafon.

The earl of Ferrers, uncle to the prefent lord of that name, about twenty-eight years fince offered a melancholy inftance of fuch a cafe by murdering his fteward, not in the heat of paffion, but in a cool premeditated manner. As he lived fome time after the wound, his lordfhip fent for a furgeon, who finding that it was mortal, informed a magiftrate of the circumftance. The earl was upon this arrefted and carried to the tower of London. As every citizen has a right to be tried by his equals, and the peers of England are a diftinct body, the Houfe of Lords are confequently fole judges in this kind of procefs. On thefe occafions they are all fummoned, not as legiflators, but as members of a judicial tribunal, and their affemblies are not convoked in the ufual place, but in Weftminfter-hall, which is more commodious on account of its fituation and immenfe fpace.

This was the auguft tribunal which took cognizance of the procefs againft lord Ferrers, and condemned him by an unanimous decree. The laws ordain that the body of a murderer fhall be anatomifed, and this circumftance afflicted him in a very fenfible manner. He heard his fentence pronounced with the utmoft compofure; but when

that

that part which mentioned his diffection was read,
he inftantly exclaimed " God forbid !" It was in
vain that he requefted to be beheaded inftead of
being hanged on a gibbet; he defired to die in the
tower where his anceftor the earl of Effex had been
executed, but he was told that he muft prepare to
fuffer at Tyburn in common with the vileft criminals.

The only favour they would grant him was to
allow the ufe of his own carriage in the journey inftead of being drawn in a cart: an indulgence which
Dodd and others afterwards experienced.

He accordingly repaired to Tyburn in a mourning coach; his horfes covered with crape, and his
fervants clothed in black. On his arrival he mounted
the fcaffold, and was obliged to remain there a
whole hour with the rope about his neck. This
period being elapfed, one of the fheriffs who accompanied him mentioned that his time was expired, and took leave of him. His Lordfhip on
this immediately took a leap; the fcaffold was
removed, and the body left fufpended in the air.

The corpfe was afterwards carried to Surgeon's
Hall, where it was expofed naked for three whole
days, that the law might be fulfilled in every point.
The hangman fhewed the rope with which he had
been executed, and fuch is always the folly of the
people, that many thoufands paid a fhilling a piece
for the fight of it. The body was afterwards de-
pofited in the family vault, and the brother of the
defunct immediately took the title.

The peereffes enjoy the fame privileges in regard
to trial as the peers themfelves, and it was in recollection of this that an illuftrious * princefs thrown
into prifon a few years fince, and dubious of her
deftiny, exclaimed, " Why am I not in my own
" dear country, where my trial would have been
" conducted

* The late queen of Denmark.

" conducted publicly, and by the moſt noble
" judges !

It was in the year 1776 that the ducheſs of
Kingſton was accuſed of bigamy, while ſhe was at
Rome. At the firſt news of it, ſhe immediately
departed for England, notwithſtanding ſhe was ſick,
and even obliged to perform the journey in a litter.
Soon after her arrival her trial commenced. I had
the ſatisfaction of being a witneſs to this ſingular
ſpectacle, which not a little reſembled the pomp
with which divine ſervice is performed in *catholic
countries*. Foreigners ridiculed the Engliſh for
treating ſuch trifling matters with ſo much importance, while engaged in an unfortunate war; it was
however impoſſible, without overturning the very
foundation of the conſtitution, to refuſe to hear her
accuſer or deny herſelf the privilege of defending
her cauſe before that tribunal which her rank aſ-
ſigned to her. The trial was public and attended
with the uſual ceremonies, but with an uncommon
concourſe of people.

The preſident whom the king appoints for the
occaſion, bears the title of the Lord High Steward,
a very eminent dignity, and which ends with the
trial, The chancellor was inveſted with this dignity, perhaps the greateſt in the world, and pre-
ſided holding a long taper wand in his hand as a
mark of his office. Weſtminſter Hall, the height
of which is ſuperior to moſt churches, allowed
ample room for the amphitheatres which were
erected on the occaſion. The ſeats and boxes appropriated to the royal family, the peereſſes, the
members of the Houſe of Commons, &c. were covered with the richeſt tapeſtry. It ſeemed to be a
general *gala*; the paſſages were guarded with ſoldiers, who do not uſually appear on theſe occaſions :
the peers, to the number of almoſt two hundred,
the biſhops and the judges in their robes, forming a
femicircle

femicircle, together with the high-fteward at the
foot of a throne erected for the king, although he
is never prefent, formed altogether a fuperb and
elegant appearance. At fome diftance a large table
was placed for the fecretaries of this great tribunal,
and the centre of the circle was referved for the ac-
cufers and accufed.

The duchefs had two of her women attending on her, a phyfician, a furgeon, an apothe-
cary, a fecretary, and fix advocates. She was
dreffed in black, and her conduct, which was at
once firm, and noble throughout the whole, gained
her the admiration of all the fpectators. She herfelf addreffed the affembly with an inimitable dignity. Neverthelefs fhe was convicted by the peers,
who gave their judgment by rifing up one after the
other, and with their hands on their breafts declar-
ing *on their honours* that fhe was guilty. The
youngeft baron begins, and they rife in order of
rank and creation.

The punifhment inflicted by the law for bigamy,
is a red hot iron applied to the hand; the nobility
however are exempted by an ancient privilege. The
counfel for the duchefs claimed this as a right, and
the adverfe party denied it: it was then that for the
firft time this unfortunate woman feemed to lofe
her refolution. She fainted and was carried away.
She was at laft allowed this favour, and efcaped
with a reprimand from the Lord High Steward,
who concluded with an obfervation " that this was
" the laft time when fhe could experience this in-
" dulgence."

Such was the conclufion of this fingular procefs,
which lafted fix days. Thefe fix days feemed to be
a feftival to the whole nation. Although the court
did not fit till ten o'clock, the hall was full by five
in the morning. There were even ladies who repaired thither by break of day, magnificently dreffed

an

and ornamented with jewels, and remained till
five at night. As it happened in the summer, a
period when all the gentry are in the country, thoufands were continually arriving from the remoteft
corners of the kingdom. Thofe who had not tickets, offered for them twelve, fifteen, and even
twenty guineas a piece. A lady, who after all her
endeavours could not procure one, being quite in-
confolable for the bad fuccefs of her attempts,
avowed in company that fhe would fooner facrifice
fifty guineas than not be a fpectator. The duchefs,
on hearing of this ardent curiofity, obferved, " If
" this lady longs fo much to be in the hall, I am
" difpofed to refign my place to her for nothing,
" and fhe will not then fail to fee and be feen
" by all the world." She well knew that it was
only the vanity of fhewing herfelf that tormented
her countrywoman, and not a wifh to behold a
fcene which, although very interefting, had nothing
agreeable in it. This kind of trial is peculiar to the
nobility, and cofts an immenfe fum to government.

It was alfo during my ftay in London that
Sayre the banker was accufed of high-treafon.
This gentleman, who is a native of America, is
well known in the north of Germany, by his intrigues there in favour of his countrymen. He is
now fettled at George-Town in Maryland. He
was an inhabitant of London, and in high reputation, when he had the audacity, at the beginning
of the American conteft, to attempt the execution
of a project at once rafh and imprudent. As
almoft the whole nation was difcontented during
that unfortunate war, he refolved to make himfelf
mafter of the perfon of the king, carry him to the
Tower, and keep him prifoner there until he had
agreed to whatever was propofed to him. For this
purpofe he makes the neceffary arrangements. He
communicates part of his plan to Richardfon, a
captain

captain of the guards, and requests his assistance. That officer promises to consider of it, and repairs instantly to the earl of Rochford, one of the secretaries of state, to whom he recounts the singular proposition that had been made to him, and confirms the truth of it by an oath. As this attempt was high treason, that minister imagined that it was his duty to take immediate cognizance of it. He accordingly issues a warrant, Sayre is apprehended and conducted to his house.

In the mean time the secretary of state having sent for Sir John Fielding, and procured the attendance of Richardson, began the examination; the prisoner however was too cunning to say any thing before the arrival of his counsel, to whom he had found means to send a note, informing him of his situation.

He was not mistaken in the zeal of that gentleman, who, throwing himself into a carriage as soon as he received the letter, made so much haste that he arrived a few minutes after the prisoner. He immediately requests to speak with Mr. Sayre; but the minister, on being informed of his business, refuses to permit an interview. This answer provokes the barrister, who immediately sends word that *be insisted* on seeing his client, and *must* speak to him that very moment. What recompense would the boldness of this gentleman have met with in any other country? Such a message to a secretary of state armed with such an extensive authority, in his own house, and in an affair of high treason! the most moderate would without doubt have ordered him to be thrown out of the window.

In England, where nobody is above the laws, and where the most powerful dare not to infringe them with impunity, they regulate their matters in another manner.

The

The council was immediately introduced, and he publicly informs the prisoner, that he ought not to answer to any interrogatories in that house. Sayre on this turning towards his Lordship observes, that he will follow the opinion of his lawyer, and that, as it was intirely useless, he beseeched him to ask no more questions. On this the minister commits him to the Tower. Bail is offered and refused. However, at the end of six days he is set at liberty, as the policy of the state did not then admit of his trial. Sayre however had no motives to prevent him from prosecuting the minister: he accuses him of having arrested him without sufficient cause, affirms that the warrant was illegal, commences an action for false imprisonment, and a verdict is found against the secretary of state for three thousand pounds.

The power of the laws and the extent of English liberty was never better illustrated than in the suit between the count de Guerchy and the chevalier d'Eon. As a particular account of this has never reached Germany, and the chevalier, with whom I was intimately acquainted, is not unknown there, it may not be improper here to mention some of the characteristic traits of this singular being.

D'Eon had already distinguished himself by his military and political talents at the courts of Warsaw and St. Petersburgh, when he was sent to London with count de Guerchy, in the year 1763, in quality of secretary of legation. Soon after his arrival, the count, who was ambassador from France, returned to spend a few months at Paris, confiding the care of every thing to the chevalier, who was invested with the rank and title of minister plenipotentiary at the court of London. His transactions in that station having given great umbrage to the ambassador, he on his return testified his displeasure. This was soon followed by an entire rupture.

Both

Both of them complain to their court. The friends of the count were more powerful at Verfailles than thofe of the chevalier; perhaps he had alfo the better caufe; however, it is certain that his antagonift was difgraced. Thinking that he had now no occafion to preferve moderation, the chevalier foon broke all thofe ties by which he was connected with France. His refentment, which knew no bounds, made him even difcover thofe ftate fecrets which had been confided to his honour. He fpoke openly concerning the late peace, affirmed that it had been purchafed for money, mentioned the traitors, and even the fums that had been paid. A fpeech of this kind muft neceffarily excite the moft lively fenfations. It was not however thought proper to inftitute a fuit againft him, and his affertion was treated as an attrocious calumny. D'Eon, to filence fuch infamous reports, offered to adduce irrefragable teftimony, and befides to particularife the very fums that had been fent from France to England for that purpofe. This intrepid conduct immediately abafhed thofe concerned in this difhonourable affair, and d'Eon was induced to concealment by a propofition not very ungrateful to the deranged ftate of his finances. It is well known that after this he lived feveral years in London perfectly at his eafe.

But his fituation was no ways to be envied. The court of St. James's and its partifans hated him as a traitor, who had been inftigated to perfidy by the moft venal motives. The people defpifed him for deviating from his refolutions on account of the moft difhonourable impulfe; they faid that he ought to have told all or nothing. The juft refentment of the court of France, which left him every thing to apprehend, added not a little to his folicitude. He was obliged to be always on his guard; and was fo fearful of being carried off, that he never went out

on

'on an evening unless accompanied by his friends. By this prudent conduct he frustrated many projects. which were formed against him with equal art and boldness.

I shall not pretend to decide whether it is true or not that they tried to take him of by poison. It is however certain that he complained loudly of the count de Guerchy, who he said had made such an attempt in his own house.

He himself applied to a justice of the peace, gave information of the circumstance, swore to the facts, and promised to adduce proofs. This was in order to commence a criminal process against the count, who unfortunately thought himself, as ambassador from a peaceful monarch, entirely out of the reach of the laws. He even ridiculed such of his friends as testified any inquietude on the occasion, imagining that his rank and high favour at court would entirely shelter him from prosecution. He was however cited before a justice, and according to custom was obliged to appear in person. This supposed insult put him into a rage, and he immediately went to the minister, whose uneasiness not a little disconcerted the poor count, who measuring the power of a king of England by that of his own sovereign, expected nothing but a little pleasantry from the secretary of state. The term when he was obliged to make his appearance was short; every thing that could be done in his favour was put in practice to prolong it, and thus the minister plenipotentiary of his most christian majesty gained sufficient time to leave London in the night and escape to Calais. The chagrin occasioned by this sad catastrophe brought him in a short time to the grave.

The chevalier d'Eon remained in London till the year 1777, when some doubts having arisen concerning the sex of this extraordinary person, several

policies

policies were opened, and a prodigious number of betts made on the subject. Piqued at these doubts, the chevalier mentioned in the public papers that he would satisfy the whole world whether he was male or female on a certain day ; and accordingly fixed the time and place.

It was a coffee-house in the city that he appointed for the exhibtion of this singular scene to the curious. The concourse was prodigious. D'Eon appears clothed in the uniform of a captain of the French cavalry, and decorated with the cross of St. Louis. He addresses himself to the assembly, and informs them that he is of the sex whose appearance he assumes, and that he comes prepared to prove his assertion either with his *sword* or his *cane*.

The boldness of this speech had different effects on the auditory, some praised and others laughed at it ; but the greatest part of the spectators heard with the utmost coldness the menace of the chevalier, who, perceiving that no person chose to accept the challenge, returned in triumph. It is nevertheless certain, that, to determine the betts, which amounted to almost a million sterling, he was promised very large sums of money if he would unequivocably unveil the mystery. I myself know that they offered him thirty-thousand pounds sterling, which they were prepared to pay in ready money. Such a proposition was very tempting ; and I am sure the chevalier would have disclosed the secret for a great deal less, if he had not been obliged to submit to the indelicate inspection of such a number of people.

As he refused to accede to the proposal, this uncertainty continued till his departure for France, when two of his countrymen swore that the chevalier was a woman, and this determined many wagers. But those who had large stakes would not allow their testimony was valid, although one of them

them who pretended to be a phyfician, affirmed,
that he had cured d'Eon of a certain difeafe ; in
fine, the generality of mankind are not even now
agreed concerning the fex of this fingular being.

Would it not be childifh to believe that a perfon,
who by nature and inclination had fuch a near re-
femblance to our fex, belonged to the other ? The
habit of a woman, which the chevalier is now
obliged to wear by order of the king of France, and
which is difgufting to him, cannot prove any thing.
the farces daily acted in courts are fo various, and
the occafion of them often fo impenetrable, that
the change of drefs is not to be regarded. I confefs
that every circumftance in the life of this fingular
perfon is wonderful and extraordinary. After having
been guilty of the moft perfidious treafon againft
his native country, and when the baftile feemed ready to entomb him in one of its dungeons, he
not only receives his pardon, but a penfion of four
thoufand livres a year, and that too at a time when,
entirely forgotten, he could no longer hurt the court
of France. It is pretended that he lived in great intimacy with Louis XV. who kept up a conftant
correfpondence with him, and that it was on condition of delivering up his letters that he efcaped
punifhment. But how can we reconcile this circumftance with his treafon ? Is it poffible that the
French minifter fhould have been ignorant of his
fex, when at thirty-fix years of age he employed
him at the court of London ? The fuccefs of a
minifterial intrigue, it is true, has often depended
on a difguife of this kind; but it is inconceivable
that in the prefent times, and during the adminiftration of a duke de Choifeul, the court of Verfailles
would have nominated a woman for her minifter
plenipotentiary to a great nation fuch as England.
It is alfo certain that d'Eon entered the college of
Mazarine at Paris at twelve years of age, and was
                                        educated

educated there. A gentleman who is at present a considerable merchant in London, and who was brought up at the same seminary with him, betted twenty thousand pounds that his school-fellow was a man. His reasons were undoubtedly convincing. The mother and the relations must certainly have known the sex of d'Eon. What mother could have been so inconsiderate as to leave a young girl at the age of twelve to the mercy of so many boys? A miracle only could conceal such a circumstance, and it seems that this miracle happened. Neither the amusements of a forward child nor the suppositions of the masters ever made this strange discovery. D'Eon was even admitted in London to a society, which, whatever regard in other respects it may evince towards the female sex, yet never entrusts them with their secrets. In the year 1770 he was deputy grand master of the French lodge of free masons, a body which at that time were quoted as a model, on account of the strictness of their rules.

I have thought it my duty to state my sentiments on this singular affair, because it seems to me never to have been before considered in the same point of view. My own knowledge, considering my intimacy with the chevalier, is very limited, and I think that the uncertainty of all impartial persons is fully justified until authentic proofs shall hereafter tear away the veil which still conceals the truth.

I cannot conclude the history of the chevalier without saying something of his antagonist Monf. de Morande; a person well known by the singularity of his adventures. Having made some mistakes at Paris for which he was sent to prison, he went to England on his release, and published a book, which at that time made a great noise, entitled *Le Gazetier Cuirassé*, or *Scandalous Anecdotes of the Court of France, written in a free country, an hundred miles distant from the Bastile.* Soon after
this

this he wrote the *Memoirs of the Countess Dubarry*, and sent a copy of the manuscript to herself, offering to suppress it for 2000 louis d'ors. That lady was so much afraid of the publication of it, that she sent the celebrated Beaumarchais to London, who concluded an agreement with the author, for a yearly pension payable in London, which was luckily for him signed by Louis XV. a few weeks before his demise. This gentleman was one of the witnesses who were examined concerning the sex of the chevalier.

The fate of the unfortunate Dr. Dodd, who was sacrificed to the laws of his country, is worthy of a place in this work. I myself was witness to two affecting scenes occasioned by this event, for I was present at his trial, and attended also when sentence of death was pronounced against him. This man was of a noble and interesting appearance, respectable on account of his profession, his eloquence, and his distinguished talents. The judges, the jury, the counsel, the spectators, all the world was bathed in tears. The prisoner also wept. " I despise," said " he, " that stoic firmness which contemns death ; " it is a pagan virtue, in which I would not glory. " I love life, and I am sorry to die."

This unfortunate man always flattered himself with the hope of a pardon, and his numerous friends interested themselves for this purpose with the same warmth as if the safety of the nation depended on his life. The jury who tried him recommended him to the mercy of the sovereign ; whole corporations, the city of London itself presented a petition in his favour ; the newspapers were every day filled with the good actions he had performed, and quoted the most interesting passages in his sermons. His writings were collected and reprinted ; the poets sung his praises, and in fine every thing was practised to excite the sympathy of the

nation

nation for a criminal fo much beloved. Having
fucceeded, his partizans drew up a petition to the
king, and never before was fuch a one feen in England. It was carried by a porter who bent under the
load, for it took up twenty-nine yards of parchment, and was figned by twenty-three thoufand
houfekeepers. It is however remarkable that the
great merchants and other people of condition would
not fubfcribe to this petition, which did not fucceed,
as the council refolved that it was not proper on this
occafion to extend the royal clemency.

Dodd himfelf attempted to procure the commife-
ration of Lord Mansfield, by a letter couched in the
moft affecting language. As it never has been
printed I fhall infert it here.

" *My Lord,*

" But a few days—and the lot of the moft un-
" happy of created beings will be decided for ever!
" I know the weight of your Lordfhip's opinion.
" It is that which will undoubtedly decide, whether
" I am to die an ignominious death, or drag out
" the reft of my life in difhonourable banifhment.
" O my Lord! do not refufe to hear what I in
" my humility dare to oppofe to the feverity of the
" laws.

" I feel how frightful my crime is; the fentence
" which condemns me is but too juft: I however
" flatter myfelf, that, amidft all the reproaches
" caft againft me on account of my crime, it will
" ftill be remembered how ufeful my charitable
" endeavours have been to that very fociety which
" I have injured. I afk for nothing but the prefer-
" vation of my life, a life which I fhall drag out
" in difhonour, and perhaps in mifery! Have
" compaffion, my Lord, on a man covered with
" infamy, without fortune, and without refource,
" but

" but not however without fear at cafting his eyes
" towards the abyfs of eternity !

"However great that mifery which will be my
" lot, yet ftill allow me to live. That very mifery
" under which I fhall languifh the reft of my days
" will forewarn all thofe who were witneffes of it,
" to beware of indulging their paffions, and to
" guard againft a fatal vanity and a fpirit of diffipa-
" tion.

" For the laft time, I conjure you, my Lord, to
" fuffer me to live; and when you fee me paffing
" from the frightful dungeon which now enclofes
" me, to an ignominious exile, be affured that
" juftice will be fufficiently fatisfied by the fuffer-
" ings of him who is,

" My Lord,

Newgate,   " Your Lordfhip's
June 11, 1777. " Moft humble fuppliant,
" WILLIAM DODD."

This letter did not prevent Lord Mansfield from
giving his opinion, that Dodd ought not to be par-
doned. The reafons which he adduced were convincing : Thofe very reafons alfo inclined the king
to refufe a pardon, in 1783, to Ryland the celebrated
engraver, whom he loved and patronifed.

The friends of Dr. Dodd, feeing that all their
folicitations were in vain, formed the project of
reftoring him to life after his execution. The delinquent was in all human probability made acquainted with the fcheme, as he befought the hangman after he mounted the ladder that he would not
draw his feet ; a ceremony which is very common,
and which the fpectators themfelves often do out of
compaffion. After he had hung the ufual time his
friends took the body, as is always allowed when
the criminal has not been a murderer. A mourning-
coach was in readinefs to receive it : it was placed

H 2

in

in a coffin without a lid, and brought with the utmoft fpeed to the houfe of one of his acquaintances,
where a phyfician ufed all the fecrets of his profeffion for its refufcitation; but all his efforts were unfuccefsful.

As my fole intention in recounting thefe tranfactions is to give, by an authentic recital of facts,
a juft idea of the prefent ftate of the laws of England, and the mode of putting them in execution,
I will here recite an event that happened in London
in the year 1778, and of which, to my great aftonifhment, I myfelf was a witnefs.

A young man of twenty years of age was condemned to death on the evidence of a highwayman, who accufed him of being an accomplice.
His own bad character and the teftimony of the
robber, accompanied with all the requifite proofs,
feemed to leave no doubt of his guilt. The unhappy wretch was in confequence of this conducted in
a cart to Tyburn, with fome other criminals. He
remained with the rope about his neck, according
to the permiffion which the law allows, one whole
hour at the foot of the gibbet. During that hour
the culprit is permitted to fay whatever he choofes
were he to utter high-treafon againft the fovereign,
or inflame the people to a revolt, it would be illegal
to prevent him. They think humanity requires that
fuch an alleviation fhould be permitted to one who
is about to be launched out of the world by a violent death. There are actually a great many men,
who on this fad occafion experience a certain pleafure in communicating thofe fentiments with which
they are affected. Lord Lovat, who after the rebellion in Scotland perifhed on a fcaffold, made ufe
of this privilege. He declared that George II. had
no right to the crown, which belonged to the pre-
tender alone; and added, it was with great pleafure

that

that he was then about to shed his blood for his lawful sovereign.

The young man whom I have just mentioned said
not a word, but, trembling with fear, sat expectant
of the awful period which was to put an end to his
existence. The fatal moment at last arrives, and
every thing is prepared; when his accuser, turning
towards Villette the chaplain of Newgate, who is
obliged to accompany the criminals to Tyburn,
declares in the most solemn manner that the poor
young man was innocent; and that he had been led
away by the spirit of revenge to fabricate a story on
purpose to procure his death. This declaration made
all the spectators tremble; but the ordinary, who
was accustomed to these kind of scenes, answered
coldly, that it was now too late to retract. In the
mean time the people began to murmur, and some
respectable persons addressed themselves to the under
sheriff, who officiated in the absence of his principal.

He having heard nothing of the confession, was
about to give the fatal signal; the conductor of the
cart had his whip uplifted in the air, and the cries
and prayers of the unhappy wretch were still sound-
ing in the ears of the assistants, when all of a sudden
somebody cried, Halt! It was then represented to
the under-sheriff, how barbarous it would be to
allow an innocent man to perish. The emotion of
this gentleman was equally great with his astonishment; for this was a case entirely new, and
without any precedent. Every body was of opinion, that this young man ought not to be executed
with the others: the cruel Villette alone insisted
that he could not be saved, as the laws do not give
to the officer the power of suspending the execution,
for a quarter of an hour. The sub-sheriff, who
was acquainted with the laws, and fully convinced
of the justice of Villette's observations, was now
about to perform his duty with an aching heart. He

H 3　　　　　　　　　　　　　had

had almoſt given the fatal order, when the high-conſtable addreſſes him as follows : " In the name " of God, ſir, is it poſſible that you can give your " conſent to the death of this guiltleſs perſon !" " What can I, what ſhall I do ?" replied he. " If " you will delay the execution, I will inſtantly " mount my horſe and go to the king." He accordingly departs, without hearing the cruel pleaſantries of the ordinary, who prognoſticated that the journey would be unſucceſsful.

Four other perſons were joined in this ſentimental embaſſy, who make towards Weſtminſter in full gallop. Tyburn is diſtant from St. James's two Engliſh miles. They ſoon arrive at the palace ; but the king was gone to Richmond, and all the miniſters were gone to the country, it being then the height of ſummer.

They then inſtantly repair to the offices of the ſecretaries of ſtate, hoping to find ſome perſon there of whom they could receive advice ; but all the clerks ſhrugged up their ſhoulders, ſaying that the officer himſelf ought to know the extent of thoſe powers which the law gave him. On this they return after an abſence of an hour and a half, and relate the event of their unfortunate journey.

The execution of the other criminals had been ſuſpended during this period, and Villette now inſiſted on the under-ſheriff's giving the ſignal ; menacing him at the ſame time with a criminal proceſs, and affirming that, if he did not execute the culprit, the jailor of Newgate would not receive him back after he had been delivered over to the executioner. The high-conſtable on the other hand aſſerted the contrary, and did not ceaſe to addreſs him with the moſt maſculine and perſuaſive eloquence, until he agreed to his requeſt. The eight other criminals were immediately hanged ; and the young man who
had

had fainted with exceffive joy, was carried back to Newgate.

The king being informed of this event, extended his clemency that very evening to the prifoner, who after having been conducted to the foot of the gibbet, found himfelf in a few hours-free and happy. His Majefty alfo granted a pardon to the under-fheriff for having arrogated a power which he did not poffefs, and he received the praifes of the whole nation for his boldnefs and humanity. To him might be applied the following line from Shakefpeare:

" To do a great right, he did a little wrong."

They have not in England a fet of men who can properly be ftiled executioners. The hangman is a perfon employed by the fheriff; and he might gain his livelihood by any other occupation, for infamy is not there attached to his employment. It is contemptible indeed, but it is not difhonourable; and this contempt is not attached to the action of hanging, but to the idea of its proceeding from a fordid defire of gain; for, if he could procure no other perfon, the fheriff would be obliged to perform the duty himfelf. Of this there was an inftance fome years fince, not indeed in London, but in the country. The two men appointed for this purpofe happened to die, almoft at the very moment when they were about to execute their office; and the fheriff not being able to procure any other, nor daring to delay the day or even the hour of execution, was obliged to put the criminal to death with his own hands.

The nobility in certain cafes have the privilege of being beheaded: murderers, however, fuch as lord Ferrers, are denied this favour. A butcher, who by his trade is beft qualified for this operation, is generally employed. The family of the culprit employ

him

him, and for this purpose commonly make him a present of a hatchet with a silver handle.

They have in Scotland a singular law in regard to criminals who will not plead to the indictment. If the prisoner obstinately persists in silence, he is not publickly executed, nor his estate confiscated, but a heavy and cruel punishment immediately follows. Of this they give him an exact detail on the last day of the session, requesting him either to declare himself guilty or to enter on his defence, and observing, that then is the time to speak, as it will afterwards be attended with no advantage. If he still continues silent, the law condemns him to the following punishment. Being conducted to a dungeon, he is stripped naked and extended on a kind of a tomb-stone, the feet being placed higher than the head. In this posture, which he is obliged constantly to retain, different parts of his body are loaded with weights of iron and stone ; he is supplied with bread and water alternately, and in such a manner that the day on which he eats he does not drink, and on that on which he drinks he is not allowed to eat. This regimen is continued till his death. After the rebellion in Scotland in the year 1745*, there were many examples of this kind: one hundred and forty-one wretches resigned themselves to this horrible species of death, to preserve their fortune to their families.

In England their are still a few of those singular laws which evince the barbarity of remote ages. For example, a husband is permitted to sell his wife, provided she gives her consent. I myself was witness to a transaction of this kind in the city of Worcester. A journeyman conducted his dear moiety to the market with a rope about her neck, as the law prescribes, and exactly in the same manner as an ox or an ass. A shoemaker, who was her lover,

appeared

---

* The author here has been grossly misinformed.

appeared according to appointment, and the bargain
was foon made. The price of the woman was five
pounds.

The laws in general are not favourable to the
fair fex in England, yet notwithstanding this, the
women reign there with a more abfolute dominion
than in any other country. They know how to
make both the men and the laws bend beneath the
power of their charms, and turn to advantage thofe
very things which are leaft in their favour.

As foon as the marriage is concluded, the fortune
of the woman is entirely at the difpofal of the hufband; but the moment that he has taken poffeffion
of it, he becomes liable to her debts, and is obliged
to pay them: fo that his dear wife may make him
fpend many an uneafy quarter of an hour. I knew
a woman who, although a foreigner, knew but too
well how to make ufe of this fatal privilege. She
and her hufband lived very unhappily together, and
their unfortunate union became ftill more miferable
by their continual broils. In this defperate fituation
fhe conceived the defign of parting from him, and
for this purpofe contracted feveral frefh debts: what
which fhe wifhed for accordingly happened; for the
poor man being unable to pay them, was conducted
to prifon.

However, it is ftill worfe to be arrefted a few
days after marriage, for the former debts of a wife,
which in that country a hufband efpoufes with her.
Senfible people, therefore, take great care to make
the neceffary inquiries; for many women never
think of marriage until they have contracted debts
which become troublefome to them. The bride-
groom has often been known to be conducted from
the nuptial bed to a prifon.

A German experienced a fingular adventure of
this kind. A rich widow, who at the death of her
hufband inherited his fortune and his debts, which
were both very confiderable, delayed the fettlement

of his affairs from day to day, till at laſt ſhe
was on the point of being arreſted. While in
this alarming ſituation ſhe happened to ſee a
young German whoſe figure pleaſed her, but
whoſe dreſs ſeemed to announce that fortune had
acted the part of a ſtepmother to him. In conſe-
quence of this, ſhe reſolved to make him an uncommon propoſition. It was that of giving him a
thouſand pounds in ready money, provided he
would inſtantly marry her; at the ſame time informing him, that in a few days he would be arreſted for the debts which ſhe would otherwiſe have
been obliged to pay. He inſtantly cloſes with the
propoſal, to which was added the promiſe of an
annuity of three hundred pounds a year during his
confinement, and a preſent of five hundred pounds
ſterling, on his quitting England after his releaſe.
The lady on her part engages to fulfil theſe conditions, and he on his to renounce all the rights of
a huſband.

Neceſſity made him agree to every thing propoſed. As the law againſt clandeſtine marriages
had not then taken place, my countryman eſpouſes
the widow immediately, receives the ſtipulated ſum,
is carried to the King's bench, where he remains
quiet and happy, and returns to his native country with a little fortune, after two years impriſonment.

To the end that the ſubmiſſion which women owe
after marriage, may be the better impreſſed on the
minds of their wives, the Engliſh have a law
which condemns to a particular kind of death, any
woman who is convicted of murdering her lawful
huſband. On theſe occaſions they are not hanged,
but burnt. However, as they are the declared
enemies of every puniſhment that favours of cruelty,
they ſtrangle them before they reduce the bodies
to aſhes; but the preparation is ſo frightful, that it
                                                    always

always produces the fame effect as the punifhment itfelf. This crime is however very rare. The murder of a hufband is regarded in England as a fpecies of high treafon; it is accordingly denominated petty treafon.

The laws allow fo much for the fubjugation which a woman is fuppofed to be under, in refpect to her hufband, that, if fhe commits any crime in concert with him, fhe needs not be afraid of being punifhed, nor even of being tried for the offence. They fay, that the duty which fhe owes to her hufband, forces her to obey him. According to the fame principle, the hufband is obliged to anfwer for all the faults of his wife; it is he, and not her, who is profecuted.

Among the number of regulations in that ftate, two may be reckoned, which, if I am not much deceived, exift no where but in England. No traveller has as yet made mention of them, and even very few of the Englifh themfelves know that fuch are in force. Would any one imagine, in a country, where the people fwear every moment, and where oaths form a part of the gallantry of the failors and the populace, that they were prohibited by law? This ftatute was enacted at a time when the Puritans were at the head of affairs. As it is impoffible, fince bigotry has ceafed to infect that ifland, to enforce this law in the prefent day, and becaufe it would be indecent to repeal fuch an act, the magiftrates have agreed to be indulgent to thofe who infringe it. They cannot however refufe to punifh any perfon, when an informer by means of an oath convicts him of having incurred the penalty. To prevent, however, the multiplication of this fort of accufations, they have fixed the fine at the moderate rate of one fhilling.

The

The second law is against those who treat animals with cruelty. Being always passive, it greatly redounds to the humanity of an enlightened nation, to protect dumb creatures from the barbarity of their masters. These accusations are very frequent, and no indulgence is shewn to the guilty. The pecuniary mulct is from five to ten shillings, and sometimes even more, at the discretion of the magistrate, and according to the exigence of the case. It proceeds from this that they treat animals almost as if they were reasonable creatures, and that horses and dogs experience the mild usage so much boasted of by the English.

Cock-fighting, of which I shall speak hereafter, is not liable to any punishment, and one would think that this was an exception to the former law. The two champions, however, encounter upon equal terms.

One may also place that body of people called constables, among the number of singularities with which that country abounds. It would be doing wrong to confound these with the officers of justice. They are all reputable tradesmen, having an occupation and a dwelling-house, whom the law invests with this authority, to watch over the order and security of the public. The office of constable is reckoned among the parochial employments incident to all the householders in the parish. No person can refuse to undertake it, although there is not any salary annexed to compensate for the trouble and attendance. The law fixes the duration of this charge for one year: the more opulent inhabitants generally employ a substitute, for which they pay a certain sum. The constables never arrest debtors; a class of men called bailiffs are employed in that occupation. Neither do they risk their lives against highway robbers: the thief-takers, who are

paid

paid by government, and act under the controul of certain magistrates, are retained for that purpose.

To these two latter employments a certain degree of infamy is attached: the bailiffs in particular are generally hated, and woe to them, if they ever arrest any one illegally, or assume powers not allowed by law! If a prisoner happens to escape from their hands, the people try all in their power to assist him. Their conduct towards the constables, whom they commonly esteem, is entirely different. A person taken into custody by one of them, is looked upon as a disturber of the peace of the community, and every body endeavours to secure him. The constable carries in his hand, while on duty, a staff on which the arms of England are emblazoned; on producing of which, all the king's subjects are obliged to support him.

The lord chancellor represents, in his own person, a court armed with high authority. He is obliged, in certain cases, to temper the too great severity of the laws, and to take care that the judges are not only just, but also reasonable in their decisions. His tribunal is accordingly called a court of equity. In it there are no juries: he himself is the sole judge. He is also the guardian of all the orphans in the kingdom; so that, in the discharge of this duty, he is frequently occupied about the interests of the lowest class of citizens. His court is always open, and there are not any vacations in it, as in the others: thus the famous *habeas corpus* act may at all times, and at all hours, be sued out in behalf of any one.

The chancellor is also speaker of the House of Peers, an office which must always be filled by a man of distinguished abilities. The ministers of England are frequently employed and disgraced by means of cabals and intrigues; but it is necessary
that

that the talents of a person elevated to that high employment should never be equivocal.

Although the party in opposition are for the most part constrained to yield to the more numerous partisans of the court, yet it often happens that they propose regulations which are acceded to, while those of the court party are rejected, because the minister does not always think it proper to shew his strength.

It is said that, when he himself does not make the proposition, he for the most part chooses to be passive, and in such a case is it no mortification to him when a bill is rejected. I was witness to an instance of this kind, which at the time it happened made some noise. The society of free-masons, which is exceedingly numerous in England, and has in the capital alone two hundred and six lodges, in the year 1771, projected a scheme in favour of their establishment, the purport of which was to build a grand general lodge in the neighbourhood of London; they also intended to augment the statues of their order, and to give them the force of laws. In consequence of this, they presented a petition to the House of Commons, praying to be allowed the privileges of a corporation. This request was delivered and seconded by members of parliament, who were at the same time free-masons and of the court party; and they lavished on this occasion, all the eloquence which a zeal for the brotherhood inspired them with.

The heads of the opposition were entirely silent, and the free-masons of Great Britain already imagined that they had effected their purpose; when one of those unquiet and discontented men, so common among those islanders, got up and observed, that it would be ridiculous to grant them such great privileges before they had been fully apprised of the design, and until parliament had received an

exact

exact detail of their rules and interior regulations. This idea, which tended to difcover all the myfteries of the inftitution, could not be complied with. The free-mafons therefore withdrew their bill; and as they were not empowered to purchafe any place in the name of the fociety, without the fanction of parliament, they were contented to build a fuperb edifice in the metropolis, where they now hold their affemblies. *

However ingenious the Englifh may be in quib-bling away the meaning of the laws, when they make againft them, they are neverthelefs always appre-henfive of a direct infringement. This fear is more prevalent in the rich and powerful than among the common people: every where elfe it is exactly the reverfe. It is, for example, uncommonly rare to fee a gentleman ftrike an inferior, although this is ufual in other countries.

The minifters themfelves, all-powerful as they are, very feldom invade the laws, even in trifles, altho' there be no danger of a complaint againft them. It is fufficient that an act of parliament has regu-lated any thing, to prevent one of them from acting in oppofition to it. I myfelf became ac-quainted with many inftances of this kind, in my firft journey to England; and I was at that time tempted to confider as mere caprice, a punctilio founded on the moft noble bafis.

* Free-mafon's Tavern, Queen-ftreet.

CHAPTER

CHAPTER IX.

The facility of procuring Credit in England—
Bailiffs—Singular Process on being arrested—Bail.
Fleet and King's-bench Prisons—Laws and Regu-
lations—Debtors—Acts of Grace--The Military
obliged to submit to the Civil Power—General
Gansel.

THE prisons for confining debtors in England,
are such as might be expected in a nation which
regards the powerful and sacred rights of humanity.
They have no view of punishing debtors, by de-
taining them in custody; the intention is solely to
keep them in a place of safety.

As it is extremely easy to contract debts in England, it must therefore necessarily follow, that the
gaols are always full of prisoners. The poorest people, provided they are not common beggars, labour
with the utmost assiduity to hire a small tenement,
and become *house-keepers*, because, besides the convenience resulting from it, there are certain privileges annexed to such situation. In consequence
of this, they prefer the most miserable cottage
hired in their own name, to more convenient apartments in another house.

From this proceeds the great number of houses in
London, which on this very account are as five to
three in proportion to those of Paris, where all the
inhabitants live heaped upon one another.

The

. The national character is difcovered in this very circumftance. It often happens, that a man has nothing in his little houfe, but a bed, a table, and fome chairs; and yet, in quality cf a *houfekeeper*, he procures a certain degree of credit, and no one makes any difficulty in trufting him. The butchers, the bakers, the taylors, the fhoe-makers, &c. &c. furnifh him with whatever he may ftand in need of, without requiring ready money; people in good circumftances generally make them wait till Chriftmas; a fhorter time is however fixed for the poor; and whenever the debt amounts to the fum of * forty fhi.lings, the creditor has a right to arreft the debtor.

Nothing is more eafy than this. He goes to the fheriffs' office, where there is no other perfon than a clerk; he informs him of his bufinefs, and afks for a writ. The clerk, whofe duty it is to diftribute thefe writs without making any inquiry, receives his fee, after having firft made him kifs the bible, the ufual manner of taking an oath in England.

The bai.iffs of whom I made mention in the preceding chapter, are afterwards employed, in virtue cf their office, to arreft the debtor. The people deteft thefe men; and it is very natural, for they lead a lazy life, and inhabit good houfes, which ferve as temporary prifons. The creditor carries the writ to one of thefe, and gives him inftructions. The bai'iff conveys the prifoner to his houfe, where he remains for twenty-four hours: during this time, he makes ufe of every art, either to fettle the matter or procure bail. If an accommodation does not take place in that time, the officer conducts him to prifon: a fee however, properly applied, will often procure an indulgence for feveral days.

The

* By a late act, no one can be arrefted for any debt below the fum of ten pounds.

The bail which the debtor is obliged to procure, when he neither chooses to pay the debt nor go to goal, is of no service to the creditor. After this he may settle the suit amicably. Two house-keepers are necessary, when security is to be given for the debt: if the sum is trifling, and the people are responsible, the officer is obliged to accept them. When the security does not appear to him sufficient, it is in his power to carry the prisoner to gaol, and refer the cognizance of the whole to the higher powers; who are by law obliged to accept the bail, when they swear in open court, that their property exceeds double the sum in contest, after all their debts are paid. When two housekeepers have made oath in this manner, the lord chief justice of England himself cannot refuse them, not-withstanding they may have all the outward marks of poverty. Nothing can vitiate such bail, but a proof of perjury.

It is possible to abuse the wisest laws, and this is the case here. There are wretches who gain their livelihood entirely by this kind of traffic. They inhabit miserable houses in the suburbs, and all their moveables consist in a few old chairs and tables, which would not produce what would pay the expences, if they wanted to sell them. The German jews distinguish themselves in this *honourable* kind of traffic; for even they, in quality of house-keepers, may be received.

The prisoners who wish to evade payment, or to procure their own liberty, purchase the services of these people, by a sum proportioned to the debt: this is generally ten pounds in the hundred.

If at the time appointed the debtor does not appear in person, the bail become fixed; but they take care to keep out of the way, and at the first notice put their goods in a place of safety. The process ends here, unless the creditor, wishing to sacrifice another fum of money, arrefts the jews, to maintain them afterwards in prifon.

Let thofe readers who are aftonifhed at fuch abufes exift, recollect that I now fpeak of London, a place of which it is difficult for a ftranger to form any conception. It often happens that the manners, the cuftoms, and the laws themfelves, are fo intimately connected with the conftitution, that it is fometimes difficult to alter a part of this mighty edifice, without deftroying the whole. It proceeds from this, that no remedy is applied to thefe glaring improprieties, which a foreigner imagines might be deftroyed with fuch facility.

If a reform could be eafily atchieved, is it to be fuppofed that the greateft lawyers in the kingdom, fuch as a Thurlow and a Mansfield, would not long ere this have obviated fuch inconveniences in the difcharge of their own duty?

Lord Mansfield has already been for many years lord chief juftice of England. As a ftatefman he is not confpicuous, but he is an eloquent and engaging orator. Whoever liftens to him in the court of king's bench, where he prefides, will imagine it is an oracle that fpeaks. He knows fo well how to mingle wifdom and dignity together, that he appears like THEMIS herfelf in every caufe where government is not immediately concerned. At the famous trial of lord George Gordon, this refpectable magiftrate entirely forgot that his houfe had been burnt, his library deftroyed, and his precious collection of manufcripts loft for ever. He behaved like a judge whofe fole duty it was to interpret the laws, and act according to their decifions. He treated this madman with a moderation and a mildnefs without parallel, collected all the proofs of his innocence, and gave a charge in his favour.

- I was

I was witness to a singular scene betwixt this nobleman and a jew who was brought before him. This rogue, in the most impudent manner, offered himself as security for the sum of three hundred pounds sterling. My lord testified some doubt concerning the fortune of the conscientious son of circumcision; but he pulling from his pocket a number of bank notes, asked his lordship if he was acquainted with that kind of paper? The judge was silent, and the bail was admitted. It is probable that one of the rich jews who were present, had slipped the money into his hand.

By virtue of the act of *Habeas Corpus*, a debtor detained in prison may be removed, whenever he pleases, to any gaol in the kingdom. The writ costs about three pounds sterling, and the smallness of the sum induces all the great debtors to make use of this privilege, when they are able to raise so much, and do not expect to be speedily liberated.

As there are two prisons, called the King's-bench and the Fleet, which are peculiar to England, and have nothing similar to them in Europe, they usually make choice of one of these. The latter is situated in the middle of the city; the other in St. George's Fields. No traveller that I am acquainted with, has ever given a particular account of these singular and uncommon gaols. They never, indeed have been mentioned among us but in some English romances, which are very justly rejected as so many fictions and improbabilities. So true it is that we have only a few vague ideas of a nation concerning which we never cease to speak; which we endeavour to imitate in almost every thing, and which is so very near to us.

It may be said, that these prisons are two republics existing in the bosom of the metropolis, and entirely independent of it. The situation and the largeness of the first render it more commodious
than

than the other. Its boundaries are marked by a wall, which contains a prodigious extent of ground. Within its circumference, a great number of houses are built for the accommodation of the prisoners; a garden where they may walk, a place where they may play at fives, public houses where beer and wine are sold, a coffee house, shops, &c. &c.

All the mechanics who follow trades which do not require much room nor long preparation, are allowed here to exercise their respective avocations, which they denote by signes at their doors and windows. You may find taylors, shoe-makers, wig-makers, &c. &c. who not only work for the other prisoners, but also for their customers elsewhere, who still continue to employ them. They generally make their families stay with them, and live very comfortably. Those who are at liberty sometimes surpass in number those who are confined, and the whole often amounts to two or three thousand. There is no guard but at the entrance; the greatest liberty reigns within; neither bars, nor bolts, nor irons, nor gaoler are to be perceived; nothing, in one word, to denote a prison.

As their doors are never locked up, the inhabitants may divert themselves for whole nights together. They have even been known to give balls and concerts. The free-masons have a lodge here. It was in the King's-bench that Wilkes was, in the year 1769, received as a member of that society.

The gates are open from seven o'clock in the morning till nine at night. Any person impelled either by curiosity or business, may go and come during those hours, without being asked any questions. During Wilkes's imprisonment, the avenues were continually choaked up by the number of carriages that were bringing visitors to him.

It sometimes happens, that persons afraid of being arrested run to this place as to an asylum, where they

they remain with fome of the prifoners whom they
are acquainted with, and never depart till they
have made terms with their creditors, or taken fome
other neceffary fteps. For, according to the conftitution of this fingular commonwealth, the perfons
who fly there for refuge, cannot in any manner be
molefted by thofe on the outfide. The infide is a
fanctuary, facred to Liberty, where the bailiff dares
not penetrate. He never goes further than the
lobby, where he depofits his prifoners. Woe to him
if he paffes one ftep beyond it !

Some years fince, one of thofe fellows having
difguifed himfelf, attempted to intice a widow
woman towards the door, to arreft her. She had
fought an afylum with her brother from the purfuit
of a heard-hearted creditor, who wifhed to have
her entirely in his power. In confequence of this,
he had promifed the officer a confiderable fum of
money in cafe of fuccefs. The bailiff rifks the attempt, and is fufpected. His retreat is cut off, and
the ufual fignal given, on the appearance of a dif-
turber of the peace of the fociety. All the inhabitants run out of their apartments, furround the unfortunate culprit, and demand the reafon of his
prefumption. The writ which they find in his
pocket explains the whole. Being unable to excufe
himfelf, he craves forgivenefs; but to prevent fimilar attempts for the future, they refolve to make
him an example. Accordingly a moft fingular punifhment is refolved upon. They condemn him to eat
the piece of parchment which contains the writ.
The wretch is obliged to obey. It is cut into fmall
pieces, and he is forced to fwallow them, one after
another.

In this prifon there are apartments which would
not difgrace a palace. Thefe are generally occupied
by rich people, who pay for them at a very dear
rate: for nothing is more common than to fee perfons

fons who poffefs confiderable fortunes conducted to this place, who remain there as long as they pleafe, and fet out whenever they choofe to make the necef-fary arrangements with their creditors. During their confinement they fquander large fums of money, and give a great deal in charity to their fellow-pri-foners.

One may here fee people dreffed in the moft fafhionable clothes; affemblies of ladies and gentle-men, apartments elegantly furnifhed, and tables delicately ferved. The genteel and polite air every where vifible, will never allow any one to think that all this is in a gaol.

The ftreets are called after particular names, and the houfes properly numbered: a chamber is thought to be very cheap, when it can be hired for half a guinea. The coffee-houfe is a very good building, and has a fine view of St. George's-fields: here all the newfpapers are taken in.

One is almoft fure of meeting good company at this place, as it is frequented by refpectable perfons, who have loft their fortunes by fome unforefeen ac-cidents.

It was here that the Rev. Mr. Horne wrote his excellent book on the government and laws of Eng-land; that Wilkes formed the plan of his prefent grandeur; and that lord Rodney lived for fome time, before, by his exploits during the late war, he ac-quired the admiration of all Europe.

The unbecoming affemblage of the two fexes, is one of the greateft abufes of this prifon. I have already faid, that according to the laws of the coun-try, the hufband is obliged to anfwer for the debts of his wife, fo that it is he only is arrefted. One does not therefore meet with married women here, but there are plenty of widows, and unmarried ladies. Thefe laft, who are all prieftesses of Venus, abound in great plenty, and fometimes exceed an hundred.

hundred. One of these must be very disagreeable, if she does not find, on her arrival, several who will offer to share their apartments with her, and even their beds. When they are tired of each other they separate, and make a fresh choice. It often happens that they remain with their lovers after they are liberated; and it is not at all uncommon to see them forming connections here, which are only dissolved by death.

. The voluptuous life which they lead in this gaol, is also augmented by the continual visits which their lovers make them. However, notwithstanding the debauchery which generally prevails, it very rarely happens that it is attended with consequences punishable by the laws.

There are certain districts in the neighbourhood of the King's-bench and the Fleet, called *rules*, which form a circuit of two English miles. The prisoner may not only ramble but even live within these, whenever he can find security that he will not escape. It is remarked that no nation is so credulous as the English.

If a person wishes to have a companion in his walks, he need only add his friend's debt to his own, and procure an indemnification for both.

There are a great many agreeable gardens in the neighbourhood of the King's-bench, where tea and coffee are sold, and which in an afternoon are full of prisoners.

The marshall has upwards of three thousand a year, in salary and perquisites; for this he has very little to do, as he never troubles himself about the interior regulations: he is obliged, however, to give large security, as he becomes liable to the debts of all those who escape. About ten years since, four prisoners, whose debts amounted to fifteen hundred pounds sterling, escaped by means of a hole in the garden wall. Before he paid so much money, the

the marfhal bethought himfelf of a very fingular expedient. He gave notice that he would give them fifty 'per cent. of the fums for which they had been confined, provided they would furrender themfelves. Three of them actually acceded to the agreement, received the ftipulated payment and returned to their former habitation.

To prevent fimilar attempts, they now take care to place guards around the outward wall, as feveral marfhals have loft confiderable fortunes, and fallen into the greateft poverty, by their negligence. It is abfolutely , neceffary, confidering the manner in which debtors are treated in England, that fome fecurity fhould be given to the creditors, without which, they would efcape daily by means of corruption.

A crowd of people belonging to the prifon, are always on watch at the door, which is conftantly kept fhut. All perfons who either enter or depart from it, are obliged to pafs through the room in which they wait. They examine the prifoners with the greateft minutenefs on their arrival ; they are not, however, permitted to vifit the infide of the prifon on any pretext whatever.

From what I have faid, it will be readily believed, that no other place of confinement in the world, in the leaft refembles the King's-bench : as yet, however, I have not mentioned a fingle word concerning thofe particulars which more eminently characterife its republican form of government.

Although the care of this gaol is entirely confided to the marfhal, yet he is not permitted to interfere in its internal regulations, and is very feldom feen within its walls. Every prifoner, whether man or woman, is a member of this commonwealth, and participates in all its privileges. They choofe a lord chief juftice, and a certain number of judges,

I   who

who affemble once a week, and decide controver-
fies.

In this ccurt they terminate all quarrels, make
laws concerning the police, hear all complaints, and
pronounce final judgment : in a word, every thing
is equally attended to as in a well governed community. Every one has a right to attend and plead
his own caufe. Thofe who are not able to exprefs
themfelves with propriety in public, fuch as women,
for example, employ others to relate their complaints, or defend their interefts.

Thefe proceedings may appear laughable to my
readers ; they are not, however, fo to thofe who
incur the difpleafure of the judges. No monarch in
the world can ever flatter himfelf to fee his laws
obeyed with fuch punctuality, as are the rules of
this fociety. The moft fevere equity dictates the
decrees, which are put in execution without a moment's delay. A colonel on half pay, who poffeffed
great eloquence and abilities, for many years pre-
fided at this court, which he governed with the
greateft propriety and decorum.

When there is a fuit commenced on account of a
debt contracted in the prifon, the action is brought
in all the proper forms. The debtor is fummoned
to appear, and is obliged to obey ; for in cafe of refufal, he is dragged by force. Twelve jurymen
being impannelled, as in the national courts, they
give a verdict, after having made the neceffary inquiries ; and from this there is no appeal. If time
is requefted, it is allowed ; if the debtor at its expi-
ration ftill wifhes to procraftinate, all his goods,
even to his bed, are then fold for the benefit of the
creditor. If he has no effects, his apartment is let
out, till either his creditor is fatisfied, or he finds
fome other way of difcharging the obligation.

Even criminal proceffes, fuch as larceny, and
breach of the peace, are here taken cognizance of.

On

On such occasions, the culprit, with a paper stuck on his breast describing his crime, is obliged to walk through every street, preceded by a herald, who with a loud voice assigns the reason of the punishment, and tells the inhabitants to beware of the delinquent. This inspires every one with hatred to the crime; and as the criminal cannot escape out of the narrow circle in which he may be said to vegetate, rather than to live, it happens very rarely that any one exposes himself to a humiliation so terrible in its consequences. It may therefore be said with truth, that the laws of this petty republic, and the punishments which they inflict, fully attain the end proposed.

The community also appoint and pay watchmen, who, according to the custom in all great towns, cry the hours during the night, and prevent fires and robberies; their occupation in the day-time is to proclaim the new laws and regulations, and, in one word, to instruct the inhabitants in every thing that it is necessary for them to know.

The families, the friends, and the domestics, of the prisoners, who settle among them, and all those who pass a single night within the walls, are under the protection of the society, and, in case of being maltreated, are entitled to receive ample and immediate satisfaction: if they, on the other hand, happen to offend themselves, they are immediately turned out of the prison, and are never more permitted to enter it.

In cases of importance, the person aggrieved may cite another before the common court of justice; and if they are destitute of money, their fellow-prisoners make a subscription to defray the expences.

According to the laws of England, a prisoner may commence a process on account of debt, without any expence: on depositing a few farthings in the

poor's

poor's box, a counsel is appointed to him gratis.
This is called suing in *forma pauperis*. If he loses
his cause, the costs are added to the debt. The
expences incurred in the court of King's-bench, by
a process not very intricate, amount generally to
about thirty pounds ; in the marshalsea to five or
six. The debt must always exceed ten pounds sterling, before a process can be instituted in the former court for its recovery.

I know not whether the privileges of this place
are sanctioned by any law ; they are however tolerated by the legislative power, and that, perhaps, as
a compensation for the loss of liberty. But without
attending to these considerations, the conduct of
government in this case is extremely wise. What
disorders, what complaints, what profligacies of
every kind, would not ensue among so many prisoners, if a well regulated police did not remedy all
these inconveniencies, by establishing order and
harmony among them !

Without this they would be obliged to use the
methods practis'd in France, where they treat
debtors like so many criminals ; crowd them in horrible dungeons, punish them by whipping, without
distinction of age, rank or sex ; and thus tormented
by their equals, devoured by hunger, and eat up
with vermin, leave the poor wretches to curse their
existence !

What a contrast is here betwixt the two nations !
nevertheless the French are not ashamed to treat the
English as a cruel and savage people ; and I am
sorry to add, that some of my own* countrymen
have not blushed to retail such absurdities, and
judge of a whole nation by the misbehaviour of the
populace.

There is a great number of shop-keepers established in the King's-bench prison, who trade in
prohibited

* The Germans.

prohibited goods, which they sell at a very low
price. Among other things they retail tea, coffee,
brandy, soap, and candles, which they procure in
large quantities; and as they are not subject to the
visits of the excisemen, they not only supply the
prisoners but others publickly. This abuse is not to
be reckoned among the number of those tolerated by
the government: it took its rise under an indolent
minister, and no one has since attempted to reform
it.

Those debtors who claim a maintenance, are
obliged to present themselves before one of the
courts of justice, and swear to their poverty; after
which, the creditor is obliged to furnish them with
the sum assigned by law.

This allowance is in consequence of a very ancient custom, and amounts to four pence per day.
Very few of the debtors have recourse to this, because the oath which they are obliged to take,
wounds their pride, and the supply itself is but
trifling.

It is necessary, while on this subject, to remark
a very singular custom. The payment of this allowance must be made every Saturday, for the following
week. If the creditor is not punctual, which may
often happen when he lives at the distance of a
league from the King's-bench, the prisoner is enlarged, and the debt cancelled. On this occasion,
all that is necessary to be done, is to prove that the
stipulated sum has not been regularly paid.

An insolvent act frequently opens all the gaols in
the kingdom, and then almost all the prisoners are
released. I say *almost all*, because there are a few
excepted from the benefit of it; these, for example,
who owe five hundred pounds and upwards to any
one person. With some there is a kind of infamy
attached to it, which prevents them: there are
others who have a great deal of money, and con-

consequently

fequently cannot become infolvent; and many are
fo fatisfied with the advantages arifing from fmug-
gling, that they never wifh to be releafed.

The names of all the debtors who choofe to clear
themfelves by means of the act, are printed in the
Gazette; and before they receive their liberty, they
are obliged to fwear in the prefence of a magiftrate,
that they are unable to fatisfy their creditors.

The Englifh do not reckon imprifonment dif-
graceful; it is however thought a great reproach
to be cleared by an act. On thefe occafions, they
are always afked if they can give any fecurity to
their creditor? when this queftion was put to the
unfortunate king Theodore, who was actually releafed in this manner, he anfwered, *Yes, the kingdom of Corfica.*

As it is expreffed in the bill, that all infolvent
debtors who appear by a certain day fhall be entitled
to the benefits of it; on thofe occafions, you may
fee people arriving from the moft diftant parts, of
Europe, to acquit themfelves of the debts which
they have contracted in England. Not only the
natives, but foreigners of every nation, profit by
the opportunity. Tenducci, the famous Italian
finger, who owed more than ten thoufand pounds
fterling, returned to England, in the year 1777, for
this purpofe. He afterwards was engaged at Drury-
Lane theatre, and ran away the very next year,
after having incurred feveral thoufand pounds of
frefh debts.

All the prifons in England would not be able to
contain the prodigious number of debtors, both
Englifh and foreigners, who furrender themfelves
at fuch times. In confequence of this, they have
adopted a fingular practice, for the accommodation
of thofe who have been fome time in confinement,
as well as thofe newly arrived. Thefe latter are not
received within the walls of the gaols, but are
allowed

allowed to be at liberty, and live wherever they pleafe. To entitle themfelves to this privilege, they are fhut up for a few moments within the prifon : after this, they give an *undertaking* to appear whenever they are called upon, which they would be fure to forget, were they afraid of the confequences.

As the military are wholly fubordinate to the civil power, and as an officer has no right to punifh a foldier for any thing but the neglect of his duty, it is not at all uncommon to find many of them confined in all the gaols of the kingdom, on account of debt, or a criminal profecution. A foreigner, and efpecially a German, who has been ufed to behold the army, on every occafion, treated as a body altogether feparate and diftinct from the people, is extremely aftonifhed at this cuftom. I have feen a bailiff arreft an officer on the parade, and carry him off. It is not to the colonel, but to a juftice of the peace, that one complains againft a foldier ; it is a foldier alone who carries his complaints to the commanding officer, who, when the offence is not trivial, does not think himfelf competent to decide upon it, but is obliged to refer it to the civil tribunal.

An old foldier, who had ferved on the continent during the war of feven years, where he had learned a great many military tricks, fome years after the peace, while a centinel in the park, happening to take off a man's hat who was fatisfying fome of his natural wants, foon found that this German cuftom was not tolerated in England. The man immediately applied to a magiftrate, fwore that the foldier had ftole his hat, and obtained a warrant. The thief was accordingly feized, imprifoned, tried, condemned, and would have been actually executed, if the king had not granted him a pardon.

No

No debtor can be arrested on a Sunday; from twelve o'clock on Saturday night, till the same hour on Sunday evening, he is in perfect freedom. During that day, he may go wherever he pleases, even among his creditors, who have been looking for him in vain during the rest of the week.

Those who have been security for any man, may, however, arrest him on a Sunday : nay, even in a church, when he refuses to surrender; and neither any new process, nor fresh bail, can take him out of their hands. This privilege is the more just, as not one in the whole world has greater confidence than an Englishman, or is more easily induced to answer even for a stranger, when the sum is not very great, notwithstanding he derives no advantage from his kindness. It therefore happens, that *running away* from bail, is looked upon among them as the most infamous of all actions.

It is necessary that the sheriff's officer should employ the utmost caution in seizing a debtor. A writ is only valid in certain districts, and beyond these they cannot go, without suing out another: for example, the city of London, and the counties of Middlesex and Surry, have each a particular jurisdiction.

There is a certain part of Westminster, in the neighbourhood of the Park, where bailiffs dare not go, and where the debtors may remain in safety. This precinct, which includes St. James's, the Green and Hyde Parks, is called the verge of the court; and is under the regulation of the board of green cloth. Before permission is granted to arrest a person resident there, he always receives twenty-four hours notice. All the houses are full of lodgers, and apartments let for more money than any where else in London.

The proverb that an *Englishman's house is his castle*, is not without foundation; for no one can be
arrested

arrefted in his own houfe, on account of debt. However, if the bailiff, happening to find the ftreet-door open, gets to the mafter of it and fhews his writ, he is obliged inftantly to follow him. There is no kind of tricks which they do not practife, for this purpofe. They drefs themfelves fometimes as men of condition, at other times like women, and on fome occafions they wear a livery.

They are not allowed to open the ftreet-door; but it is not at all uncommon to fee them pafs the bounds prefcribed by law, hoping in general, that the debtors have not money enough to inftitute an action againft them.

They are, however, fometimes deceived. It is now about twenty years ago, that general Ganfel commenced a procefs on this account. That gentleman had not a houfe of his own, but hired a firft floor in which he lived. As he owed a large fum of money, his creditors wifhed to feize him. The bailiffs, in confequence of this, having unlocked the outward door, made towards the general's apartments, who wounded one of them with a piftol from the infide; but, being obliged to yield to numbers, he was dragged to prifon, and there commenced an action againft them.

All England was attentive to the decifion on the queftion, whether a lodger enjoyed the fame rights as the owner of a houfe? The twelve judges to the great fatisfaction of the whole nation, decided in the affirmative. In confequence of this, the fheriff's officers were immediately conducted to gaol, and the general, who was greatly in debt, was removed to the Fleet, where he died a prifoner fome years afterwards.

CHAPTER X.

The Police of London—Highwaymen and Footpads—
House-breakers—Anecdote—Thieves—Women of
the Town—Seduction—Bagnios—Singular Excess
—Unnatural Crimes held in great Abhorrence.

THE English have not a single word in their
whole language, to express what we term the
police; if one however concludes from thence, that
the thing itself does not exist among them, he will
be grossly deceived. Foreigners more especially,
who cannot separate the idea of London from that
of the highwaymen, who infest the great roads in
its neighbourhood, imagine that it is the worst regulated metropolis in the world.

London is nevertheless as well governed as any
city can be, which contains such an amazing number of men, who enjoy the most uninterrupted
liberty. The human soul can never be more elevated than when a philosophical mind surveys this
million of men crowded together, whom neither
the soldiery nor the sceptre of despotism, but the
invisible power of the laws preserves in unity, by
infusing the order and harmony necessary for the
regulation of such a gigantic body. If the wealth
of this great city, the voluptuousness of every kind
with which it abounds, and the luxury of the present
age are considered, ought we not rather to be astonished that this prodigious mass does not, by continual

nual friction, fometimes emit the moft dangerous fcintillations ?

It appears to me wonderful, that the crowds of poor wretches who continually fill the ftreets of the metropolis, excited by the luxurious and effeminate life of the great, have not fome time or another entered into a general confpiracy to plunder them.

The thefts and rogueries practifed there, confidering every thing, are but few in number. A wife precaution might ftill diminifh the evil; for it is not poffible that human wifdom fhould be able totally to deftroy it; while the metropolis is fo extenfive, while it remains without walls, and wi hout gates, and while the kingdom preferves its prefent conftitution.

I fhall here give fome account of its prefent police. The poor, in every parifh, are maintained out of a certain provifion to which every houfe-keeper is obliged to contribute.

A great number of hofpitals, which are the *ne plus ultra* of that kind of eftablifhments, by their order, their arrangement, and their cleanlinefs, are open to the fick of all nations and religions, whom they entertain by means of annual fubfcriptions.

The ftreets are moft excellently lighted every evening, towards the dufk, without having any regard to the moon, which is often obfcured by clouds, although it is often ridiculoufly allowed for in the economical calculations in other countries. Thefe lamps are placed for fix or even feven miles along the great roads, on purpofe to light the paffengers. You alfo meet with a watch-box, at the end of every hundred yards, containing a man, provided with a gun and bayonet, who, by means of a bell, gives an alarm at the approach of any fufpicious perfon. There are in London itfelf two thoufand watchmen, each armed with a long pole, and carrying a rattle, with which they affemble

their

their companions, at the appearance of any tumult. When they find either doors or windows open, they inform the proprietors; they also cry the hours, tell the weather, and give notice of fires.

The precautions which are taken in respect to conflagrations, those horrible scourges of the human race, are also very wife. At the first notice of a fire, you perceive a multitude of men, running from all quarters, with the engines which are entrufted to their care. For the first of these brought to the spot, they receive a recompense of five guineas, the second is entitled to three, and the third to one. The others are not paid any thing; however the hope of gaining one of the three premiums, makes them use the utmost industry and dispatch.

All the houses and furniture are infured. Every street, whether large or small, courts, alleys, &c. have their names painted at each corner. All the doors are numbered, and, befides this, generally have the names of the owners engraven on brafs plates. Every house in that immenfe city is provided with water by means of pipes which are carried under ground. The pavement, which is of the best kind, is rendered still more excellent, by the great care that is taken of it; one is also astonished at the neatness of the streets, and the great attention to prevent the accumulation of dirt.

The hackney-coaches, of which a certain number is assigned to every quarter of the metropolis, are ready at a moment's notice, during the whole day, and dare not, on any pretence whatever, refuse to carry passengers wherever they please, either in town, or within a certain distance from it. The number is painted on two tin plates affixed to the doors; if it is ever taken off, the proprietor is fined. The hire of these carriages is regulated according to the time and the distance; and if the

coachman

coachman takes more than his fare, he is liable to be-
feverely punished.

It is the fame in refpect to the wherries that ply
on the river, which are not only numbered, but
alſo have the names and places of abode of the
watermen painted on the infide. When any complaints are made againſt the boatmen, an immediate
deciſion may be expected.

The juſtices fit during the whole day; if any
preſſing bufineſs ſhould oblige one of them to be
abſent, another may be found at every hundred
yards. The aldermen of the city attend Guildhall
in rotation, hear all difputes, and fettle petty differences on the ſpot; this is all done *gratis*, and in
open court: the judges, therefore, can neither be-
corrupt nor unjuſt. The lord mayor alſo fits daily
at the Manſion-houſe.

After this defcription, it will be eafy to decide, whether London is well governed or not. The French
and their partifans will determine in the negative,
becauſe it is not the cuſtom there, to impriſon and
maltreat twenty innocent people, to deter one that
is guilty.

The laws are peculiarly fevere againſt highwaymen, whofe guilt, when fully proved, is puniſhed
with death. To prevent them from forming affociations, they very wifely allow a culprit to efcape,
on accufing and convicting his companions. This
advantage, which thofe rogues often make uſe of,
infpires them with diftruſt, and prevents them from
uniting in affociations which would be exceedingly
dangerous. The magiſtrates alſo often entrap them,
by means of the thief-takers, who difguife themfelves, and travel in a poſt-chaife, along the moſt dangerous roads in the neighbourhood of town. Thefe
fire their piſtols the moment that they are attacked,
jump out of the carriage, and are often lucky
enough to feize their prey. The highwaymen principally

cipally truſt for their eſcape in the ſpeed of their horſes, and their knowledge of the bye-roads. This claſs of men are generally very polite, they aſſure ycu *they are very ſorry that poverty has driven them to that ſhameful recourſe*, and end by demanding your purſe, in the moſt curteous manner. They often reſtore to thoſe, who in their fright have given all their money, a trifle to continue their journey. Some of them converſe with the utmoſt phlegm, and ride off without any ceremony. Some, beſides the caſh, take alſo the watch; others refuſe it, well knowing that it often leads to a diſcovery.

Thoſe who are too poor to procure a horſe, commit robberies in the ſtreets. The town is their place of action, as the country is that of the highwayman's.

If one does not travel either very early or very late, there is no fear of being attacked even in the moſt ſuſpicious places; and on ſuch occaſions, a perſon or two on horſeback will prevent any danger. The nobility, and all people in affluent circumſtances, are generally attended by ſervants well armed, and are never ſtopped, but when they have omitted this ſlight precaution. They highwaymen are not in the leaſt dangerous, as they never proceed farther than a *menace*, never making uſe of their piſtols, but in caſe of reſiſtance. On this account, no perſon is imprudent enough to attempt defending himſelf, or he might eaſily do ſo in a cloſe carriage, againſt a man on horſeback. I never uſed to carry fire-arms, when it was my fortune to travel in the neighbourhood of town, at any critical hour, being contented with taking the neceſſary precaution, in reſpect to my money. This conſiſted in dividing it, and putting in a purſe the part which I deſtined for the collectors; for as prudence will not allow them to ſtop long, they are in a hurry to depart with their ſpoil, without ſtop-

ing

ing to examine it. Among the Englifh, indeed, the prize is never very great, for they think it inconvenient to carry much ready money. You will never fee among them a heavy purfe, becaufe they think it looks as if they boafted of their wealth, or might be fufpected of fome defign in fhewing it; thofe who are attached to ancient cuftoms; never carry one at all, but keep their money loofe in their pockets.

The trade of a thief is divided into different claffes, each having its particular maxims, cuftoms, and denomination. The poorer fort, who ftop paffengers in the ftreets and neighbourhood of London, during the night, are called *foot-pads* ; thofe who are mounted on horfeback, and attack travellers in the high-roads, are called *highway-men* ; and thofe who, by flight of hand, find means to get into apartments, and commit depredations, are called *houfebreakers*. The *pick-pockets* are different from all thefe, and are the moft poor and defpicable of any, unlefs they are very eminent in their art, and referve themfelves for great attempts alone.

Thefe different kinds of thieves remain faithful to their particular tenets. A highwayman will never condefcend to become a pick-pocket: he would think himfelf difhonoured, in attempting to empty any one's pockets, by a low trick. Of fuch a *falling off* there are hardly any examples. I have feen one of thofe thieves, who efcaped the punifhment inflicted by law, on account of turning *king's evidence*, fo much defpife the idea of *filching*, that he would not take a handkerchief, part of which happened to be out of a gentleman's pocket, and which he might have eafily fnatched, without being perceived: on the contrary, he warned him of the circumftance, and defired him to conceal it.

I pafs on to the other fpecies of rogues, who, notwithftanding the multitude of watchmen employed

ever

every where in the metropolis, steal out from their
wretched apartments, and plunder houses in the
night time. These break open the shutters, force
the windows, or saw the iron bars, with the greatest
dexterity, and little or no noise. If they are surprised by the watch, or perceive that the inhabitants
are alarmed, they immediately throw their tools
away, and take to their heels. They melt down
silver plate, for fear of being discovered by the cy-
pher or the arms, and are acquainted with people
who purchase it in ingots, and buy from them all
their booty. As these, who are termed *receivers*,
encourage theft, by this kind of traffic, they are
doubly punished, and find it impossible, notwithstanding their wealth, to escape from the hands of
justice. They used formerly to be transported for
fourteen years, to America, while thieves were
only banished for seven. This has been lately
changed into imprisonment; the same proportion is,
however still observed.

It very often happens, that women, on whom
Nature seems to have been prodigal of her favours,
league with these wretches. They act as spies during the day, and at night disguise themselves, and
assist in profiting by the discoveries which they have
made. By frequently visiting the courts of justice,
I have had occasion to hear very singular transactions of this kind. I one day, at the Old-Bailey,
saw a young woman, fair as Venus, present herself
before the astonished judges and spectators. Her
dress was in the most elegant taste, and she captivated every heart, by those graces, and that air of
dignity which she displayed during her defence.
This ravishing creature, happening to be very
much attached to a young man, who belonged to a
gang of thieves, had been so imprudent as to join
them. She had assisted at one of their nocturnal
expeditions, and helped to carry away the plunder.

The

The houfe where they commited the depredations ftood by itfelf, and the owner being in the country, no body was in it. As they had not waited for the night, but fimply till it was dufk, the robbery was hardly accomplifhed, when an alarm was given, and the thieves were purfued, Although the fair accomplice had taken the precaution to throw away every thing in her flight, yet fhe was obftinately followed to a houfe into which having run, fhe immediately fhut the door—But how did fhe appear to thofe who purfued her? Reprefent to your imagination an old beggar-woman, covered with dirty rags, her face blackened, her hair difhevelled, and, in one word, the moft hideous figure in the world: fuch was the appearance of this handfome female, when fhe faved herfelf from the fury of the populace,

The miftrefs of the houfe was a widow, of an unfufpected reputation, fhhe lived eccnomically on a little income, which fhe however knew how to increafe, by a thoufand ftratagems. In this critical momert fhe acted her part admirably; for, as fhe refufed to let any body enter until a conftable was brought, fhe had fufficient time for preparation.

On hearing that a thief had taken refuge in her houfe, fhe pretended the greateft fear and aftonifhment. Her officious neighbours helped to fearch every corner after this frightful creature, which fome of them had feen enter; they found nobody, however, but a beautful young woman, in an elegant undrefs, fewing in the beft apartment, whom the landlady, on entering, called her relation. She took particular care to fearch in every part of the room where fhe fat, and then retired, after making many apologies to her handfome coufin; fo that after an ineffectual fearch, the crowd departed without the leaft fufpicion. However, a few days after, fome of the gang being feized, information

was

was given againſt the young woman, and ſhe was
involved in the proſecution. Her charms, and her
no leſs bewitching eloquence, made a great impreſſion on the minds of the judges and the ſpectators,
but the inexorable law felt no compaſſion, and ſhe
was condemned to four years impriſonment.

The pick-pockets, as I have already obſerved,
form a claſs entirely apart. It is by trick and ſtra-
tagem, and not by force, that they attain their
ends; therefore they never have occaſion for arms.
They do not unite in bodies, each perſon acts for
himſelf; and they immediately convert every thing
they acquire into ready money.

There are ſome of them, who, by means of
faſhionable clothes, inſinuate themſelves into the
firſt company, and their impudence is often crowned
with ſucceſs. A fellow of this kind, called Bar-
rington, renowned in London, on account of his
great dexterity, elegant manners, and boldneſs un-
paralleled, ſtill carries on his trade with great reputation *. Some years ſince, having ſlipt into the
ſtage box at Drury-lane Theatre, he found means
to ſteal from Prince Orlow a gold ſnuff-box, adorned
with the Empreſs of Ruſſia's picture, ſet round
with brilliants. His Highneſs having perceived the
theft, requeſted that the culprit might be immediately puniſhed; but when he was informed, that it
was neceſſary that he himſelf ſhould appear in perſon,
he ſtifled his reſentment, and the offender was re-
leaſed.

Nothing is more aſtoniſhing than the fidelity, I
may even ſay the probity of theſe wretches, in regard to one another: this appears in the mutual
dangers that they run, the fair diviſions that they
make of the ſpoil, and, in fine, is perceptible thro'
their whole behaviour. This phœnomenon fully
                                                  juſtifies

---

* He is at preſent in Newgate.

juftifies the Englifh proverb, that, " *there is honour*
" *among thieves.*"

This fhameful trade has been, if I may be allowed the expreffion, immortalized by Gay, in his
Beggar's Opera, which is fuch a favourite with the
public, that it is reprefented in London, at leaft
thirty times a year. In this dramatic entertainment,
you may fee a band of thieves, with piftols in their
hands, celebrating their revels, and finging fongs in
honour of their profeffion. Of courfe, much may
be faid againft the morality of fuch an entertainment; but it is lucrative to the theatre, on account
of the witty fallies with which it abounds, its fingularity, and the excellence of its mufic.

All the juftices of the peace for the county of
Middlefex, befought Garrick, in the year 1771, to
ftop the performance; but the Englifh Rofcius did
not choofe to deprive himfelf of a piece, which
feemed to be a mine of wealth.

Criminals are never carried to the King's-bench,
or the Fleet, which are deftined entirely for the
confinement of debtors, but to other prifons, cf
which Newgate is the principal. They are there
put in irons, but, except this, which prudence
evidently dictates, are never maltreated. Their
friends may vifit them, and are generally allowed
to give them any relief, to alleviate their unhappy
fituat: n, There is however, a great difference between their dungeons, and the places where debtors
are enclofed, who can fcarce indeed he confidered
as pr foners.

At an execution, the thieves, that they may fee
their companions die, always prefs as clofe as poffible to the place of punifhment: the fpectators,
however, have never more occafion to look to their
pockets than at that moment. A remark of a highwayman, in which there is fome pleafantry, is often
quoted. An acquaintance of his being carried to
Tyburn,

'Tyburn, after having gravely surveyed the gallows, and all the preparations for his fate, exclaimed, " O, *what an excellent trade would ours be, if this* " *d—n'd machine was out of the way!*" " *Fool!*" replies the other, " *this gibbet, which you curse, is* " *the best support of our trade, for, were it not for* " *it, every pick-pocket would turn highwayman.*"

Cheats ought to be mentioned entirely by themselves. They never steal, but employ all the stratagems that can be devised, to *trick* people out of their property, and convert the wealth of others to their own use. Half of their business is to be well acquainted with the laws, for they always take care to carry their projects just short of that point where the magistrate would interfere. They associate together, hire noble houses, furnish them with magnificent furniture. and keep the most shewy carriages. The valet de chambre and the footmen are all in the secret, and share the earnings of their employer. Sometimes the master puts on a livery, to quiet a clamourous creditor, who, duped with the brilliant appearance, has left his goods, without ever having seen the master of the mansion.

Concerning this subject, I could relate a thousand anecdotes, of a very uncommon kind, which I heard during my stay in London; but as these agree so little with the manners and customs of all the other countries in Europe, they would be accounted so many fables.

I am now arrived at a subject unfortunately inexhaustible, I mean the *women of the town.* It is well known how handsome the English ladies are, and I am sorry to add, that the greatest part of this class of women abuse, in the most shameful manner, the charms with which nature has so prodigally endowed them. London is said to contain fifty thousand prostitutes, without reckoning kept-mistresses. The most wretched of these live with

matrons,

matrons, who lodge, board, and clothe them. The dress worn by the very lowest of them is silk, according to the custom which luxury has generally introduced into England. Sometimes they escape from their prison, with their little wardrobes under their arms, and trade on their *own bottoms*, when, if they are unfortunate, or happen not to be economical, they are soon dragged to gaol by their creditors.

The uncertainty of receiving payment makes the house-keepers charge them double the common price for their lodgings. They hire by the week a first floor, and pay for it more than the owner gives for the whole premises, taxes included. Without these, thousands of houses would be empty, in the western parts of the town. In the parish of Mary-le-bone only, which is the largest and best peopled in the capital, thirty thousand ladies of pleasure reside, of whom seventeen hundred are reckoned to be house-keepers. These live very well, and without ever being disturbed by the magistrates. They are indeed so much their own mistresses, that if a justice of the peace attempted to trouble them in their apartments, they might turn him out of doors; for as they pay the same taxes as the other parishioners, they are consequently entitled to the same privileges.

Their apartments are elegantly, and sometimes magnificently furnished; they keep several servants, and some have their own carriages. Many of them have annuities paid them by their seducers, and others settlements into which they have surprised their lovers in the moment of intoxication. The testimony of these women, even of the lowest of them, is always received as evidence in the courts of justice. All this generally gives them a certain dignity of conduct, which can scarcely be reconciled with their profession.

The

The higher claffes of thefe females are uncommonly honeft ; you may entruft them with a purfe
crammed with gold, without running any rifk whatever. They can never be prevailed upon to grant
favours to the lover of one of their companions,
even if they are fure that the circumftance will be
kept a profound fecret. One of my friends made
a propofal of this kind, and was refufed; he re-
doubled his prefents his careffes, but in vain: " I
" am, fir," fays fhe, " an unhappy female,
" obliged to live by this difhonourable profeffion ;
" and Heaven is my witnefs, that I am in want of
" money ; but I will never confent to have any
" connection with the acquaintance of my friend.
" If you were an Englifhman, I might not be fo
" difficult ; but as you are a foreigner, I cannot.
" What opinion would you have of us, if I were
" to gratify your wifhes ?" Not fatisfied with the
excufe, he ridiculed her delicacy, and tempted her
with more money ; but, notwithftanding her poverty, fhe perfifted in her refufal, and all this from national pride.

During the elections for members of parliament,
it is not unufual to fee thefe ladies refufe to barter
their favours for large fums of money, and referve
their charms for the purchafe of votes, in favour of
certain patriots, whom they efteem.

Such virtues greatly leffen the infamy of their
profeffion. I have feen many people of rank walk
with them in public, and allow them to take hold
of their arms, in the moft familiar manner. I have
even beheld more than one minifter plenipotentiary
converfing publickly at Vauxhall, with females of
this defcription. Although their rank requires a decorum, which would be unneceffary among the
Englifh nobility ; yet thefe gentlemen eafily accede
to the cuftoms of a country, when they are in favour
of liberty.

One

One of thefe ladies, called Kitty Fifher, was very celebrated, about twenty-five years fince, on account of the elegance and delicacy with which fhe facrificed to Venus. She was indebted to nature for an uncommon portion of beauty, judgment, and wit, joined to a moft agreeable and captivating vivacity. The union of fo many perfections procured the efteem and fafcinated the defires of thofe who prefer Cyprian delights to all the other pleafures of life. This lady knew her own merit ; fhe demanded a hundred guineas a night, for the ufe of her charms, and fhe was never without votaries, to whom the offering did not feem too exhorbitant. Among thefe was the late Duke of York, brother to the king ; who one morning left fifty pounds on her toilet. This prefent fo much offended Mifs Fifher, that fhe declared that her doors fhould ever be fhut againft him in future ; and to fhew, by the moft convincing proofs, how much fhe defpifed his prefent, fhe clapt the bank-note between two flices of bread and butter, and ate it for her breakfaft.

The idea of the pleafures to be enjoyed in the capital infpires the girls in the country with the moft longing defire to participate in them. Imagination inflames their little heads, and prefents every object under an exaggerated appearance. The young people of both fexes, who have been educated at a diftance from town, imagine the metropolis to refemble that paradife promifed to the Mahometans, by their great prophet. Is it to be then wondered at, that they form fo many little projects to abandon their homes, and refide in the centre of pleafure ? Or that a maiden, without experience, fhould be eafily deceived, when the propofition comes from a lover ?

When an amorous couple has no hopes of getting their parents' confent to their union, they
foolifhly

foolishly think that they are obliged to run away, and they accordingly make for London. This fatal elopement raises the indignation of the young woman's relations, who are deaf to her prayers, and the young man becoming more pressing every day, she yields to his desires, in the hope of being more happy. The ungrateful lover, after being satiated with her charms, abandons her: thus left without any help, alone, unknown, she remains in the midst of an immense city, where trick and intrigue every day produce the most atrocious and singular scenes.

Some severe censor may here say, that in this deplorable situation she might take the high road, and beg her way to her father's house, or having received some education, she might get into service. These two resources are impossible in England. The amiable professor Moritz has already proved, by his own example, that journies on foot are entirely impracticable in that island. But if they were, could a young and beautiful creature venture to travel by herself? In the second place, who would employ a person, whose character could not be ascertained, and who has no one to speak in her behalf? And if she were willing, and fortunate enough to overcome so many disadvantages, would she be permitted? Her hostess, her creditors, the true or sham officers of justice; the most infernal schemes, and most scandalous practices, are employed against the poor wretch, till, yielding to necessity, she is constrained to consent to whatever is required of her.

One need not be astonished, after this, to hear that there are so many unfortunate women, who often possess all the virtues, and all the good qualities which we admire and cherish in their sex; youth, beauty, mildness, education, principle; and even that delicate coyness, which is the most powerful attraction to love. The ladies of pleasure in London actually give us an idea of the celebrated

Grecian

Grecian courtefans, who charmed the heroes of
Athens, and whom the fage Socrates himfelf often
honoured with his vifits.

Let it be recollected, however, that I now fpeak
only of a few, for it is very uncommon, not to fay
impoffible, to find fuch precious qualities among
thofe vile proftitutes, whofe kind of life ftifles in
their breafts every feed of virtue, if any indeed
ever exifted therein. At all feafons of the year,
they fally out towards the dufk, arrayed in the
moft gaudy colours, and fill the principal ftreets.
They accoft the paffengers, and offer to accompany
them: they even furround them in crowds, ftop
and overwhelm them with careffes and entreaties.
The better kind, however, content themfelves with
walking about till they themfelves are addreffed.
Many married women, who live in the diftant parts
of the town, proftitute themfelves in Weftminfter,
where they are unknown. I have beheld with a
furprize, mingled with terror, girls from eight to
nine years old make a proffer of their charms; and
fuch is the corruption of the human heart, that even
they have their lovers. Towards midnight, when the
young women have difappeared, and the ftreets become deferted, then the old wretches, of fifty or
fixty years of age, defcend from their garrets, and
attack the intoxicated paffengers, who are often
prevailed upon to fatisfy their paffions in the open
ftreet, with thefe female monfters.

Befides the immenfe number of women, who live
in ready furnifhed apartments, there are many
noted houfes, fituated in the neighbourhood of St.
James's, where a great number are kept for people
of fafhion. A little ftreet called *King's Place* is in-
habited by nuns of this order alone, who live under
the direction of feveral rich abbeffes. You may fee
them fuperbly clothed at public places; and even
thofe of the moft expenfive kind. Each of thefe

convents

convents has a carriage and servants in livery;
for the ladies never deign to walk any where, but
in the Park. They pay for their lodgings and their
board, and are entirely on the footing of *penfioners*,
being governed by the rules of the house.

The admission into these temples is so exorbitant, that the mob are entirely excluded: there are
indeed, only a few rich people who can aspire to
the favours of such venal divinities. The celebrated Fox used to frequent these places often before
he became a minister; and even afterwards, drunk,
as it were, with the pleasures which he had enjoyed,
he went from thence to move, astonish, and direct
the House of Commons, by means of his manly
and convincing eloquence. It is very singular, that
this man, while he sacrificed to Venus, and parti-
cipated so often in her orgies, was always regulated
by the maxims of an unimpeachable probity, and
true patriotism; the moment, however, that he
devoted himself entirely to the study of politics, he
stifled the spirit of libertinism, and with it these two
virtues.

There is in London a species of houses called
BAGNIOS, the sole intention of which is to procure pleasure. These are magnificent buildings,
and the furniture contained in them is not unworthy
of the palace of a prince. They there procure
every thing that can enrapture the senses. They
do not, indeed, keep women, but they are instantly
brought in chairs; and only those who are celebrated for their fashion, their elegance, and their
charms, have the honour of being admitted. The
English preserve their national phlegm in the midst
of their very pleasures. It is impossible to form an
idea of the gravity with which every thing is conducted even in these houses. Noise and riot are
banished

banifhed; the domeftics fpeak in a whifper; and old men, and debauched youths, put every fcheme in practice to reftore the proper tone to their nerves, which have been weakened by too much enjoyment.

This kind of entertainmant is very expenfive, and yet fometimes the *bagnios* are full all night long. For the moft part, they are fituated within a few paces of the theatres, or are furrounded by taverns. The profufion of wealth wafted in them, occafioned Beaumarchais, who was not unacquainted with the luxuries of Paris, to affirm, " That more " money is exhaufted during one night in the " taverns and bagnios of London, than would main- " tain all the SEVEN UNITED PROVINCES for " fix months."

A young gentleman, a native of Hampfhire, whofe father never would give him permiffion to vifit London, had fcarce buried the old gentleman, and become matter of his own perfon, and a for- tune of forty thoufand pounds fterling, when he fet out for town. His paffion for debauchery was fo very great, that, inftead of alighting at an inn, he went directly to a bagnio, and there demanded a lodging. They had never been afked for this before; but his inexperience, and his wealth, made them agree to every thing; and they immediately began to project plans, which he was eager to ex- ecute. Continually furrounded by fharpers, and women of the town; intoxicated with mufic, love, and wine, days and nights imperceptibly glided on, and followed each other without being perceived. The fcarceft wines were drank by them, in the utmoft profufion; they even made baths for their feet with champaign. For eleven days this luxu- rious young maniac led this kind of life; when he thought proper, at length, to make his arrival known to one of his friends. This gentleman's furprize was extreme: he, however, immediately

repaired

repaired to the inconfiderate youth, and painted the dangers and the difagreeable confequences of this kind of life in fuch lively colours, that he confented to depart immediately. It was, however, firft neceffary that the bill fhould be fettled: the hoft demanded for thefe eleven days of wild debauchery, no lefs than twelve hundred guineas. The new MENTOR however refifted the charge with indignation: the young man was arrefted, bail was given; and, to punifh the perfidious addrefs with which he had attempted to ruin an inexperienced lad, a court of juftice reduced the demand to a mere trifle.

Were this abufe, the natural confequence of luxury and fuperabundance, attempted to be reformed, fuch a reformation, in a country like England, would be attended with the moft pernicious confequences to trade and commerce. If they were to eftablifh a tribunal of chaftity in London, as was formerly done at Vienna, that great city would foon be depopulated; the melancholy of the English would become intolerable; the fine arts would be frightened away; one half of the inhabitants would be deprived of fubfiftence, and that fuperb metropolis converted into a fad and frightful defert. If any proofs are wanting, enter the fhops of the citizens, and afk them who are their beft cuftomers, and who pay them the moft regularly? They will immediately anfwer, that they are the unfortunate women, who deny themfelves almoft the neceffaries of life to purchafe fine clothes, and fpend in one moment the the whole gains of a week. Without them, the theatres would be empty: they not only repair to all public places in crowds, but draw after them thoufands of young men, who frequent thefe places, merely to fee and converfe with them. Every one who knows London, muft be of my way of thinking.

A young

A young unmarried Englishman, with a large fortune, spends but a small share of it on his common expences; the greatest part is destined to his pleasures, that is to say, to the ladies. A tavern-keeper, in Drury-lane, prints every year an account of the *women of the town*, entitled, *Harris's List of Covent-garden Ladies*. In it, the most exact description is given of their names, their lodgings, their faces, their manners, their talents, and even their tricks. It must of course happen, that there will sometimes be a little degree of partiality in these details: however, notwithstanding this, eight thousand copies are sold annually.

The English women are so handsome, and the desire to please them, and to obtain their favours, is so ardent and so general, that it is not in the least surprising, that those islanders should hold a *certain unnatural crime* in the utmost abhorrence. They speak in no part of the world with so much horror of this infamous passion, as in England. The punishment by law is imprisonment, and the pillory.— With this accusation, it is, however, better to suffer death at once; for, on such an occasion, the fury of the populace is unbounded, and even the better sort of people have no compassion for the culprit. It is very uncommon to see a person convicted, and punished for this crime; not on account of the paucity of the numbers charged with perpetrating it, but because they never yield to such a brutal appetite but with the utmost precaution.

A criminal prosecution was commenced, on a charge of this kind, against Foote, the celebrated comedian, about a year before his death. The intrepid actor soon after appeared upon the stage, in one of his gayest characters; but the noise from the pit, and the *epithet* made use of, and repeated from box to box, entirely disconcerted him. At length he obtained liberty to speak. He then assured

K 3

the:

the audience that he was innocent, and befought them not to condemn him unheard: he promifed to demonftrate before a court of juftice the falfity and the malice of the accufation; and added that, until he had fully eftablifhed his innocence, he would not afpire to the continuance of that favour with which the public had always had honoured him. The fpectators were appeafed. He acted his part and received the ufual plaudits: he alfo gained his caufe.

The cuftom fo common in other parts of Europe, of men's *faluting* each other, is looked upon with the utmoft indignation in England. A foreigner who would attempt fuch a thing in the ftreets of London, would in all probability be infulted by the populace. Inftead of embracing, they *fhake hands*. This ceremony repeated more or lefs often, expreffes the different degrees of good will, friendfhip and efteem. People fometimes act this *pantomime* in fuch a *forcible* manner, that they make each others hands and arms ache.

If *kiffing* is not allowed among the men, this prohibition is amply recompenfed by the right of publicly embracing the ladies. The hufbands themfelves are not vexed at this agreeable cuftom. Neither jealoufy nor fhame can prevent it: practice has thus rendered a fafhion entirely indifferent, which in Italy, would be regarded as a prefumption which the offender could only expiate with his blood.

CHAPTER

CHAPTER XI.

The manner of living in England—Coffee houfes—
Lloyd's—Affurance Offices—Domeftic Cuftoms—
The Contraft between French and Englifh Dinners.
Cookery—Liquors—Drefs—Singular Requeft to
the King—Servants--Sunday—Good-nature of the
People—Boxing—Marfhal Saxe's Difpute with a
Scavenger—The King of Bath.

THE Englifh live in a very remarkable manner.
They rife late, and fpend moft of the morning,
either in walking about town or fitting in the coffee-
houfes. There they not only read the newfpapers,
but tranfact bufinefs. Affociations, infurances, bets,
the trade in foreign bills; all thefe things are not
only talked of, but executed in thefe public places.
They there form connections, conclude bargains,
talk of the intrigues and cabals of the court, criticife
works of genius and art, and enter patriotic refolutions concerning the good of the ftate.

Each profeffion has its own particular coffee-
houfe; fuch as lawyers, the military men, the
learned and men of wit.

There are feveral dozens of thefe around the
Royal Exchange, where more bufinefs is tranfacted
than in the Exchange itfelf. That of Lloyd's in a
particular manner deferves to be noticed; I do not
think that there is another equal to it in all the
world. Thofe merchants who fpeculate in infurances, and who in 1778 amounted to fix hundred,

K 4   affemble

aſſemble there. They ſubſcribe ten guineas a piece per annum, and, by means of that ſum, carry on an immenſe foreign correſpondence with all the countries in Europe.

This ſociety accordingly receives the earlieſt and moſt authentic intelligence, reſpecting the politics or the commerce of all the nations inhabiting the four quarters of the globe. They often inform government of circumſtances that they would not know till long after from their miniſters and their agents; and which, perhaps, they would never otherwiſe hear of. The ſpirit of order and exactneſs, introduced into their intereſting regulations, is ſo perfect, that the moſt extraordinary news receives a certain degree of authenticity by coming from that place.

As theſe gentlemen, in common with the reſt of the nation, are famous for their *public ſpirit*, they are not barely contented with informing their particular friends, but tranſcribe their intelligence into a book, for the inſpection of the nation at large. They alſo publiſh the arrival of all veſſels, whether Engliſh or foreign, that come into any of the ports of England. There is not one of theſe, whoſe good or bad properties they are unacquainted with. They alſo know their age, the character of the captain, &c. &c. Being compoſed almoſt entirely of rich merchants, there is no danger of loſing the ſum aſſured, but in caſe of a *general bankruptcy*; and ſuch is their known probity, and reputation, that they are often, in doubtful caſes, appointed umpires by foreign ſtates.

An Engliſh coffee houſe has no reſemblance to a French or German one. You neither ſee billiards nor backgammon tables; you do not even hear the leaſt noiſe; every body ſpeaks in a low tone, for fear of diſturbing the company. They frequent them principally to read the Papers, a taſk that is abſolutely neceſſary in that country.

The

The dinners of the English, like all their domestic customs, have something peculiar to themselves. By supposing every thing to be entirely opposite to what it is in Paris, one may form a just idea of these houses in London, where the old fashions are still kept up. The number of people who live in the Anglo-Gallic style is very small.

Soup, which is the first dish in France, never appears on any table in London. The French eat a great deal of bread, and very little meat; the English much meat, and little bread. Joints, in France, are either roasted or boiled to rags; they eat them almost raw in England. Ragouts, sauces, and *made dishes*, are the delicacies of the French; the English are for what is simple and natural; they even push this taste too far. The tables of the former are often too small for the dishes; the entertainments of the latter consist of two or three large pieces of meat, or of prodigious pies, in which some hundreds of birds are entombed.

The desert, in France, is composed of fruits and confectionary; in England, of large cheeses. Among one nation, they eat more than they drink; among they other, they drink more than they eat, and regard their liquors as the chief article in a repast.

The English are in a hurry during their meals, that they may sooner indulge this passion. The ladies then leave them to enjoy themselves with greater freedom. Politics immediately commence, and *healths* continually go round; each guest proposes a toast in his turn, the master of the house having first given his. They then fill their glasses, and, naming either a minister or a beauty, empty them in a moment.

Napkins, which have been disused for twenty years, are now beginning to be introduced. Those who are attached to the old customs, ridicule the

use

we of them. This precaution, they say, is only
neceffary for children; grown perfons have no occafion for them, as they can cover themfelves with
the table cloth, which is of an extraordinary length.
They change the knife and fork with every plate.
They do not ufe thefe inftruments indifferently in
either hand, as in all the other nations in Europe ;
the fork is always in the left, and the knife in the
right hand. It is by this method, which is infinitely
more commodious than ours, that you may immediately know an Englifhman before he has fpoken a
fingle word.

'The difcredit into which Englifh cookery has
fallen among foreigners, proceeds entirely from the
prejudices entertained againft their manner of dreffing victuals. But who, in the whole world, would
not prefer flefh full of fucculent and nourifhing juices,
to thofe roafted meats which are infipid to the tafte,
if not eaten with an unwholefome fauce ? I have
known ladies brought up very delicately, and ufed
to all the elegancies of foreign tables, who, on their
firft arrival in London, have been difgufted with
the victuals; but they foon changed their minds, and
found them very agreeable afterwards. It is the
fimplicity in the dreffing, that alone generates fuch
prejudices in the breafts of ftrangers.

Their drinks alfo are remarkable, on account of
the fingular mixtures of which they are compofed.
Sillabub for example, is a compofition of red wine,
milk and fugar. The common people enjoy themfelves, during the winter, with warm * beer mixed
with bitter effences, and with ale in which gin,
fugar, and eggs have been boiled together. It is
their attachment to ftrong liquors, that makes them
fo very fond of port-wine, which is fold at a high
price. Burgundy and champaign, are exceedingly
dear, on account of the duties: notwithftanding
this,

* Purl.

this, the confumption of thefe wines is very great in London, where they like every thing that is *powerful* and *beady*. Although cyder is allowed to be equally agreeable, yet it is drunk only in the diftant counties.

They are peculiarly attached to porter: on this account, there are no lefs than eight thoufand ale-houfes in the metropolis and its neighbourhood. In thefe all ranks are mixed and confounded together: it is not uncommon to meet with even perfons of quality there.—It is well known that Swift and Stern frequented them, to ftudy the human heart.

The impoft on coffee is fo great, that it pays a duty of more than feven pence a pound. This does not, indeed, leffen the confumption; the exorbitant price, however, occafions it to be drunk very weak. This cuftom is fo prevalent, that even the richeft people will not ufe it when ftrong; the moft contemptible tradefman in all Germany drinks better coffee than they do. In refpect to tea, the Englifh are, on the other hand, uncommonly nice: and it is calculated, that they confume more of this commodity than all the reft of Europe. Thoufands of people live on this beverage, and bread and butter, which is faid to correct its bad qualities; but they take care that the one is good, and the other ftrong. Our manner of drinking it, would not in the leaft agree with them; for that they may the better enjoy the flavour of the herb, they colour it with only two or three drops of milk.

They generally eat wheaten bread. The prodigious fwarm of Germans fettled in London, have prevailed on fome bakers to make *rye bread*; the fale of it is, however, very confined, for my countrymen themfelves foon prefer the other. I have offered it to their beggars, and even they have rejected it.

It

It is furprifing, that mankind generally have an invincible diguft to all the viands which they have not been ufed to during their infancy. This fingular averfion, which we perceive in all nations, can never be overcome but by the moft preffing want. *Sour crout*, a compofition long unknown among the Englifh, has been very beneficial to their failors during diftant voyages; and yet, it was neceffary to take infinite pains to reconcile them to this anti-fcorbutic nourifhment.

It was not until Captain Cook's fecond expedition, that, exhorted and encouraged by the two Forfters, the feamen ufed themfelves to it. During that tedious and dangerous navigation in the unknown feas, one man alone perifhed; and it was to this compofition that the fortunate circumftance, of which, till then, there had been no example, was generally attributed. Government have therefore taken the proper precautions, that no fhip of war, deftined for a long voyage, fhould be unprovided with this excellent preventive.

It is abfolutely neceffary that travellers fhould conform themfelves to the manners of every climate, in refpect to diet. Difeafe, and even death itfelf, are the fad confequences of this neglect; and I could cite a number of examples to this purpofe. The Eaft Indies become graves to thoufands of Europeans, merely becaufe they chcofe to live there in the fame manner as in their native country. Without this caprice, the projected journey through Arabia would have fucceeded, and NIEBUHR had not returned alone.

A foggy air, and nourifhing food, make it neceffary to drink ftrong liquors in England. Thofe who ufe water often lofe their health, and fometimes their lives. The fame effects would attend the ufe of the Englifh regimen in Italy, where the burning heats require fherbets, cooling liquors, and other cuftoms, and, in one word, a different manner of living.

living. It is very common to hear ftrangers blame the climate, inftead of the unhappy confequences of impolitic negligence.

The Englifh are unfortunately led away, beyond all the other countries in Europe, by the luxuries of drefs, which every day feems to increafe. Twenty years ago, gold and filver lace was not worn but at court, and the theatres; perfons elegantly attired always rode in carriages. The people crowded about a gentleman who walked in full drefs, either in the ftreets or the park; they never ufed fwords, and the beaus wore their hats. Except the laft cuf-tom, none of the others prevail. One now often meets with laced clothes; even the common people fometimes appear in embroidered vefts. In general, however, the Englifh ftill wear plain broad cloth, both in fummer and winter, but it is of the fineft kind: a common tradefman will ufe no other. They do not cover themfelves with *peliffes*, but great coats, which guard againft the cold in winter, and the rain in the fpring and autumn.

It is in this fimple drefs that the minifters of ftate walk about the ftreets and public places, without being followed by a fingle domeftic.

The Englifh in general, even thofe of the mid-dling clafs, wear very excellent linen, and change it daily. The finenefs of the fhirt and ftockings, a good hat and the beft of fhoes, diftinguifh a man in opulent circumftances; no attention whatever is paid to the coat. The richeft citizens frequent the 'Change in clothes very old, and much worn. The cuftom of wearing rich buttons prevails more than ever within thefe few years; fo that a fimple frock often cofts more than a laced one.

It is almoft in fpite of themfelves that the Englifh have adopted the cuftom of dreffing their hair; the people employed in that bufinefs are the moft inex-pert of any in Europe.

Some

Some years fince, the wig-makers of London prefented a very fingular petition to the king, befeeching the fovereign to cut off his hair, and wear a wig: " Your majefty's example," faid they, " will " be followed by every one ; and our trade, which " is now ruined, will foon acquire its wonted con- " fequence and celebrity." The king laughed at this pleafant requeft, but did not think proper to grant it.

I have already more than once had occafion to mention fome charaƈteriftic treats of the Englifh nation. The great difference betwixt them and the reft of Europe, proceeds entirely from the liberty which they enjoy, and which gives occafion to a thoufand extraordinary and fingular cuftoms.

It is not according to our ideas that we ought to calculate the fpace that feparates the different claffes of men in that monarchico-republican government. This obfervation extends even to fervants. The firft man in the kingdom is cautious of ftriking his domeftics; for they not only may defend themfelves againft him, but alfo commence an aƈtion in a court of juftice: in fuch a cafe, a pecuniary recompence, and many difagreeable circumftances, are fure to follow. They obferve with a great deal of reafon, that as poverty and dependance contribute very little to the happinefs of this life, it would be extremely cruel to aggravate the lot of thofe who are obliged to live in fervitude, by a conduƈt unauthorifed by the laws. If a fervant commits a fault not punifhable by the magiftrate, his mafter can only difmifs him.

Thofe will be much deceived, who may from thence imagine, that an Englifh footman will confequently be impertinent. On the contrary, I am convinced, that no part of Europe abounds with better domeftics. The noble condefcenfion with which they are treated, the fear of not receiving a

charaƈter,

character, and the largenefs of their wages, all tend
to keep them in good order, and infpire them at
once with zeal and activity.

One is alfo aftonifhed at the politenefs and promp-
titude with which he is attended at taverns and
coffee-houfes; a circumftance which but ill corref-
ponds with the pride of the nation: it muft however, be recollected, that the waiters always expect
a gratification, and that, in fome of the principal
houfes, this amounts to a great fum in the courfe of
the year.

The fcandalous practice of giving *vails*, fo much
in vogue twenty years ago, is now almoft entirely
banifhed: it exifts no where but among the lower
orders of the people. Formerly a vifitor was obliged
to diftribute a great deal of money among the fervants, when he dined with a man of quality; fo
that it was much cheaper to go to a tavern, than to
accept of fuch an invitation. It is to Lord Chef-
terfield that the Englifh are indebted for the abolition of this cuftom: his reprefentations had fuch
weight with the nobility, that they unanimoufly
agreed to difcountenance it.

The appearance of the female domeftics will
perhaps, aftonifh a foreigner more than any thing
in London. They are in general handfome and
well clothed: their drefs has the appearance of fome
tafte, and their converfation fuch as if they had
kept the beft company. A ftranger is apt to be
embarraffed at firft, and can fcarce imagine that
they are not gentlewomen. They are ufually clad
in gowns well adjufted to their fhapes, and hats
adorned with ribbands. There are fome who even
wear filk and fattin, when they are dreffed. All
their work confifts in keeping the houfe neat; and
dufting the furniture. To this employment they
attend for a few hours in the morning; and after
that,

that, all the reft of the day is entirely at their own
difpofal.

As to a *lady's maid*, the eye of the moft fkilful
connoiffeur can fcarcely diftinguifh her from the
miftrefs. The appearance of a waiting-woman is
that of an opulent and a fafhionable perfon; fhe
ufually accompanies her lady in public, expects particular attention to be paid to her, and, after fome
years of fervice, generally receives a fmall annuity,
which makes her comfortable for life.

When out of place, fervants of all denominati-
ons apply to a regifter-office; a fingular inftitution,
known only in that country, by means of which
they are immediately provided with employment.

Sunday is very ftrictly obferved in England; and
as all kinds of work, even mufic, are prohibited,
that day is therefore ufually deftined to the pleafures
of the country. All the citizens who have country-
houfes, repair to them on Saturday afternoon, to
make preparations for their friends on the following
day. The prodigious number of ale-houfes and
taverns, fituated near the capital, is then full of
perfons of both fexes; and, contrary to the general
ufage, an *ordinary* is kept for their reception. All
the great roads around London are alfo crowded
with carriages, horfes, and foot-paffengers; and I
may fairly affert, that three-fourths of the inhabitants of the capital keep the *Sabbath* in this manner.

It is very fingular, that thefe weekly revels
never occafion any difturbances, or exceffes of any
kind.

It feems to me, that no better proof need be
alledged of the good nature of the Englifh, than
their deportment on all public occafions. One is
aftonifhed to obferve compaffion, benevolence, ge-
nerofity, and, in one word, all the focial virtues,
carried to fo high a degree of perfection, among
the

the lowest of the people. If a stranger loses his
way, and happens to ask for any particular street or
house, the first person whom he meets will point
out his road, and even accompany him, without
the hope of any recompence: no one ever experienced a refusal.

When any embarrassment is occasioned by the
jostling of coaches in a narrow street, the people
immediately fly to relieve them, and restore order;
they are perfectly satisfied with thanks. In Paris,
it is not unusual to see blood spilt on such occasions;
the magistrates, therefore, distribute soldiers in all
parts of the city, to preserve tranquillity. Such a
precaution is never made use of in London; yet
the greatest regularity prevails at Ranelagh, the
Pantheon, and other public places, notwithstanding
the multitude of carriages which are assembled
there.

The king of England, in 1784, gave an amiable
instance of the humanity so general in that kingdom. Happening to stroll in one of the agreeable
walks in the neighbourhood of Richmond, without
any other company than that of some of his sons,
he met with a poor villager, who had been selling
provisions in the town. His cart was stuck in a
ditch, and having no help, he was attempting in
vain to get it out. Without deliberating a moment,
the monarch, aided by his children, went to his
assistance, and immediately relieved it with his own
hands. The peasant, unacquainted with the rank
of those who had come so generously and opportu-
nately to his succour, in the joy of his heart, proposed to carry them to the nearest ale house, and
treat them with a pot of beer. His offer produced
a few pieces of gold in return, and their departure
gave him time to recover from his astonishment.
The present which occasioned this charming
action

action to be known, at the same time betrayed its author.

On any public commotion, when the people run into the streets, and assemble in crowds, the greatest care is taken left any accident should happen to the women and children, whom they either make room for, or carry in their arms, that they may be better seen.

A lady of fashion, the wife of a minister from one of the German courts, when coming out of the play-house, happened to get into a crowd, where the pressure was extreme, and the danger of her situation the more alarming, as she expected in a few days to become a mother. At the moment when she was about to faint, a person who supported her with his arm, cried out, " Gentlemen " make room, I beseech you, for a *lady with child,* " who is suddenly taken ill." She herself has often assured me, that a *thunder-bolt* could not have more quickly dispersed the mob, than this exclamation. Every one immediately gave way, and she luckily got to her carriage without any further delay.

In the year 1780, when the dregs of the people acted the GORDONIAD, and made conflagrations their pastime, these wretches never carried their violence so far as to attack a woman ; even those of the catholic religion were in perfect safety. When the populace, who were enraged against the archbishop of York, were about to set fire to his house, Mrs. Markham, his wife, appeared at the window, and addressed them in the following terms : " Gen- " tlemen, a lady has this very moment been taken " in *labour* here ; and as it is impossible to remove " her and the infant, I hope that you have too " much humanity to occasion their death." This ingenious petition had the proper effect, and the crowd instantly dispersed.

When

When a quarrel happens in the streets, the passengers immediately interfere. Persons of the highest rank do not hesitate for a single moment to become mediators. The day after my arrival in London, I had an opportunity of being a witness to this practice in an affair where I myself was interested. A young jew, a native of Germany, having attempted to cheat me in the most bare-faced manner in the world, I felt myself so much piqued at the fellow's impudence, that I could not contain my resentment. The customs of the English being entirely unknown to me, I acted exactly in the same manner as I should have done in my native country, on finding my honour wounded. I accordingly seized the culprit by the collar, who, fearful of my resentment, cried out with all his might, and soon gathered a crowd around us. As I was not ignorant of the language, I immediately recounted the circumstances which gave occasion to such violence. Some of the people, however, informed me, in the most polite terms, that, according to the laws of *that* country, no offence whatsoever could warrant my behaviour. The jew, who was conscious of his guilt, did not choose to prosecute me, but escaped as fast as he could, and gave me time to profit by the just observation of these worthy people, and to return them my thanks.

In similar disputes, when the parties agree to terminate their differences by a *boxing-match*, the spectators, far from opposing them, encourage the idea. This custom, which proceeds from certain false principles of courage and equality, is not, however, so much in fashion as formerly. Even persons of quality were not heretofore ashamed of engaging in such quarrels. They have of late, however, left the glory of them entirely to the populace

lace, who, being no longer animated by their example, begin now to have lefs relifh for them.

The two combatants ftrip to the waift, and attack each other with their *fifts*; a *ring* is then immediately formed by the populace. His *fecond* affifts the perfon who falls, wipes the fweat from his body, and re-animates his courage. When they fight on a ftage, each is alfo attended by a *bottle-holder*, who wafhes his friend's face, and ufually fqueezes a lemon into his mouth. The fight often lafts half an hour, and fometimes longer, till one of the parties declares that he is vanquifhed:—this they call *giving in*. The victor, who is often more hurt than the perfon whom he has conquered, is then conducted home in triumph by the fpectators.

It is not in the power of prejudice itfelf to ftifle, in the hearts of that people, the efteem which a courageous conduct always infpires. I myfelf happened to be prefent at a *fight* betwixt an Englifhman and a Frenchman. The firft was looked upon as a mafter in the fcience of boxing; the other was ignorant of the firft principles of the art; he therefore entirely confided in his ftrength, which, indeed, fo effectually befriended him, that he ftruck his adverfary to the ground with the firft blow, and rendered him unable to continue the combat. It feemed as if this *blow* had deftroyed the national hatred, fo forcibly impreffed in the breafts of the fpectators; every one was eager to overwhelm the victorious Frenchman with praifes and careffes; they afterwards joined to treat him at an ale-houfe.

The *art of boxing* has certain rules, from which no one ever departs: whoever attempts to infringe them, becomes immediately expofed to the fury of the populace. For example, when one party falls, his adverfary muft not ftrike him; and the combat is immediately to ceafe, on either of them acknowledging himfelf to have been beaten.

On

On the event of thefe battles, which are fometimes attended with fatal confequences, confiderable
betts frequently depend ; it is not uncommon, however, to hear the combatants who are generally in-
fligated by hatred alone, cry out, on thefe occafions,
" That they fight for love !"

The celebrated Marfhal Saxe was once challenged
in this manner, by a fcavenger who was employed
in fweeping the ftreets. He, relying on his amazing
ftrength, accepted the propofal ; the fcavenger,
therefore, began to ftrip according to cuftom ; but
he had fcarce taken off his fhirt, when the Marfhal
feizing him by the arms, to the great aftonifhment
of the fpectators, threw him with the fame eafe as
if he had been a trufs of ftraw, into his own cart ;
where he ftruggled along time with his hands and
feet, and was very near being ftifled in the mud.

The Englifh ufed formerly to fight duels in the
fame manner as other nations ; but the Puritans dif-
countenanced this barbarous cuftom. Thefe enthu-
fiafts, who would allow no other rule of conduct
than that prefcribed by the bible, having found nothing therein to authorize this fpecies of combat,
took a decided averfion to it. At laft, Cromwell,
by enacting fevere laws againft this practice, abo-
lifhed it entirely. This was, perhaps, the firft
time that fanaticifm ever produced fuch happy confequences.

Within thefe laft fifty years, however, duels have
begun to be again in vogue, in the fame proportion
that boxing has declined. But as every thing in
that country is different from what it is elfewhere,
it fo happens that this cuftom, which in other kingdoms is confined to a certain rank, has no bounds
among them. You may there fee priefts, merchants,
and clerks terminate their differences with a cafe of
piftols.

Some years since, two negroes in livery fought each other in this manner. As the stage continually satirises such extravagancies as these, this ridiculous practice is now discountenanced.

The English are still very fond of cold baths. There are a prodigious number of these in London, where one may bathe daily at the rate of a guinea per annum. This practice is much recommended by the best English physicians. The ancient Romans were also very much addicted to it. It was by these means that Antonius Musa, restored the health of the emperor Augustus. The senate, on account of this cure, remunerated him with a magnificent present, and erected a statue to his memory, which was placed with that of Esculapius. Septimus Severus made use of the cold bath daily; and as he resided a long time in Britain, it is probable that he introduced the practice into that island. The Saxons borrowed the custom from the ancient Britons.

England possesses many mineral springs, a great number of which still retain the names of the saints after whom they were formerly called. The fountains where the first christian preachers baptised their converts, inspired a certain religious veneration, and were esteemed *holy*. The monks, taking advantage of such prejudices, attributed in their legends certain miraculous virtues to these places, after they had first discovered their natural effects.

Of all the *waters* in England, those of Bath are the most remarkable; they were known even by the Romans, who consecrated them to Minerva. The Britons call this place EAER PALLADDUR, or the City of Pallas.

Bath is a handsome town, and the public buildings which it contains are really magnificent. It is not only resorted to by the sick, but even by those in health,

health, whom the variety of pleasures to be seen there, attracts from every part of the three kingdoms. The *season* when it is most frequented is the beginning of the winter.

To regulate the diversions, and preserve order and regularity amongst such a prodigious number of people, who are at the same time rich and free, it has been thought proper to choose a person who is stiled KING OF BATH; to whom the most entire obedience is paid, in regard to every thing that concerns the general good. This convention is made and agreed to by the first people in the kingdom, who regularly frequent the place, and maintain their sovereign in his prerogatives. This situation is equally honourable and lucrative, for it produces a revenue of sixteen hundred pounds sterling annually. It is for life, unless great and forcible reasons oblige the subjects to dethrone their monarch.

This eminent post is usually given to some gentleman, who joins to much experience a considerable portion of wit, gaiety, and knowledge of the world. All these qualities, together with an extraordinary talent for inventing new pleasures, and aranging elegant entertainments, were united in an Englishman of the name of Nash, who for many years ruled Bath with an unlimited sway. He died in 1761, and was greatly lamented by his whole kingdom.

The throne is at present filled by a gentleman who was formerly a captain in the army.

CHAPTER

CHAPTER XII.

*Character of the English Ladies—Of the Nobility—
Whimsical anecdotes — Hon. Mr. Montague —
Lotteries—Insurance offices—Betts—Sir Watkin
W. Wynne—Lord Baltimore—May-day—Voyage
to New Zealand—Otaheite—Charles I.—Anec-
dote of a Spaniard—National Hatred—Aversion to
Anatomical Operations—Mrs. Phillips—Ballads.*

OF all the remarkable objects which England
offers to the eye of a foreigner, no one is more
worthy of his admiration, than the astonishing
beauty of the women.

It produces such a surprising effect, that every
stranger must acknowledge the superiority of the
English ladies over all others. The most exact
proportions, an elegant figure, a lovely neck, a skin
uncommonly fine, and features at once regular
and charming, distinguish them in an eminent
degree. Their private virtues also render them
capable of enjoying all the felicity of the marriage
state.

The proneness of the whole nation to melancholy,
renders the women grave and serious; their minds
are less occupied about pleasures, than in solicitude
for the happiness of their husbands, and the management of their domestic concerns. Even women of
quality suckle their children; they think that the
name and duties of a *mother* have nothing in them
which they ought to blush at, and that no station

on

on earth is comparable to the pleasures of maternal
tenderness, and the agreeable reflections which result
from it.

Notwithstanding vice is often pushed to the extreme
in the capital, it is very uncommon to see a married
woman become profligate, and give way to infamous pleasures. To this there is always an insur-
mountable bar in her love for her family, the care
of her houshold, and her own natural gravity. I am
of opinion, that there is not a city in the whole
world where the honour of a husband is in less
danger than in London.

It is to this serious and melancholy disposition that
we ought to attribute the attachment of the English
catholics to the cloister, and which has induced so
many of them to retire to France, and still more
to Flanders. They have even established a species
of convents in England, for those who do not like
to leave their native country. A certain number
of ladies live there in common, perform divine service together, and conform to all the institutions of
that order to which their *house* belongs. Like other
nuns, they take the vows, and their dress is always
plain and modest.

I have already mentioned the prodigious attachment of the English to politics. This passion is
actually among them an inducement to marriage.
A husband who can talk of nothing but public affairs,
is always sure to find in his wife a person with whom
he may converse concerning those topics which interest him most. He has no need to go abroad, to
satisfy his appetite for this darling subject.

The English are not ungrateful to Nature for her
prodigality towards them. The children are never
bound up in swaddling-clothes, but covered with a
thin dress, which gives a perfect freedom to all their
motions. The great advantages arising from inoculation, become every day more perceptible.

L

The

'The schools for the education of young people of
both sexes, are almost always in the country. In
walking through the charming villages which sur-
round the metropolis, one is delighted to see three
or four houses together, dedicated solely to this purpose. These support a prodigious number of lan-
guage-masters, dancing-masters, music-masters, &c.
&c.

The ladies trusting perhaps too much to their natural charms, often neglect the means of setting
them off to advantage. But a very few, even of
the women of the town, make use of *rouge*. Many
women of fashion, when dressed in the most elegant
manner, do not use hair-powder; *neatness*, however,
which seems actually to be a *rage* amongst them, is
never neglected.

The most elegant part of an Englishwoman's
apparel is her hat, which is usually adorned with
ribbands and feathers. No female, of whatever
rank, dares appear in the streets of London on foot,
without one of these; the very beggars wear them.
The art with which they place them, is but imperfectly imitated by foreigners, who know not how
to derive from them all their magical advantages.
The charming effect which they produce, made
Linguet observe, that if Homer had been acquainted
with this enchanting dress, he would not only have
given a cestus to Venus, but also a hat.

The fair sex in that country have a number of
customs peculiar to themselves, and among others,
that of riding on horseback; in this situation, they
may be seen galloping by hundreds along Hyde-
Park. On these occasions, they are always dressed
like Amazons; a practice introduced by queen Anne,
the consort of Richard II. and which has continued
to the present time. The ladies also think it indecent to shew themselves at the window. It is only an
extraordinary circumstance that will make a woman
of

of character open it, to fatisfy her curiofity. The women of the town, however, are entirely above fuch a prejudice.

The education among the Englifh, as far as it regards health, is excellent: I cannot, however, fay fo much in refpect to morals. The abufes which prevail in the great fchools are well known; I fhall therefore be filent concerning them. After a long contention concerning the advantages and difadvantages of a public or private education, it feems at laft to have been decided in favour of the former. The young duke of Bedford, who is the richeft peer in the kingdom, was for feveral years at Weftminfter, where he was brought up as other young men. His table and his bed were entirely the fame as theirs. Two guineas a week were allowed him for pocket money; and out of his income, which amounts to fixty-thoufand pounds per annum, five hundred only were expended in his education.

All the exercifes which tend to bring the mufcles into action, and to make the body healthy and robuft, are the daily recreations of thefe public fchools, which, notwithftanding their numberlefs difadvantages, do not, however, make youth effeminate.

A great number of children of good extraction are deftined from the earlieft age to commerce, and educated accordingly. This practice, fo wife in itfelf, and which was the fource from which the Genoefe nobility derived their opulence, and by which the illuftrious houfe of Medicis were raifed to a throne, where they became the benefactors of mankind, was not introduced into England until about the middle of the feventeenth century.

The Englifh nobility during the civil war, being almoft entirely attached to the king, were banifhed from all employments by the Houfe of Commons, whofe power then preponderated; they therefore

had

had no refcurce but in trade. Thofe who poffeffed
abilities amaffed immenfe riches, and contributed by
their examle to remove the ancient prejudices
which ftill fubfifted in their country againft the employment of a merchant. Soon after this, fome
of the firft people in the kingdom became the moft
zealcus partizans of commerce, and embarked their
fortunes in it, by which means they at once gave
activity and vigour to trade. This it is affirmed,
was the oiigin of that fplendour and opulence which
England foon after acquired. In our own time, we
have feen the fon of Sir Robert Walpole, formerly
prime minifter of England, a private ban..., and
the brother of lord Oxford, a citizen of London.

People of rank not only become merchants, but
fome of them have even condefcended to learn
trades. It is cnly however from whim, that a perfon of quality ever takes fuch a ftrange refolution.
I fhall mention, for example, the honourable
Wortley Montague, brother-in-law to lord Bute,
who, when a child, ran away from his father's
houfe to become a chimney-fweeper. The rags
with which he was covered, the coarfe fare, and the
tlows which he received daily, feemed preferable,
in his eyes, to all the advantages appertaining to his
birth. For nine months he followed this profeffion,
and remained in the capital unknown: at length,
however, he was difcovered and brought home,
where every thing was practifed to cure him of his
fingular attachments but in vain. He foon afterwards
eluded the vigilance of his relations, embarked as
a cabin-boy in a veffel that failed for Lifbon, and
then travelled over Spain as an affiftant to a mule-
teer. The life of this man, who died fome years
fince in the Eaft, is one of the moft melancholy and
remarkable examples of the waywardnefs of human
nature.

Thefe

These fantastical actions are very frequent in England; and they there pass under the denomination of *whims*.

In the year 1776, a person died in London, who by means of trade amassed the sum of sixty thousand pounds sterling. By his will, he appointed one of his relations his sole heir; with this particular condition, however, that he should repair every day to the Royal Exchange, and remain there from two till three o'clock. Neither the weather, nor his own private affairs, nor any thing but bad health, of which he was to produce a certificate, could excuse him from this task. If he omitted his attendance for a single day, he was to lose the fortune by an express clause in the will, and a certain charitable foundation was to become entitled to the whole estate.

The testator, by this means, intended to pay a compliment to commerce, by which he had procured his riches; but this *whim* made a slave of his heir. It was on Sunday alone that he could leave London, because the Exchange was then shut. I have seen this man, and been witness to his extreme discontent.

An English nobleman in the decline of life, having passed a very restless night in one of his country-houses, formed the resolution of marrying; and, that he might avoid trouble, resolved to espouse the first woman that he should see the next morning. Full of this idea, he rose at break of day and rang his bell. His *valet-de-chambre* appeared immediately, and having received orders to call up one of the women, he ran for the house-keeper. Scarce had she entered his apartment, when his lordship said, " Go and dress yourself immediately to accompany " me to church, for I intend to make you my bride " this day." The housekeeper smiled, and imagining that her master only meant to joke with her,

L 3   departed.

departed without saying a word. Half an hour after, his lordship rang again, and enquired of the servant, whether she was not yet dressed? On being informed that she was employed about the domestic affairs, he ordered any other female to be sent him, and accordingly one of his scullions was produced. She immediately accepted the proposal, and in an hour afterwards became his wife. A son, who afterwards filled one of the first offices of the state, and who is still alive, was the *fruit* of this singular whim.

I was once acquainted with an Englishman, who was extremely amiable in his character, and remarkably polite in his manners, but who had a most fantastical passion, which he assured me was deeply imprinted in his very soul. His greatest pleasure in life was to comb the hair of a beautiful woman. He kept a charming mistress solely for this purpose. He cared but little whether she loved him, or was faithful to his bed; all that he wanted was to please his senses by means of her long and beautiful locks. He has often assured me that this employment produced the most voluptuous sensations.

The execution of a criminal, interests in the most lively manner the celebrated George Selwyn, who is generally loved and admired on account of the goodness of his heart, and the readiness of his wit. Such a spectacle has inexpressible attraction to him, and affects his senses in a manner equally powerful and inexplicable.

One of his friends, after reproaching him with his *whim*, betted a large sum that he would be present at an execution which he named. Mr. Selwyn, accordingly was led away by an invincible impulse; which not being able to conquer, he actually paid the wager, and repaired to Tyburn. When Damiens, the regicide was broken on the wheel at Paris, the wit did not fail to be present: he even

gave

gave a fum of money to the executioner to permit him to ftand on the fcaffold, to contemplate this horrid fcene in a more familiar manner.

A love for what is fingular and extraordinary, alfo occafions that fpirit of gambling which is fo general in England, more efpecially during the drawing of the lottery. At that time a prodigicus number of infurance-offices are opened in all parts of the capital, and policies are made upon particular numbers. In the evering, a large bowl of punch, which is conftantly replerifhed, is placed on a table, around which many unfortunate wretches, becoming intoxicated with the fumes of the liquor, and their paffion for gambling, ruin themfelves and their families.

Such is the paffion of the Englifh for play, that every difpute is generally decided by a bett. I knew an Englifhman who laid five hundred pounds, that during a whole year he fhould fleep every night in a different houfe in London. The three firft months, however, had fcarce elapfed, when he repented of his engagement, and chcfe rather to pay the money than be expofed to the inconvenience of fuch frequent removals,

In the year 1778, juft before the war commenced between England and France, two wealthy Englifhmen made the following agreement :—One of them, who did not doubt that hoftilities would foon commence, but who imagined the period at a greater diftance than was expected, gave a hundred guineas to the other, on condition that he fhould pay him one guinea a day until war was proclaimed. It fo happened however, that, from reafons of ftate, the war begun and finifhed without ever being *proclaimed*. The lofer has fince offered to pay his antagonift one thoufand pounds ; which the other however refufed, and he now actually receives three hundred

L 4   and

and fixty-five guineas per annum, in confequence of this circumftance.

There are a number of people in England, who take a fecret fatisfaction in breaking the laws of their country. Some, notwithflanding they are not in want, feem to be impelled by an irrefiftible defire towards their neighbour's property, in which covetoufnefs has nothing to do. I myfelf knew a very beautiful woman, who put any thing in her pocket which fhe happened to fee; it was, however, always returned next morning.

Another lady, both young and charming, had the fame propenfity, without poffeffing the fame honefty. If fhe ftopped any where to make a purchafe, fhe was always fure to *fteal* more than fhe bought. A fhopman having conceived violent fufpicions againft the fair plunderer, refolved to be on the watch; and having caught her one day ftealing a piece of Flanders lace, he left it to her choice either to be carried before a magiftrate or a clergyman; fhe accepted of the latter, and the young man at the fame time became mafter of a handfome wife, and twelve thoufand pounds fterling.

Another offender of the fame kind was not fo lucky. His name was Ayre: he was a man about fixty-five years old, and was poffeffed of thirty thoufand pounds fterling in the public funds, which he had procured in bufinefs. Being incited folely by avarice, he ftole every thing that he could lay his hands upon. One day, while attempting to make off with two quires of paper from the ftamp-office, he was caught in the fact, tried for the offence, and, as it was fully proved, was fentenced to be tranfported to America for feven years. This miferable wretch, however, at length, became the juft victim of his own fordid avarice; for his friends having privately agreed with the captain of the fhip for a cabbin and other neceffaries during his paffage,

he

he was scarce at sea when he repented of the bargain. He therefore rather chose to sleep on straw with the other criminals, that he might save his money, than on a good bed which he was obliged to pay for. Being soon after seized with a fever, this old man, overwhelmed with age and infirmities, died before his arrival in America,

The conduct of Sir Watkins William Wynne well merits the denomination of a *whim*. This baronet, who is the richest commoner in Wales, when he came of age, gave an entertainment to the nobility, gentry, and farmers of that district, which lasted for three days, and by its magnificence was not unworthy of a sovereign. The guests, who amounted to eighteen thousand of both sexes, ate, drank, and danced in the open air.

The annals of England are full of whimsical occurrences. In the county of Essex, there is a village called Dunmow, into which the lord of the manor, who died in the thirteenth century, introduced a singular custom, and at his death left a fund for perpetuating it. By this, any husband becomes entitled to a flitch of bacon, who can solemly swear that he has not, for a whole year, disputed with his wife, and never once, during that period, repented of his marriage.

The records of that place notice only three men, who, during the space of more than three centuries, have been able to take such an oath.

But none of the English of the present age have become so remarkable by their singularities, as the famous Lord Baltimore, whose whole life was one uninterrupted series of innumerable oddities.

His follies, however, never hurt any one: on the contrary, they were generally attended with uncommon marks of goodness and benevolence. His fortune was immense, for it amounted to nearly forty thousand a year, the greatest part of which

was

was tranfmitted to him from the province of Maryland alone. He had laid it down as a principle, to live entirely according to his own fancy; in confequence of this, he never folicited thofe employments and dignities, to which, both on account of his fortune and his abilities, he had a right to afpire. He never went to court. An attachment to the *fair-fex* was his ftrongeft paffion: a circumftance which was greatly augmented by his travels in the Eaft. On his return to England, he built a fuperb houfe, in the moft pleafant part of London, after the mode of a celebrated HARAM in Conftantinople. The edifice being finifhed, he formed it into a feraglio, which he furnifhed with handfome women, to whom, except the permiffion of going out, he refufed nothing. They were, however, regulated by certain rules, and to thefe he exacted the ftricteft obedience. His lordfhip lived in this manner, in the capital of a chriftian country, exactly as if he had been a muffulman. If he difliked any of his fultanas, they were loaded with prefents, and allowed to depart: fome of them actually received portions, and were enabled to marry in confequence of his liberality.

Although this kind of life did very little harm, and the Englifh, as we have already faid, are extremely indulgent towards *whims* and *caprices* of every kind, yet the inhabitants of London could not bear thofe Turkifh cuftoms. Songs and fatires were daily compofed on this Englifh bafhaw, and the moft trifling anecdotes of his domeftic life were wrought up into novels and romances. The courtiers, who never could pardon the contempt with which he treated their manner of living, alfo endeavoured to ridicule his conduct.

In a fhort time, one of the young women whom he entertained, was prevailed upon to accufe him of having committed a rape upon her. A criminal
procefs

procefs was inftituted in confequence of this accufation; but his lordfhip vindicated his innocence,
and triumphed over the malice of his enemies.
This affair, however, made a lively impreffion on
his mind; he difmiffed his miftreffes, fold his
houfe, which is at prefent occupied by the duke
of Bolton, gave away the magnificent furniture,
and in a fhort time left his native country. He
died foon after at Naples, in the thirty-fixth year
of his age.

The immenfe riches poffeffed by the Englifh,
enable them to indulge the moft uncommon caprices. A wealthy individual, fome years fince,
built a houfe not far from Hyde-Park, merely to
ridicule the gothic ftyle. All that was difagreeable and fantaftical in that *tafte* was here *carica-
tured*.

A young prodigal, having formed the project of
laughing the free-mafons into contempt, who ufed
to walk in proceffion through the capital, on St.
John's day, affembled about eighty chimney-fweep-
ers, whom he decorated with the enfigns, and
badges ufually worn by that fraternity, and obliged
them to march in a folemn manner through the
principal ftreets.

One may eafily conceive the great number of
people who were attracted by this pleafantry; and
from that time, that fociety have never publickly
celebrated the feaft of their patron faint.

I myfelf affifted at a fatirical proceffion, but of a
kind entirely different from the former. The people of England, in the year 1770, were extremely
difcontented with the adminiftration which at that
time governed the affairs of the kingdom, becaufe
they imagined that they intended to overturn the
conftitution. In confequence of this, about a hundred perfons, clothed in deep mourning, affembled
together, to accompany a hearfe covered with black,
and

and followed by attendants in the same manner as at
a funeral. In the inside of this the GREAT CHAR-
TER was placed, surrounded with all the emblems
of LIBERTY, the *obsequies* of which they celebrated
in the most solemn manner. The procession, followed by an innumerable crowd, passed the palace
of St. James's; and this farce, which terminated
without any bad consequences, conveyed a very
proper lesson; at least, the event shewed that it was
an useful and a necessary one.

This taste for the EXTRAORDINARY some years
since gave rise to a very uncommon project. It
never was heard of in Germany, and is but little
known even in England.

A Scotchman of the name of Herries, who lived
in one of the Hebrides, or Western isles, had been
disappointed in love. This circumstance had such
an effect on his mind, that he conceived a disgust
for a civilized and social life. He therefore resolved
to seek for other men, and other countries: in consequence of this he sold his estate, and with the
money equipped two vessels, on board of which he
embarked, with about sixty of his tenants. His
sole intention in this expedition, was to sail for New
Zealand, a description of which he had read in
Captain Cook's Voyage, and then, to gain the affections of the inhabitants, marry a native of the
country, introduce agriculture, and become sovereign of the whole island!

A gentleman of fortune conceived the strange
idea of going to reside in Otaheite; five of his
friends offered to accompany him, with their wives
and families; and actually applied to the younger
Forster, who had been there, for his opinion of the
enterprize.

The history of England affords, even in remote
periods, a number of the most fantastical anecdotes.
During the civil war between Charles I. and his

parliament, at the time when the royalists began to despair of overcoming their enemies, the equestrian statue of the monarch was put up to auction. A cutler, who had a mind to *speculate* on this circumstance, bought it for a trifling sum of money. Being asked what he intended to do with it, he replied, that it was his intention to melt it into *handles for knives*. Accordingly, he furnished his shop with a prodigious number of knives and forks, with *bronze* mounting. In a short time his warehouse was full of customers; persons of both parties ran to purchase knives, the handles of which were made from a statue of a king of England. To the royalists, it afforded a melancholy but precious remembrance of their dear master; and as to their antagonists, this extraordinary circumstance was not a little flattering to their republican pride. The mechanic, in the mean time, profited by the enthusiasm of his countrymen, and doubled the price of his commodity, notwithstanding the rapidity of its sale; so that in two or three years, he realized a considerable fortune.

All this time, however, the public had been duped. The statue had not been melted, as the cutler had asserted, but only buried in the ground, and was actually, on the restoration of Charles II. dug up and restored to that prince, who ordered it to be placed on a new base at Charing-Cross, where it remains to this day.

The emblem on the pedestal is well appropriated to the subject : it consists of two Genii, who, with sorrow imprinted on their countenances, sustain a crown of thorns.

At that unfortunate period, when the English forces, under the command of general Braddock, were beat in America by the French army; when Minorca was taken by the latter power; and Admiral Byng, by the intrigues of the ministry of the
former,

former, had experienced a violent, and as some
ftill affert, an unmerited end; the nation became
furious. In this unfavourable difpofition, the populace having obferved a foreigner dreffed entirely
in the French ftyle, near this ftatue of Charles I.
immediately furrounded him. As he had juft arrived in London, and was entirely ignorant of the
Englifh language, it was impoffible for them to
tell what countryman he was.

The mob, in the mean time, held a confultation,
and at laft it was refolved to place him on his majefty's horfe. A ladder was accordingly procured in
an inftant; the unhappy ftranger was obliged to get
on behind the monarch, and, after the moft infult-
ing language, was about to be pelted with dirt.

Luckily, however, at the moment when they
commenced the affault, a gentleman happened to
be paffing that way, who having afked the reafon
of this ftrange behaviour, and learned from the
ftranger himfelf that he was a Spaniard, immediately informed the people of this circumftance.

No fooner did they know their miftake, than they
teftified the utmoft repentance for their precipita-
tion, helped the rider from his uneafy feat, and
delivered him into the hands of his preferver.

The Englifh populace call every foreigner a
Frenchman, whether Swifs, German, or Italian.
They in general have the greateft hatred that can
be imagined to the whole French nation. Of late
years, however, this prejudice feems to be entirely
banifhed from the better fort, who now think the
language of that polifhed people a neceffary part
of their children's eduation. It was otherwife formerly. The late Lord Suffolk, one of the promo-
tors of the American war, actually employed a
mafter to inftruct him in the French grammar, after
he became a fecretary of ftate for the foreign depart-
ment.

The

The averfion of the Englifh to anatomical dif-
fections, is another of the prejudices which characterize that nation. The furgeons have great difficulty in procuring dead bodies; they are obliged to
pay large fums for them, and are forced to carry
them to their houfes with the utmoft fecrecy. If
the people near of it, they affemble in crowds around
the houfe, and break the windows.

What greatly augments the general averfion to fo
ufeful a fcience, is, that the fextons are oftentimes
induced, by the certainty of a reward, to dig up
corpfes from the church-yards.

I am aftonifhed that government does not take
advantage of this national prejudice, and deliver to
the furgeons the bodies of all foot-pads and highway
robbers. Murderers, after execution, are always
allowed to be diffected.

The Englifh, far from being felfifh in regard to
the happinefs and independence refulting from their
liberty, on the contrary, wifh to fee all the kingdoms
of the earth partake of the fame blefling: this is
another of the traits that characterize them.

At the time that PAOLI and his brave countrymen
were obliged to yield to the power of France, the
whole nation affirmed, that it was their duty to aid
thefe iflanders in the recovery of their liberty. The
government, who were not willing at that time to
gratify the wifhes of the people, were neverthelefs
obliged to appeafe their murmurs, by granting a
penfion of a thoufand pounds a year to the Corfican
chief, which he enjoys at this very moment.

Every thing in London is made known by means
of hand-bills or advertifements in the newfpapers.
One perfon informs you that his MAD-HOUSE is
at your fervice; a fecond keeps a boarding-houfe
for ideots; and a good-natured man-midwife pays
the utmoft attention to ladies in *certain fituations*,
and promifes to ufe the moft fcrupulous fecrecy.

Phyficians

Physicians offer to cure you of all manner of dif-
orders, for a *mere trifle*, and as for the money to
pay them, you need never be at a lofs; thoufands
daily making tenders of their fervices to procure you,
at a moment's warning, any fum that you may ftand
in need of.

A lady of the name of PHILIPS is very folicitous
in advertifing her goods, which are undoubtedly very
fingular in their kind. Thefe confift of ware which
are to be met with in a very few great cities in
Europe. The voluptuaries of Italy are but imperfectly acquainted with them; and it is only in
Paris, and in London. that they are manufactured
and ufed.

I beg leave to mention the BALLADS, among
the fingularities to be met with in this nation. Thefe
it is true, are alfo common in France, but not fold
publicly as in London.

It is ufually females who are employed in this
avocation. They wander about the moft populous
ftreets of the capital, ftop now and then and draw a
crowd around them, to whom they fing their fongs,
which they fometimes accompany with mufic. In
thefe, witty expreffions and humourous fallies are
often contained; and one is fometimes forry to fee
fuch talents as the writers muft undoubtedly poffefs,
employed in celebrating the trifling occurrences of
the day. The fubject is generally fome political
event, which has novelty and intereft to recommend it. Thefe ballads, being printed on coarfe
paper, are fometimes fold for a farthing, and fometimes for a halfpenny a piece; the quicknefs of the
of the fale, however, amply repays the printer, as
they are vended by thoufands, if they happen to be
popular. The populace purchafe thefe with the
utmoft eagernefs, and confider them as fo many delicious morfels.

In

In other countries, the vulgar imitate the higher ranks; there, on the contrary, the great are only solicitous to diftinguish themfelves from the mob. A rich tradefman thinks that he is entitled to the privilege of being *original*, and to live after his own manner.

Thefe originals, whofe manners are as favage as they are uncommon, are generally called *John Bulls*, and one fometimes meets with a *John Bull* among people of fashion.

John Bull is a favourite fubject for the fatire of dramatic writers. The people are never more happy than when they fee their own follies perfonified in this character; they are then fure to receive every farcafm with the loudeft applaufe.

CHAPTER

CHAPTER XIII.

*The Theatres—Italian Opera—Jubilee in honour of
Shakespeare—Kelly the Poet—The Contrast betwixt
the English and French Theatres—Foote—Garrick.
George Alexander Stevens—Mrs. Cornelys—Pantheon—Masquerades—Debating Societies.*

THE two principal theatres in London, open
during the winter, are those of Drury-lane, and
Covent-garden; in the Haymarket play-house,
which is under the direction of Mr. Colman, they
act only during the summer months.

The Italian Opera generally commences in the
month of December, and shuts in June: the representations are twice, and sometimes three times a
week. As the English in general have no great
attachment to this exotic entertainment, and are,
for the most part, entirely ignorant of the language,
this theatre is treated with the utmost contempt by
the more sensible part of the people. The nobility
alone support it; and they merely because—*it is the
fashion.*

There is not any place of entertainment in Europe where the audience *yawn* so much as there;
its decorations, machinery, and wardrobe, are altogether unworthy of the nation. There is nothing
tolerable but its music. The great sums given by
the managers to the *castratos,* who are better paid in
England than any where, prevent them from laying
out any money on the necessary decorations. The

latter confequently enrich themfelves, and the former have been conftantly involved in difficulties.

It is very fingular, that the manners, cuftoms, and pleafures of other countries, can never become popular in England. This fingularity extends to mafquerades, and is vifible in regard to operas; for although the opera-houfe is a noble building, and has coft immenfe fums. It has never yet been able to produce one work whofe merit rofe above me-diocrity.

Every thing that can charaƈterife the Englifh nation, is to be met in their national theatres alone: there all the efforts of art, the elegance of compofition, and the flights of genius, are united. Drury-lane and Covent-garden are rivals to each other, and it is difficult to decide, which of them poffeffes that fuperiority for which they both contend.

Thefe two play-houfes, for forty days before Eafter, perform oratorios on certain days, and fometimes double the price of admiffion. Thefe are generally HANDEL's compofitions. The fingers are all Englifh; and it has been obferved by fome judicious connoiffeurs, that they only want Italian names, and a few journeys to the continent, to procure uncommon reputation.

The greateft part of the foreign muficians who vifit London remain there; for as that great city is aƈtually a PERU to them, they do not choofe to deprive themfelves of the lucrative monopoly which they thereby enjoy, in regard to their own profeffion.

The Englifh theatre is faid to have attained its greateft degree of perfeƈtion, during the laft years of GARRICK's life; and without doubt, this was its moft brilliant period. The principal works of the immortal Shakefpeare, and other celebrated dramatic poets, were then reprefented with a juftice, a dignity, and a magnificence, before unknown.

It

It is true, that even then there was but one
GARRICK, but he was seconded by the efforts of
other actors, who, without equalling him, were yet
worthy of being his associates in immortalising that
celebrated epoch. Among these were Barry, Wood-
ward, Weston, &c. The retreat of the English
Roscius, in 1776, was followed by the decline of
the stage; the other three died in the same year.
Mrs. Abington, the Athalia of England, wished also
to retire, and could not be prevailed upon to remain
without the most earnest entreaties.

Mrs. Siddons and Mr. Henderson supplied, but
in an indifferent manner, the public loss; they were
the only two who distinguished themselves among
the crowd of actors, who were at that time candidates for the favour of the public. They made
their first appearance at Drury-lane, and were loaded
with applause. The audience, however, began in
a short time to see them with a greater degree of
coolness, and became consequently more sparing of
their praises.

Among the number of *peculiarities* belonging to
the English playhouses, may be reckoned the after-
pieces, called ENTERTAINMENTS. These, for
the most part, consist of a happy mixture of dia-
logue, song, and dance; the decorations are amazing, and the machinery is carried to the most astonishing perfection.

The people are uncommonly attached to this
kind of diversion. All the great events that occur
to the nation are dramatised and represented on the
stage; for example, the coronation of the present
King, the Prince of Wales receiving the order of
the garter; the grand review at Portsmouth, in
1774; the camp at Coxheath; and the siege of
Gibraltar. These representations often last for an
hour and a half, and are usually given after one of
Shakespeare's plays.

The

The Englifh do not diflike entertainments, however long, provided they have variety to recommend them.

I have feen the Peak of Derbyfhire, its grottoes, caverns, and adjoining mountains, and, in fine, every thing that is marvellous in that fpot, reprefented with an art that feemed to equal magic.

But the moft remarkable of all thefe, is SHAKE-SPEARE's JUBILEE: that in honour of Voltaire, at the French Theatre in Paris, in the year 1777, was a paltry imitation of the Jubilee of the Englifh Poet.

When this is acted, the fcenes are painted to reprefent the market-place at Stratford. At a certain fignal, the ftage is filled with a mob of country people, whom they actually take out of the ftreet on purpofe; and then begins a proceffion, the like of which has never been feen on any theatre.

A troop of dancers march firft with a folemn ftep; after them come nymphs, who ftrew flowers around. The principal characters in each comedy then make their appearance, preceded by a flag, on which the name of the play is infcribed; a triumphal car, in which THALIA is drawn by *grotefque* figures clofes the firft part.

This is fucceeded by the Mufes, Venus, and the Graces; Cupids, Nymphs, Fawns, and Dryads, who carry the ftatue of Shakefpeare, and keep time to the found of inftruments of mufic.

Tragedy clofes the proceffion, attended by heralds and ftandard-bearers, who walk before her: then not only the principal characters in each piece, but alfo the moft ftriking incidents make their appearance.

In Macbeth the forcerers and their cauldron; in Coriolanus the tent of that general adorned with the *fafces*; and in Romeo and Juliet the tomb of the

Capulets

Capulets forcibly imprefs the mind with the recollection of the principal incidents in every play.

When the perfons of the drama arrive on the stage, they reprefent, in *dumb-fhew*, the principal paffages of the tragedy.

King Lear exhibits the madnefs with which he is fuppofed to be afflicted; and Richard III. that fury with which he is tranfported in the midft of the battle.

Macbeth appears with a bloody poniard in his hand, and his lady, as defcribed by the poet, purfued by the avenging furies, and wandering about the palace with a lighted torch. Juliet ftarts from her lethargy, and lifts her head from the bier. The lictors and the eagles precede Julius Cæfar; a number of Roman ladies proftrate themfelves before Coriolanus, and implore his protection. The proceffion clofes with Melpomene, who is drawn in a chariot, and holds an uplifted dagger in her hand.

The laft fcene reprefents a fuperb temple, the altar of which is adorned with the principal fubjects mentioned by the poet, depicted in tranfparent paintings.

This was a real *apotheofis*, for it was not a literary fanaticifm, but a juft admiration of every thing that is truly great and fublime, which placed the ftatue of this immortal genius in the temple of immortality.

The actors conftantly pay the fame, if not a greater, attention to the galleries than the boxes, Before the curtain is drawn, there is a great deal of noife; and afterwards the players are fometimes pelted with orange-peel: it is very rare however, that any difturbance is attended with dangerous confequences. In 1772, Hugh Kelly, who, from writing in favour of his country, at length defended the minifter, having prefented a comedy called, *A Word to the Wife*; the audience were so exasperated, that they would not allow it to be acted. Garrick made his appearance, but for once even he begged in vain: the play therefore was withdrawn, and they instantly became quiet.

The *action* of the English stage is entirely different from that of the French. When one makes a comparison between the good actors in London and Paris, the dissimilarity of their tones, their gestures, and their expressions, appear to be wonderful.

The marriage of FIGARO, which was represented in the month of December 1784, almost at the same time in Paris and London, afforded a wonderful instance of this observation. However, an intimate knowledge of both theatres, and even of Nature herself, will easily discover to us, that there is more than *one way* to arrive at perfection.

The English make use of a great deal of action and vivacity on the stage, and are not very strict in adapting these to the propriety of their characters. Very few of them, indeed, ever acquire a dignified manner.

In original plays, taken from their own history, and which consequently exhibit the manners and the customs of the nation, this fault is not so perceptible as in translations, such as Zara, Iphigenia, the Horatii, &c. in which, it must be confessed, that they do not excel. The women's parts are however, better sustained. The actresses support the honour of the theatres, by means of a nobleness and a dignity which charm the beholder.

Mrs. Abington is the greatest ornament of their stage, and unites all parties in her praise. She attempts comedy alone, but with such a happy combination of nature and art, that I may affirm, without fear, that so many talents were never united in any other female performer in Europe. She is now more than fifty years of age, and yet is able to re-

present

present, with the same ease and propriety, either a
country girl or a woman of fashion.

The Hay-market theatre was established by the
celebrated Foote, the late duke of Cumberland having procured a patent from George II. for that
purpose. This actor was styled the *English Aristo-
phanes.* Besides a satyrical humour which was natural to him, and discovered itself the moment that
he opened his lips, he had the advantage of success-
fully imitating the Greek poets, by bringing his
cotemporaries on the stage, and making them the
butt of his sarcasms, and the public ridicule.

He may be said to have invented a middle kind of
dramatic entertainment betwixt comedy and farce.
It must be confessed, that his productions have the
merit of being so many interesting pictures of the
manners of the age. He usually chose some temporary subject, spun it into three acts, and made
but little alteration even in the names of those who
had the misfortune to fall under his lash. He knew
how to imitate with great exactness the gait and
conversation of any one, and never forgot to place
his hero in the most foolish and ridiculous point of
view. When he played, the house, during the
whole representation, was affected with a continual
and convulsive laughter.

His satirical vein made him feared by all who
approached him, as he spared no one, and his
witty sarcastic expressions were never forgotten.—
But no person dreaded him so much as Garrick, who
was more affected by any pleasantry against himself,
than by the highest eulogiums in his favour. He
made use of every stratagem to procure Foote's
friendship, but in vain, for his natural temper could
not be confined by any restraint.

Lord Sandwich, who had been greatly offended
at some of his jokes, happening to meet him one
day,

day, afked, " whether he was moſt likly to be firſt
" ***** or hanged?" " That entirely depends, my
" lord," replied the wit, " whether I embrace
" your lordſhip's miſtreſs, or your principles."

The profeſſion of an actor is not thought diſho-
nourable in England; on the contrary, he is regarded and eſteemed on account of his talents. Both
Garrick and Foote not only lived in the moſt familiar manner with the firſt nobility in the kingdom,
but actually went to court, and were well received
at St. James's. The funeral of the former afforded
the moſt convincing proof, how much they reſpect
perſons who among us are treated with ſo much
contempt. A great number of peers not only accompanied the corpſe of this great man, but actually
ſupported the pall. Perhaps it may be here thought
that I allude to ſome inconſiderate young men of
faſhion, who, forgetting the reſpect due to their
rank, were actuated merely by their enthuſiaſm for
Garrick.—It was far otherwiſe. Men illuſtrious on
account of their merit, and among others lord Camden, who ſome years before had been chancellor of
England; paid this mark of reſpect to their immortal
countryman.

The friends of Garrick, after his retreat from the
ſtage wiſhed him to become a member of parliament.
It depended wholly on himſelf, to aſpire to and receive this honourable mark of diſtinction; but his
advanced age made him rather anxious to enjoy the
great fortune which he had acquired, amidſt the
calm and tranquillity of a country life.

When ſhall we ſee our German actors honoured
in this manner? If great talents could procure ſuch
a diſtinction with us, they would long ſince have
met with their reward. It is not neceſſary to be
inſpired with the zeal of patriotiſm, to rank
SCHRODER among the firſt actors now in Europe.
To compare him to Le Kain, would be doing the

M   greateſt

greateſt injuſtice : it is only neceſſary to ſee theſe
two perform, to be of my way of thinking. The
plays of Shakeſpeare, on which Garrick founded
his reputation, loſe nothing of their force or beauty
in the mouth of Schroder ; but his own country
men, ſo liberal in the praiſe of every thing foreign,
have not yet been ſo juſt, either ſufficiently to ap
preciate his merits, or thoſe maſter pieces of the
Engliſh theatres.

A perſon of the name of Stevens, who died in
1783, was the inventor of an entertainment equally
ſingular and original, which he called *Lectures on
Heads.* This conſiſted in comical and ſatirical
obſervations, upon all ranks and claſſes in the
nation.

The author diſplayed a thorough knowledge of
the world, much wit, and a great deal of gaiety in
his repreſentations. To animate his narration, and
to give force to his ideas, he procured a prodigious
number of portraits, the phyſiognomy and dreſs of
which were expreſſive of theſe characters, and occupations, which he ridiculed.

He knew how to imitate their voice, their looks,
and their manner, with the moſt happy adroitneſs.
Women of the town, barriſters, phyſicians, clergymen, merchants, officers, men of learning, artiſts,
ladies of faſhion, and billingſgates ; in one word,
all the profeſſions, copied by Stevens, were carica-
tured before the public with the utmoſt humour and
gaiety.

It was very ſeldom that this performer was trivial ;
every thing that he ſaid was full of that *practical
philoſophy,* which is as inſtructive as neceſſary. He
uſually ended his lecture with a ſatire againſt himſelf, in which he never ſpared his own foibles.

It has been often attempted, but always without
ſucceſs, to eſtabliſh a French theatre in London.
The laſt effort was in 1752. A great number of
French

French actors were then engaged at a prodigious expence; and a play-house was fitted up in the most costly manner for their reception. When the first representation was announced, an uncommon number of people of all ranks and descriptions assembled on the occasion.

The comedians expected a disagreeable reception; but the noise and the catcalls of a tumultuous populace soon made them loose all their courage. It was in vain that they attempted to begin: the clamours and the uninterrupted hisses of the pit and galleries, joined to showers of orange-peel, always prevented them. Not one of the actors had the boldness to appear a second time on the stage; and no other resource was left them, but to escape through a private door.

Some days afterwards, they risked another attempt. A great number of young men of fashion, armed with swords, placed themselves in the boxes, while their servants, and several people hired for the purpose, occupied the centre of the pit, to second them in case of need. When the curtain drew up, this served as a signal for the attack. The stage was instantly covered with oranges; the actors took to their heels, and the champions from the boxes and pit joined each other sword in hand. In a short time the affray became general: the gerandoles and the crystal branches were broken in a thousand pieces. The ladies fainted away, and the gentlemen who had the rashness to draw upon the people, had their swords broken in pieces, and were obliged to retire, beaten and covered with blood. The tumult was concluded with the entire destruction of the play-house, after several persons had been killed, and many wounded, who might truly be said to have suffered martyrdom on account of their attachment to the French theatre.

After

After·this unfortunate attempt, who would have thought that such an abfurd projeɛt would have been again revived? However, in 1778, a fociety of perfons of quality, headed by the duchefs dowager of Bedford, projeɛted the renewal of the fame fcheme, and, having formed the plan, perfifted in its execution.

French comedians were already fent for from Paris, an agreement was entered into with them, the moſt advantageous promiſes held out, and money advanced for the journey: in one word, all the arrangements were completed. In a few days, however, the news-papers were full of fatires, both in verfe and profe, againſt this undertaking: fongs were fung in every ſtreet, ridiculing the French ſtage; and, what was undoubtedly more difadvantageous than any thing elfe, Palmer an aɛtor belonging to Drury-Lane, addreſſed the public in a prologue, in which he befought them not to patronife a foreign, at the expence of the national theatres. His petition was received with uncommon applaufe,- and the difpofitions cf the people made evident by the general enthufiafm of the audience.

This Anglo-gallic fociety accordingly concluded, that it would be very dangerous to perfift in their fcheme; and, in all human probability, it will never be revived.

The concerts in London are allowed to be very grand, and the Englifh in general prefer them to the mufic of the opera-houfe; but as the price of a ticket is half-a-guinea, none but the higher ranks can receive any gratification from them.

Ranelagh is incomparably fuperior to any thing of the fame kind in Europe. Its immenfe faloon and magnificent illuminations, the continual motion of the people of fafhion who affemble there in crowds, and the delicious mufic, make this a moſt
fafcinating

fascinating and enchanting spectacle. It must however be confessed, that there is a certain sameness and melancholy in this place of entertainment, which, with all its grandeur, gives disgust : people of rank accordingly never spend more than two hours there.

. Vauxhall Gardens are situated in a pleasant village of the same name, on the banks of the Thames, about two miles distant from Westminster-bridge; and part of the company go there by water. One shilling only is paid for entrance, and it is not at all uncommon to see six thousand persons there at once. The walks are but badly lighted ; in some places, however, the lamps, which consist of a great variety of colours, are distributed with great taste. The orchestra, which is in the open air, is placed under an amphitheatre, erected in form of a temple, surrounded with elegant porticoes, and brilliantly illuminated. In the most agreeable part of the garden, there is a statue erected in honour of Handel, and this is the only one in the whole place.

About forty years since, a new association, under the name of the *Attic Society*, was formed in the capital. This was held in a noble hall, where sometimes vocal and sometimes instrumental music, but always of an exquisite kind, was introduced between compositions in poetry and prose, which were recited in the most elegant and engaging manner.

A foreigner occasioned the annihilation of this rational entertainment, soon after its institution. One may with great justice affirm, that this person has in an eminent degree contributed to the progress of luxury in England ; and it is not a little remarkable, that a woman who has occasioned such an extraordinary revolution in the manners and the pleasures of a nation, should be at this moment languishing amidst all the horrors of wretchedness.

This

This lady is a native of Germany; an honour, however, which none of her countrymen has ever claimed, either in her affluence or adversity. She arrived in London about twenty-five years since, at an age when a person of her sex has no right to flatter herself with making conquests. Indeed she possessed n ither youth nor beauty, and was so ignorant that she could only speak bad German, and a few words of French.

Who could have imagined, that a person of this kind would have *set the fashions* to the most capricious and phlegmatic nation in Europe?

At first so far was she from forming sanguine expectations, that her utmost efforts were exerted in supplying her daily wants. Her means of existence depended entirely on her voice, which had nothing extraordinary in it; with it, however, she resolved to captivate the public. In consequence of this determination, she procured three musicians, and gave concerts at one shilling a ticket. Being successful in her undertaking, she augmented her orchestra, and raised the price of entrance.

Soon afterwards, her happy stars made her acquainted with a lady of quality, who became captivated with her talents; for although Mrs. Cornelys could neither sing nor speak with elegance, she nevertheless possessed a sound judgment, an uncommon taste, and an imagination inexhaustible in inventions.

From this moment, she conceived the idea of gratifying the English nobility by entertainments, such indeed as had never before her time been seen in Europe. In consequence of this plan, she hired Carlisle-House, furnished it in a most magnificent stile, and procured two thousand seven hundred subscribers. On the anniversary of the institution, she was allowed to give a masked-ball, to which any one could be admitted by a ticket, the price of
which

which was two guineas. She herself has often affured me, that on thefe occafions fhe has had upwards of eight thoufand vifitors.

The magical genius of this woman knew how to vary her entertainments in a thoufand different fhapes. Sometimes fhe exhibited colonades, and triumphal arches, grandly illuminated; at other times fhe metamorphofed her apartments into gardens, planted with walks of orange-trees, and adorned with fountains, infcriptions, and tranfparent paintings, furrounded by garlands of flowers, and variegated lamps of a thoufand beautiful tints. A whole *fuite* of rooms were richly furnifhed, fo as to imitate the manners and luxury of foreign nations, in the Indian, Perfian, and Chinefe ftiles, while nine thoufand wax-candles, placed with great art, produced a fine effect to the fpectators.

The fairy queen of this enchanted place knew no other avarice than *glory*; money had few or no charms for her, and fhe thought herfelf amply recompenfed by the praifes that were lavifhed on her tafte.

Far from amaffing riches, fhe contracted immenfe debts. She owed to her wax-chandler alone, three thoufand pounds.

This carelefsnefs and prodigality at laft occafioned her to be arrefted, and afterwards fent to the King's-Bench prifon. Her fituation was then truly fingular; fhe obtained permiffion, during *term time*, now and then to fpread pleafure and joy throughout the capital, and was obliged next day to return to gaol.

In a fhort time her creditors feized on her effects; and after having for twelve years, by her luxurious and voluptuous entertainments, merited the appellation of the *Queen of tafte*, fhe is now actually obliged to fubfift on the cafual affiftance of her former benefactors.

M 4

The

The conftruction of the Pantheon, which in grandeur and extent exceeds that of Rome, proves that Mrs. Cornelys's leffons were not thrown away upon the Englifh. The fubfcription, which amounted to feventy thoufand pounds fterling, was not fufficient to complete fuch a noble edifice. Every thing that is great, majeftic, and magnificent, has been difplayed in this temple of Comus.

At a mafked-ball, at which I was prefent, the looking-glaffes with which the dome and the other apartments were furnifhed, coft thirty-fix thoufand pounds fterling; they were not, however, bought, but only hired for the occafion. The moft brilliant concerts are generally given here; and this is one of the few public places, except the theatres, that the royal family honour with their prefence. The managers recompenfe in a noble manner the muficians who perform at this place. The celebrated Ajugari fung here during the winter of 1777, and had one hundred pounds fterling a night, although he gave only two ariettes each time.

Mafquerades are fometimes given at the Pantheon, and fometimes at the Opera-Houfe. This kind of diverfion, however grand it may appear, in other refpects does not feem in the leaft congenial to the national character, which is grave, and but little allied to the follies of dancing and grimace. The crowds of mafks, and the ingenious and magnificent dreffes difplayed on thofe occafions, are the only circumftances that can give any pleafure to a native, or even a foreigner.

The King is a great enemy to this diverfion, and it is faid that his majefty was acquainted with general Luttrel's project, in the year 1771, to difturb an entertainment of this kind by going there in *character* of a corpfe.

The Englifh ftill continue to take a great delight in the public gardens, near the metropolis, where
they

they affemble and drink tea together, in the open air. The number of thefe in the neighbourbood of the capital is amazing, and the order, regularity, neatnefs, and even elegance of them, are truly admirable. They, however, are very rarely fre-quented by people of fafhion; but the middle and lower ranks go there cften, and feem much delighted with the mufic of an organ, which is ufually played in an adjoining building.

Of all the nations in Europe, the Englifh are moft fufceptible of the pleafures of *walking*. It is on account of this, that London poffeffes fo many charming places for indulging that propenfity. St. James's-park, the Green-park, and Kenfington-gar-dens, are frequented by a prodigious concourfe of people, and on a Sunday are vifited by thoufands. The Royal Gardens at Kew, Richmond, and Hampton-court, alfo draw a number into the coun-try during the fummer.

The pleafures of the chafe, of which the Englifh are ftill very fond, are followed with great avidity during the autumn. It is not at all uncommon to fee an hundred men on horfeback, leaping hedges, ditches, and five-barred gates after a fox. The laws in regard to hunting are ftrictly obferved, and fhelter the farmer from the injuries fo ufual in other nations.

Among the diverfions moft common in the coun-try, may be reckoned *fives* and *bowls*; the fpectators are always interefted in the game, by means of betts. It is very fingular, that *fhooting at a mark* is never practifed in any part of England: the reafon, how-ever, is plain; they have not fortified towns to de-fend, and are in no fear of an invafion. Of courfe there is nothing to induce them to an exercife, from which no utility cou'd refult.

Horfe-races are among the number of thofe di-verfions peculiar to the genius of the nation. The

ancient

ancient Greeks were also fascinated with the same
amusement, and similar sports were celebrated by
the poets of that famous people. A foreigner can
never feel himself so much interested in these, as an
Englishman; he will be fully satisfied with having
seen them once. About twenty years since, a famous
horse called *Childers*, who is said to have been the
best courser ever seen in England, died. On this
occasion, a thousand portraits were engraved of him,
and his praises were sung in every street. On an
inscription below the print, it was asserted that, after
an exact calculation, this animal had been proved
to be *fleeter than the wind.*

The passion for betting, that prevails on the race-
grounds of Newmarket, and Epsom, is astonishing.
It is not uncommon to see persons risk all their fortunes there on a single match.

Ass-racing is also very frequent, in the neighbourhood of country towns: they cannot, however, be
placed among the number of the national diversions;
yet wagers are frequently laid, even upon them.

The passion of betting is so very strong among
the English, that the pensioners of Chelsea and
Greenwich Hospitals, being unable to indulge themselves in either horse or ass-races, have been known
to wager on the *speed* of vermin.

I shall finish this sketch of the favourite diversions
among these people, with some account of their
Clubs, which are generally a source both of pleasure and utility: these clubs add very much to the
society, and serve to propagate their republican
genius and public spirit. The number in the capital is astonishing. Every rank and situation of
life has one peculiarly adapted to itself, and each
has its own proper and distinct name.

The members of some of them are so opulent,
and so numerous, that they often subscribe large
sums, by means of which they carry their plans of
patriotism,

patriotiſm, or chaṗty into execution. Among theſe
are the *Humane Society*, which gives premiums tor
preſerving the lives of their fellow-creatures; the
Whig Club, which guards againſt the uſurpations of
the ſovereign; and the *Bill of Rights*, which watches
over the privileges of the nation: this latter was one
of the chief ſupports of Mr. Wilkes.

But of all theſe, the moſt extraordinary without
doubt are the *Debating Societies*, whoſe members
meet merely to diſpute. Such inſtitutions exiſt in
no other city in Europe. There is one called the
Robin Hood, which has continued from the beginning of the preſent century, and has had the honour
of being frequented by Swift, Goldſmith, Foote,
Garrick, and a crowd of celebrated men.

It is in this ſociety, that a great number of famous lawyers and orators, among whom may be
included lord Mansfield, firſt diſplayed their talents
to the public.

I have been often aſtoniſhed in theſe aſſemblies
(for they are now very numerous in London) to ſee
the loweſt of the populace evince a perfect knowledge
of ancient and modern hiſtory. The application
which they make of this, and the arguments which
they oppoſed to their adverſaries, appeared to me
very wonderful.

Thoſe of my readers, who are prejudiced againſt
the Engliſh nation, and who, conſequently, may
be tempted to accuſe me of partiality in delineating
their character, and praiſing their noble, generous,
and diſintereſted manner of thinking and of acting
are requeſted, after the almoſt infinite number of
facts which I have recited in the courſe of this
work, to read the following, as it will ſpeak very
forcibly in favour of my argument.

I happened one evening in the month of December, 1778, to viſit the Debating Society in Foſter-
lane, Cheapſide. The war had juſt broke out between

tween England and France; and it is well known
that the English had good reason, at that time, to
be irritated against all their enemies. The national
antipathy therefore, against the French, was carried
to its utmost extent among all ranks and degrees of
the people.

It was at this critical period that a Frenchman
had the rashness to venture into the assembly, and
to rise to defend the conduct of his countrymen in
regard to the American war. I could scarce believe
my eyes, and I know not whether I was most
astonished at the imprudence of the Frenchman, or
the liberality of the English, who allowed him to
proceed. Let any one represent to his own imagination, this foreigner appearing in the middle of a
hostile nation, and in a barbarous and disagreeable
accent abusing them: will he not be astonished when
I inform him that he was heard with the utmost
attention, and so far from being treated with contempt, thanked by the chairman " for having so
" much confidence in the generosity of the English
" nation, as to deliver his sentiments with candour,
" and frankness, on the most delicate and interesting
" subjects ! ! !"

CHAPTER

CHAPTER XIV.

*Reflections on the Finances—The English Liberty and
Constitution—Marine—Pressing of Seamen—Green-
wich Hospital—Sailors—Admiral Keppel--Army.
Militia—East-India Company—Arts and Sciences.
British Museum—Style of the English Gardens—
Conclusion.*

IF the reader will give himself the trouble to
weigh with care the great number of facts and anecdotes with which I have been anxious to interfperse
my Obfervations on England, he will find that the
pretended declenfion of that empire, foretold and
announced by fo many contemporary writers, has
not as yet taken place.

That kingdom, however, is at this very moment
in a critical, if not a defperate fituation, notwithftanding her foreign connections, her riches, her
commerce, and her influence.

Great Britain, which cannot naturally be confidered, in the balance of Europe, but as belonging
to the fecond order of kingdoms, has been elevated
to the rank of one of the firft powers in the world
by bravery, wealth, liberty, and the happy confequences of an excellent political fyftem. For many
years that ifland wielded the trident of Neptune in
her victorious hand, and, abfolute miftrefs of the
ocean, covered every fea with her fleets. It will be
a problem for pofterity to folve, how that ftate has
created and maintained fuch an extenfive commerce,
and amaffed fuch immenfe riches, at a time when
the

the spirit of industry had made so great a progress among her neighbours, and even Holland herself had procured a decided superiority over all the other powers on the continent.

But although the sun of English greatness is not yet set, it is probable that in a few years we shall see the power of that people extinguished; not insensibly, but all at once. The very first war that they are so rash as to engage in, will, perhaps, whatever may be its event, precipitate this fatal and too certain catastrophe. In the political, as in the national world, death has planted the seeds of destruction along with those of existence; and, though those may discover and unfold themselves, either sooner or later, yet in the end they will never feel their effect.

Let us recollect that, but a very few years since, a national debt of a hundred millions gave the utmost tention that it was then susceptible of, to the spring of this political machine. The facility, however, with which they found means to pay off the interest of this immense sum, made them believe, that they possessed an inexhaustible source of riches, and begat the most dangerous security. They are now, however, though perhaps too late, recovered from this fatal error: a national debt, amounting to the immense sum of two hundred and sixty millions, has at length opened their eyes: the annual revenue is at present incompetent to supply the annual expenditure, which, even in time of peace, amounts to more than fourteen millions. If we add to this, the interest of a debt of one hundred millions, which England must contract the first war she is involved in, it will be politically impossible for the nation to sustain such an additional burthen without becoming bankrupt.

If any unforeseen circumstance should occasion this war, the consequence would be terrible. The
ruin

ruin of the richeſt and moſt diſtinguiſhed familes
would inevitably enſue: the commerce and the maritime greatneſs of the Engliſh would be attacked in
their moſt mortal parts; and that nation, now ſo
powerful, would be reduced for ever among the
ſecond order of European ſtates.

It is perhaps impoſſible to avert this frightful ca-
taſtrophe; the ſageſt precautions could ſcarce di-
miniſh the evil, or render the conſequences leſs terrible. This awful moment is approaching with the
moſt rapid and alarming celerity; no one, however,
has the reſolution to oppoſe it, and all ſeem to allow
themſelves blindly to be led towards the horrid abyſs.

I do not, however, know whether a national bankruptcy would involve the bank of England in its
ruin. That machine which is conducted with a
complicated, but an excellent mechaniſm, is the
chief ſupport of the credit of the ſtate, of all the
great trading companies, and of the principal merchants in the capital, and the provincial towns, both
of England and Scotland. Its buſineſs is carried on
not by means of gold, but paper; which will be no
longer eſteemed, than during the opinion which the
public entertain of its value.

To ſee the excellence of the ſyſtem adopted by
this great people, in its full extent, it ought to be
recollected, that notwithſtanding the immenſe commerce of England, in every part of the globe, and
her riches, which have become proverbial, yet it
is probable, that the *quantum* of ready money circulated throughout the kingdom is very ſmall. According to the beſt calculation, it does not exceed
twenty millions of pounds ſterling.

This ſum, which ſcarce ſerved to carry on the
American war for a ſingle year, is but little more
than what the economy of a certain German ſovereign
has hoarded up in a ſhort time, and that too in a
country not famous for its riches. Similar compari-
ſons

sons will give occasion to many reflections; and I dare affirm, without either being absurd or ridiculous, that a single city in the Empire possesses a larger portion of *specie* than all Great Britain.

The spirit of activity and industry, which animates the whole nation, is the reason that this deficiency of *coin* is not perceptible. As sums of any consequence are generally paid in bank notes, and every object of trade is accomplished by means of paper, it necessarily follows, that *ready money* is never employed but in regard to trifling demands. This occasions that astonishing and continual circulation, of which Paris and Amsterdam furnish us with a very faint idea, but which, however, is merely *illusive*, when compared to real wealth.

Bank notes, of which the number and the amount are equally unknown, but are said by estimation to exceed more than a hundred millions sterling, together with the astonishing quantity of manufactured commodities, compose the national wealth of England: as long, therefore, as her *paper* maintains its credit, and her warehouses remain furnished, no person will, I think, be inclined to refuse to that island the first rank amongst the richest nations in Europe.

Foreigners have but a very small share in the national debt; the English themselves are the greatest creditors of the state. The liquidation of this debt has given rise to the schemes of a multitude of projectors, each of whom affirms, that nothing in the world is more easy. But even their most ingenious plans have proved the great difficulty of such an enterprise. Sometimes even political miracles are performed: but then they must be at least probable; and unfortunately, the payment of two hundred and sixty millions sterling, to which the first war will add another hundred millions, is among those things that may be reckoned impossible. It has been calculated,

culated that if a circle of half crowns was to be formed around the circumference of our globe, this almoft inconceivable fum would not be fufficient to pay the national debt.

However unfortunate the confequences of a nation bankruptcy would be to England, they might ftill be fupporable, if they did not affect its political conftitution and civil liberty: the lofs of two fuch ineftimable bleffings would be fatal indeed.

Both France and Germany ftill contain a great number of vifionary men, who, milled by the turbulent and unquiet genius of the Americans, have attempted to prove that the Englifh conftitution abounds with a number of the groffeft impeifections. They hoped to fee on the other fide of the Atlantic ocean, the idea of a perfect republic realized. They imagined that fo many great men, inftructed by the experience of paft ages, and capable of pointing out to their fellow-citizens the true road to happinefs, would give grandeur, liberty, and ftability, to this new confederation. They have, however, been difappointed in their hopes: the fpirit of anarchy feems to diftract the councils of America; and the opinion which the illuftrious Montefquieu formed, concerning the Englifh government, is now confirmed.

It is after this great man that I dare to affirm, that there exifts no-where a conftitution better adapted than that of England for a powerful fociety, in which all the individuals are to partake of freedom.

After having read this work, it will be impoffible I think, to forget the value of Englifh liberty: all that I could add further on this head, would be ufelefs: let me however be permitted to mention one more obfervation, concerning the government,

The equilibrium, or balance of the three bodies who poffefs the exercife of the legiflative power, is truly admirable. The King, the Houfe of Peers,

and

and the Commons of England, are three diſtinct powers, entirely independent of one another, each enjoying privileges and rights peculiar to itſelf, mutually obſerving theſe, and watching conſtantly againſt the infringements of them. The king is the ſole ſource, from whence all honours and dignities flow; but as he can neither make new laws, nor add to old ones, his preponderance is not ſo great in the ſcale as might be expected.

The Houſe of peers, beſides poſſeſſing a ſhare in the legiſlative power, is alſo the ſupreme court of juſtice in England: it is on this account that the twelve judges, who as ſuch are not peers of parliament, and who are not permitted to deliver their ſentiments, unleſs when called upon, ſit among them.

The Grand excluſive privilege of the Houſe of Commons, is the poſſeſſion of the key of the public treaſury. Money being in our planet the prime mover of all things, it follows that this laſt body does not yield in point of importance to the two former. The Commons alſo have a right to impeach ſtate criminals, even if they ſhould be members of the Upper-houſe. On ſuch occaſions, a miniſter, though protected by the monarch himſelf, cannot eſcape a trial. Therefore, when an accuſation for high treaſon is brought into the Houſe of Peers, no defence which may be brought, nor protection which can be exhibited, will prevent the ſuppoſed culprit from being committed to the Tower.

According to Monteſquieu, the movements of the political machine in England occaſion a continual diſplay of envy, jealouſy, avarice, and ambition, which the national liberty allows to appear in their full extent. From the oppoſition of theſe paſſions, factions are produced, which, ſtriking againſt each other, like the waves of the ocean, reunite and ſeparate anew. Theſe factions, which at a certain
distance

diftance appear to be hurtful, will, , when more
nearly confidered, be found to produce that alternate
fucceffion of good and evil which preferves the conftitution of every free ftate.

Sir Robert Walpole adopted two maxims, feemingly very ftrange: " That every man has his
" price, and it is only neceffary to know that, to
" be able to procure his fupport: And, that an
" Englifh minifter is often under the neceffity of
" purchafing the voice of a member of parliament,
" not to vote againft, but according to his con-
" fcience."

As there is no political object concerning which
it is poffible to conceive fo many erroneous ideas as
the Englifh conftitution, we need not be aftonifhed
at the prejudices and falfities with which the writing of fo many learned foreigners abound. It is
not long fince the author of a certain critical work,
publifhed in Germany, pretended that Schlozer had
given a proof of the moft flagrant partiality, by
affirming, that the Americans commenced the war
againft England without being impelled by fufficient
motives; and that, now it was finifhed, they had
not reaped thofe advantages which they expected.
This profound and philofophical hiftorian has advanced nothing concerning an event, perhaps the
moft remarkable in the prefent age, without the
matureft reflection. But in what confifted the pretended oppreffion of that people? Was it not an
oppreffion by which they enjoyed an equal degree of
liberty with the freeft nations in Europe, England
excepted, and by which, in a few years, they acquired a degree of fplendour till then unexampled in
hiftory?—Their complaints were undoubtedly juft,
but furely not fufficiently ftrong to authorife them
to have recourfe to arms, as neither their privileges
nor their religion were attacked. If they now retain
but fome feeble traces of their former greatnefs, if
their

their national happiness is only a vague and chimerical idea, it will perhaps be allowed, that the long and bloody contest with England has been at once equally unsuccessful and disadvantageous.

Great Britain possesses no fortresses; for one surely cannot give that name to some ramparts, and bastions, erected at the entrance of her harbours, or to the Tower of London, that celebrated state prison, formerly the source of so many horrible cruelties. This is now no more than a fort, to stop a tumultuous populace. Its arsenals are less celebrated on account of the warlike stores which they contain, than for the antique and uncommmon pieces of armour, guns, mortars, &c. to be met with there. On a platform next to the river, is a battery of sixty large cannon, which, however, are of no service, but to fire a salute on the birth-day of the sovereign, or that of any of the royal family.

An Englishman who has never visited the continent, can have no adequate idea of a fortified place. The ocean, and the floating castles which it sustains, are the sole and indeed the proper bulwarks of the kingdom, and have for more than a thousand years baffled the enterprises of its enemies. If it had been possible to effect a landing in Great Britain, that project would have been attempted during the American war, at the time when the English fleet, dispersed through the four quarters of the globe, allowed the combined fleet to attempt any thing in the channel. Notwithstanding the great preparations made on purpose, such a dangerous experiment was not tried.

In the year 1761, a project of this kind was formed by the duke de Choiseul, who was then prime minister of France. Six thousand flat-bottomed boats were prepared, the coast sounded, the place of landing determined upon, and, in one word, all the precautions taken likely to infure the moft certain fuccefs. The Englifh government, however, having received a circumftantial detail of the whole plan, took fuch effectual meafures, that the idea was abandoned. The difcovery was made in Paris, by means of an Irifhman, of the name of Mac Allefter, who by a bold and fuccefsful attempt made himfelf mafter of the fecret. In confequence of this, he fet off for London, and fortunately arrived fafe with the neceffary documents. At the peace, this gentleman was gratified with a confiderable fum of money as a recompenfe for his fervices.

The excellence of the Englifh navy can only be difcovered by thofe perfons, who, being acquainted with the ftate of the fleets belonging to the other European nations, are enabled to judge by comparifon. It is only on board an Englifh man of war, which is handfome, commodious, and even magnificent, that a proper idea can be formed of the character and the riches of that people. An abundance, unknown in the veffels of other nations, prevails there; and a number of happy inventions, which can only be imitated by foreigners in a very imperfect manner. Thefe veffels are fheathed with copper, provided with ventilators, ovens, machines for calculating the longitude, alembics for frefhening falt water, &c. &c.

The Englifh, in fine, have contrived, by a thoufand different expedients, to obviate the dangerous accidents and difagreeable circumftances attendant on long voyages.

The fubordination on board their navy is extraordinary; it furpaffes the difcipline of a Pruffian army. Even the firft lieutenant, who is the fecond perfon on board, dares never to approach the captain without faluting him with the moft profound refpect, and paying the moft implicit obedience to his commands.

mands. The firſt thing that the officers do on a morning is, to inform themſelves *what humour the captain is in*; his authority being ſo extenſive, that it is abſolutely in his power to make the lives of all thoſe around him either happy or miſerable. An old ſailor, who attended me almoſt conſtantly during my ſtay at Portſmouth, expreſſed this in one ſhort and emphatic ſentence: "A ſhip of war," ſaid he, "is either a heaven or a hell, according "to the character and temper of the com-"mander."

Notwithſtanding the ſituation of England, which has laid her under the neceſſity from time immemorial to have recourſe to a navy for ſupport, her marine was very contemptible in former times. Every maritime town was then obliged to furniſh a certain number of veſſels in time of war, and theſe, which were always merchantmen, were filled with ſoldiers. The city of London fitted out twenty-five veſſels, containing ſix hundred and ſixty-two men, to aſſiſt Edward III. in the conqueſt of France. The epoch of the Engliſh marine was the reign of Elizabeth; and ſince that time it has increaſed to the aſtoniſhing degree of greatneſs and perfection, which it has attained in our days. At the end of the American war, it conſiſted of three hundred and forty-ſix ſhips, great and ſmall. Some of theſe carried one thouſand ſeamen; every one of whom coſt the government four pounds per month.

It is almoſt impoſſible to conceive the prodigious quantity of proviſions, and ammunition, with which the ſtore-houſes belonging to the navy are filled. The principal magazines are undoubtedly at Portſmouth and Plymouth; but even in the ſmalleſt, ſuch as thoſe at Chatham, Deptford, Sheerneſs, and Woolwich, there is ſuch an abundance of every neceſſary, that in one of theſe, more naval ſtores are depoſited than in all the arſenals of Italy.

The

The manner of *manning* the navy in time of war, is of all the cuftoms in England the moft blame-able, the more efpecially as it is not warranted by the laws. As the failors are forced into the fervice, and as they on fuch occafions generally make a ftout refiftance, the moft bloody fcenes are frequently occafioned by thefe encounters. Every friend of humanity muft revolt at the idea cf a prefs gang in a free country; a practice that entirely overturns every principle of Englifh liberty. Some of the moft elegant writers have decried this mode of pro-curing feamen, and the greateft orators declaimed in parliament againft fucn a fcandalous perverficn of power; but the doctrine of *neceffity* has hitherto ftifled every other confideration. It was in vain that, during the laft war, bounies were held out to the feamen; avarice tempted but a few; the greater number rather chofe to enter on board merchant-men, where there is neither danger nor fubordi-nation.

Greenwich hofpital is well calculaled to encourage the navy. It is one of the nobleft and moft beauti-ful buildings in Europe. Its fituation on the banks of the Thames is extremely agreeable, and it is finely embellifhed with majeftic domes, colonades, ftatues, pictures, &c. This eftablifhment ferves as an afylum for many thoufand invalid failors, and a ftill greater number of out-penfioners eat in com-mon, are allowed two clean fhirts a week, and have new beds every year. Each perfon fleeps by him-felf. The neatnefs which reigns throughout this edifice is truly admirable, and worthy of imi-tation.

The Englifh feamen form a particular clafs by themfelves. From their moft tender infancy, they are more accuftomed to the fea than the land, and never fail to become as boifterous as the elements with which they have been familiar. Add to this,

the

the prejudices common to the reſt of the nation, and you may eaſily conceive that this body of men have ſomething original about them. The manner in which they ſpend their prize-money, got in time of war, and the hardſhips which they endure without grumbling, ſeem to realiſe and confirm the proverb ſo common in England, " that their ſailors get their " money like horſes, and ſpend it like aſſes."

The higher claſſes of officers in the navy are greatly reſpected, on account of their knowledge their valour, and their experience. Of between ſeventeen and eighteen who commanded ſquadrons during the American war, not a ſingle one could be taxed with incapacity.

A great number of their admirals are actually models of honour and probity. Among theſe, I beg leave to mention admiral Keppel, who, in the year 1779, by the intrigues of Lord Sandwich, was tried by a naval court-martial.

The captain of a man of war is generally a perſon of ſome conſideration in England. I knew an old gentleman called captain O'Brien, who had the honour of entertaining the kings of Portugal and Sicily on board his ſhip. The pay allowed in the navy is very conſiderable, and foreigners, on that account, wiſh for employments in the ſervice; but the jealouſy of the people prevents it. Commiſſions in the ſea ſervice are never *venal*, and men of the firſt rank and quality are obliged to riſe from the loweſt ſtations.

The great attention paid to the navy occaſions the land forces to be neglected. In the army, commiſſions are bought and ſold: a barbarous uſage, and diametrically oppoſite to all the principles of a military eſtabliſhment. The ambition of a land officer is entirely ſtifled by the little reſpect paid to his profeſſion: he therefore neglects his duty, and loſes all reliſh for the ſervice. There are ſome

English

Englifh generals, to whom the fubalterns of a
Pruffian regiment could give leffons on the art of
war.

As a free people are, with great reafon, jealous
of nothing fo much as a large army in time of
peace, all the good patriots declare againft it. In
the commencement of the year 1785, the regular
troops in England amounted to only 29,345 : fome
members of parliament, however, fpoke of this as
an *abufe*, and wifhed the number to be confiderably
decreafed.

A ftanding army is now become a neceffary evil,
in all the European ftates; and the Englifh have at
length been conftrained to adopt this cuftom : they
are, however, extremely careful to provide againft
the bad confequences refulting from it. The troo ps
are paid and maintained by an act of parliament,
called the mutiny bill; but as it remains in force for
only twelve months, it muft be renewed, at the expi-
ration of that period, by the three branches of the
legiflature; elfe the army is of courfe annihilated.
As long as this law continues unrepealed, the Englifh need never be apprehenfive of arbitrary power.
The incredible celerity with which the laft revolution in Sweden was effected, cannot encourage,
much lefs ferve as a model for, a king of England.
The better, nay, the moft numerous part of the
Swedifh nation defired to fee the monarch more
independent in refpect to his authority, and lefs
reftricted in the exercife of his prerogative : they
therefore longed for a fignal to fecond his intentions.
In England, on the contrary, a fimilar wifh could
exift in no other heart, than that of a defpicable
courtier, or an inhabitant of Bedlam.

The liberty of the nation is alfo fupported by a
ftill more potent auxiliary, which the people acquired under the wife adminiftration of lord
Chatham.—This mafter-piece of policy, like a

N   thoufand

thoufand other interefting circumftances concerning England, is either unknown or undervalued in Germany.—I now allude to the militia; an idea original in its kind, and refpectable by its confequences in the eyes of the philofopher and the ftatefman. Although it fomewhat refembles a fimilar eftablifhment on the continent, it muft however be allowed by every impartial man, that the militia of Switzerland cannot be compared with that of England.

As it was determined that thefe troops were not to ferve in foreign countries, but were only intended to defend their families, their houfehold goods, and the altars of their religion, all the people in the kingdom, refpectable on account of their wealth, their rank, and their employments, offered their fervices, and were enrolled in troops levied folely for the defence of the nation. Lord Rochford who had been ambaffador in France, the duke of Richmond, at this prefent moment a minifter of ftate, and a lieutenant-general in the army, the marquis of Lanfdowne, the dukes of Devonfhire, Manchefter, &c. all thought it an honour to ferve in this patriotic body. The duke of Grafton, after he had been difmiffed from his fituation of prime minifter of England, accepted the command of a regiment of militia, and actually fubmitted to the orders of general (now lord) Amherft, whom he had a few months before obliged to wait his leifure in an antichamber.

The duke, decorated with the order of the garter, was feen during the review at Coxheath, confounded in the ranks with the other officers. This review was one of the moft fingular fpectacles that I have ever beheld during the courfe of my travels. The camp confifted of eighteen thoufand foldiers, all of whom, but two or three battalions, were militia. For many years there had not been fuch a

great

great army in the neighbourhood of the capital. Prodigious crowds were, therefore, attracted by the novelty of the circumstance : the sovereign himself, to whom it was also new, having never before seen but a few regiments in Hyde Park, was so transported with the scene, that he cried out to the commander in chief, "O Amherst, what a fine sight " this is !" This exclamation, as the king was at that time very unpopular, gave occasion to many sharp and satirical remarks.

A body of eighteen thousand men has not any thing in its appearance that can excite the wonder of a soldier, more especially a German one ; it was something more worthy of the eye of a philosopher than that of a military man, which attracted my attention.

There is no difference either in the discipline, evolutions, or exercise of the militia and the regulars ; at least, my eye, although accustomed to the Prussian exercise, could not perceive any. On the contrary, the former distinguish themselves by their activity, and attachment to their duty. It seems to me, that those men who serve the state by choice, serve it also with pleasure.

The army is, in general, a strange mixture of men, commanded for the most part by officers whose necessities oblige them to follow that profession : the nobility prefer the militia.

A certain great monarch of the present age had not a proper idea of this establishment, else he would not have been offended with the court of St. James's, for sending a minister plenipotentiary to him, who had only the rank of major in the militia.

The duke of Manchester, a colonel belonging to the same body, was actually at that time in the quality of ambassador at the court of Versailles.

The

The national militia, in the year 1778, formed an army of twenty thousand men; since that time, it has been proposed to increase them to forty thousand.

The East-India company may be looked upon as a political phenomenon. This society of merchants possesses territories, the inhabitants belonging to which amount to sixteen millions. England, Scotland, and Ireland, hardly contain half so many. During the last war, they maintained at their own expence an army of eighty thousand men. The revenues of their dominions amount to more than six millions of pounds annually, and some of their servants have, in a few years, realized fortunes of little less than half a million sterling! To give a proper idea of their immense riches, I have only to remark to the reader, that if the sovereigns of Denmark, Sweden, Naples, Sardinia, and Poland, were to unite the sums yearly levied in their kingdoms, they would not amount to so much as those received by the East-India company.

It sacrifices about two millions per annum, to support its military establishment in time of peace; and in time of war the expence is nearly doubled: for they do not possess the talent in Asia, as in Europe, to persuade, or rather to force, the soldier to encounter all the horrors of war, for a morsel of bread, and a drop of water. Not only the English troops, but the sepoys, receive large pay in that part of the world.

The debt of the East-India company, in 1785, amounted to seven millions; a moderate sum when compared with their revenue, and which, by the adoption of a proper system of economy, they might soon pay off. It is the want of this economy, which at such an immense distance from Europe it is very difficult to enforce, joined to the insatiable avarice of their servants, both civil and military,

that

that has repeatedly brought the proprietors to the verge of bankruptcy: it is certain, however, that Mr. Pitt's bill put an end to many abuses.

In the year 1776, the company had a fleet of forty-nine ships, each carrying twenty guns, in their service, without including a prodigious number of small vessels employed in trading on the coasts of Asia. Sixteen of the larger vessels have since been deducted from this number, on account of the representation of the lords of the admiralty, who pretended that so many vessels of their dimensions occasioned a scarcity of timber, which could not be supplied by any other part of the world but their own forests.

The present state of the arts and sciences in England, is too well known to my countrymen, for me to pretend to say any thing new on that important head. I shall, however, take the liberty to make a few reflections on that subject.

The foundation of literary society in that country, is liberty; that liberty which the natives have continually before their eyes, and which they never lose sight of in any of their pursuits. They do not know what it is to be excited to study by means of pensions, which are indeed little less than honourable fetters, that prevent us from saying and writing what we please.

The Royal Society includes amongst its members the greatest part of the English peerage, as does also the Antiquarian Society, which first made us acquainted with the celebrated ruins of Palmyra, Balbec, and Athens. The nobility do not in general contribute by means of their writings to the splendour of letters, and the progress of science; they willingly, however, employ their riches in defraying the expences of these establishments.

The learned in other parts of Europe form a class by themselves, and are in general either perse-

cuted

euted or defpifed. In England, the minifters, the magiftrates, the barrifters, the phyficians, the clergy, the artifts, the merchants, and even the military, all in one word, think it a glory to be thought men of letters, and to forget, when they affemble together, every circumftance that appertains to their rank or their occupations. The Royal Academy has a certain part of Somerfet-houfe affigned to the purpofes of their inftitution. In this noble manfion, which may be called a palace (for it is one of the nobleft efforts of modern architecture) they have an annual exhibition of the works of the greateft painters.

It is well known that, in England, diftinguifhed merit may afpire to honours and dignities with more certainty of fuccefs than in any other country. I could quote examples of this without number; fuch as thofe of Prior, Addifon, and a great many more, whofe writings raifed them to the moft diftinguifhed offices in the ftate. Locke was appointed to the honourable and lucrative fituation of Mafter of the Mint, and was fucceeded in his employment by the immortal Newton. Bacon, Clarendon, and Chatham acquired their fortunes and their titles folely by their perfonal merit, and their attachment to the fciences.

Services done to the nation never fail being remunerated in a manner worthy of a great people. The elder Forfter is, perhaps, the only inftance to the contrary. He had the misfortune to incur the hatred of a minifter unworthy of his high rank, and who, notwithftanding that he had once treated him with the warmeft regard, perfecuted him afterwards with a decided and unmerited averfion. The deftiny of this learned man was peculiarly unfortunate: at a time when his affairs were very much deranged, he had of his own accord prefented the Queen with a great many birds from the iflands in the Southern Ocean, which it had coft him much labour and many years to collect and preferve, and which he

could

could have fold at a very high price in England.
Her Majefty accepted the prefent, and, to the aftonifhment of every one, forgot to recompenfe this
celebrated traveller.

His fon feems to have been enveloped in the
unhappy deftiny of his father. England loft him
while very young, and Germany, to this day,
laments his death. Never did any other foreigner
write the Fnglifh language with fo much elegance
and precifion. Many of the critics rank the hiftory
of his voyages among the number of their claffical
works.

Baretti, a learned Italian, who has refided more
than twenty years in London, has alfo attempted to
write in Englifh, but without fuccefs.

This author does not belie the character of his
his nation. Entirely unacquainted with every thing
that concerns the people among whom he has lived
for fo many years; not devoid, however, of fenfe,
but yet fuperftitious in the extreme; this perfon has
not entirely forgotten the ufe of the poignard; for
fome time fince he affaffinated an Englifhman, in
the open ftreet, who according to his account, had
attacked him.

Such an attrocious action fubjected him to a
criminal profecution: he, however, efcaped punifhment, becaufe there was no witnefs to the tranfaction; and the *dead man,* who alone knew the truth,
could not appear to contradict him*.

N 4　　　　　　　　　　The

---

* The tranflator here begs leave to obferve, that he fhould
do violence to his own feelings, if he did not ftate, that an
Englifh jury, after a full inveftigation of this tranfaction,
acquitted Mr. Barretti, who, inftead of affaffinating an
unoffending man, as is implied by the text, only defended his
own life againft the affaults of a ruffian. Some of the firft
characters in the kingdom attended the trial, and gave the
moft honourable teftimonies of the worth and goodnefs of a
gentleman, whofe life was fhortened by the moft cruel neglect,
and whofe very memory has been loaded with unmerited
obloquy.

The British Museum is rather a monument of the progress of the arts and sciences, than the means of giving them a higher degree of perfection. The cabinet of natural history, and the collection of manuscripts, medals mechanical inventions, &c. are very interesting, and in point of value almost inestimable. To these, the nation every year makes new additions, not unworthy of the wealth and the greatness of the people.

Sometimes whole cabinets are bought, and incorporated with this immense collection; there was one year, for example, when the parliament purchased the cabinet of the celebrated Sir William Hamilton, for the sum of eleven thousand pounds sterling. In the museum, a copy of Magna Charta is preserved. The printed books are contemptible in point of number, and but ill agree with the rest of this magnificent establishment. They ought to be augmented.

The house itself is undoubtedly one of the finest, the most spacious, and most agreeable mansions in the metropolis; it was built by Montague, the favourite of Charles II. To this noble enterprise, he set apart a large portion of an immense fortune. The most famous painters belonging to the court of that magnificent and voluptuous monarch, such as La Fosse, Rousseau, and Monnayer, here exhausted all the charms and the secrets of their art. Their works are viewed even at this day with rapture. The order and the arrangement which prevail in this institution, are not, however, equal to the other parts of such a noble establishment.

The greatest collection of coins and medals, perhaps in the whole world, belongs to a private gentleman of London. It is to Dr. Hunter, a famous physician, who amassed great riches by his profession, and who died some years since, that the nation is indebted for this superb cabinet; to the

furnishing

furnishing of which he dedicated fifty years, and more than one half of an immense fortune. It is now still more valuable, as it has been greatly augmented within these last ten years.

An Englishman of the name of *Duane, possessed a collection almost equal to the former. A great number of coins struck by the Parthians, and many other nations celebrated in ancient history, rendered this cabinet uncommonly interesting. Hunter purchased and added this to his own.

The immense cabinet of natural history, belonging to Sir Ashton Lever†, is another proof of English magnificence. Never, perhaps, has human industry formed such a complete collection of rare and valuable birds !

The manner of laying out their gardens, is the sole art in which the English have not taken some model for their guide. The disgusting sameness, and tedious uniformity, which all Europe had adopted, was despised by them: they therefore followed Nature step by step, and only called in Art now and then to their assistance. This method, for a long time the subject of raillery and disdain to other nations, begins every day to find new partisans.

The traces of labour are almost imperceptible in the formation of an English garden: and yet, nevertheless, the expences are very considerable: the lawns, which resemble so many verdant carpets, must be constantly cut, and attended to with uncommon care. The gardeners also receive great wages.

It is singular, that there is not, throughout the whole kingdom, one garden in the French style; they are all entirely in a taste peculiar to themselves.

The

---

* Mr. Duane is since dead.

† Sir Ashton Lever is also dead, and his collection is now in the possession of Mr. Parkinson.

The moſt remarkable, on account of their beauty
and extent, are the Marquis of Buckingham's at
Stowe, the Duke of Devonſhire's at Chatſworth,
and the King's at Kew.

Other parts of the country abound with parks, ſo
charming and romantic, that nothing ſeems wanting
but ſhepherds, to make the beholder imagine himſelf in the midſt of one of the moſt delicious provinces of Arcadia. The principal of theſe are ſitu-
ated at Richmond, Windſor, and Greenwich.

I HAVE now given a ſketch of that famous
Iſland, the people of which, according to Boſſuet,
like the ocean that ſurrounds them, are in perpetual
commotion; an obſervation which a hundred years
experience ſeems to confirm. In England, events
are continually taking place, which merit the attention of every philoſophical obſerver, and elevate
the annals of the preſent age to the hiſtorical dignity
of ancient times. LIBERTY, that inexpreſſible
bleſſing, is, and has always been, the ſource of all
theſe heroical and ſublime actions, which only excite
our barren admiration.

Long before the people had acquired, or, if you
will, conquered their great charter, Alfred inſerted
theſe remarkable words in his laſt will, " The Engliſh
" ought to be as free as their thoughts." No people abhor deſpotiſm, and every thing that may lead
to it, ſo much as theſe proud Iſlanders. This aver-
ſion juſtifies the exclamation of Macaulay, the celebrated female hiſtorian : " The ſight of a deſpot,"
ſays ſhe, " has never ſullied the purity of my
" regards."

No nation can boaſt of having for ſo long a period
of time poſſeſſed ſo many ſocial and political
bleſſings.

bleffings. To fee fo many millions of men, enjoying an uninterrupted poffeffion of rights, worthy of the dignity of human nature, is a circumftance unexampled in hiftory.

It is in that fortunate ifland alone, that the accumulation of riches, luxury, pleafures, and all their dangerous confequences, has not given fo any one clafs of citizens a pernicious and dangerous afcendancy over the laws.

F I N I S.